The Book of

ROADWATER, LEIGHLAND AND TREBOROUGH

An Exmoor Valley Discovered

CLARE AND GLYN COURT

HALSGROVE

First published in Great Britain in 2004

British Library Cataloguing-in-Publication Data
A CIP record for this title is available from the British Library

ISBN 1 84114 342 1

HALSGROVE

Halsgrove House
Lower Moor Way
Tiverton, Devon EX16 6SS
Tel: 01884 243242
Fax: 01884 243325
E-mail: sales@halsgrove.com
Website: www.halsgrove.com

Frontispiece photograph: *Fred Inkerman Bond with his father John's 'boneshaker' by the level-crossing gates in Station Road, c.1905. This penny-farthing is now on display in Roadwater Village Hall.*

Printed and bound by CPI Bath.

Contents

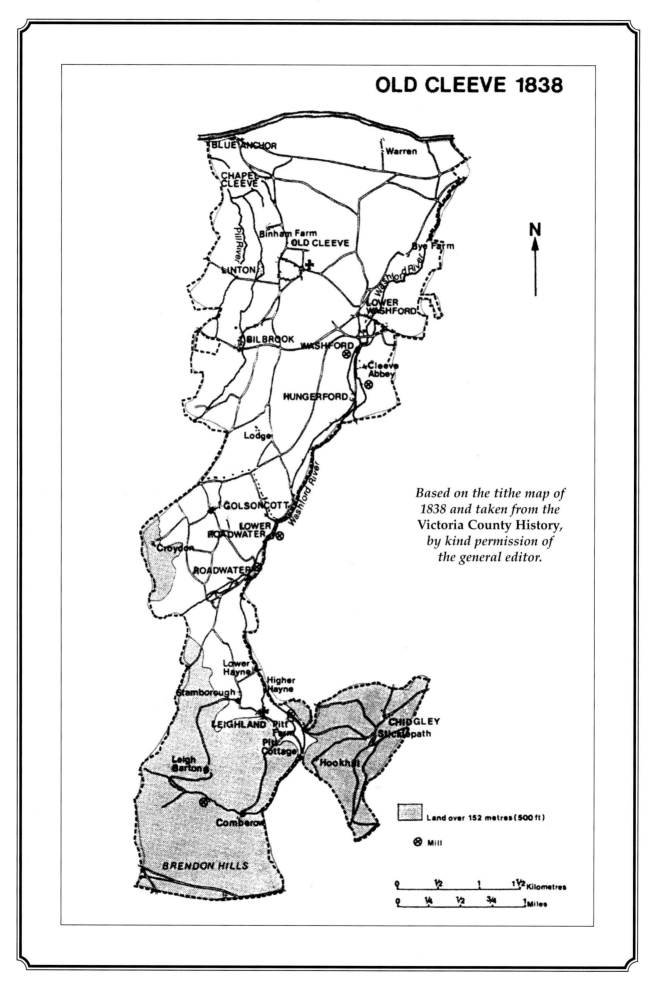

OLD CLEEVE 1838

Based on the tithe map of
1838 and taken from the
Victoria County History,
by kind permission of
the general editor.

Land over 152 metres (500 ft)

⊗ Mill

Preface

This book is not a traditional history. Such a one, with its record of manorial transactions, economic activities and the like, supported by thorough research and hundreds of footnotes, appeared as part of the *Victoria County History* in the early 1980s. In addition, some 30 years earlier, the Women's Institute had produced an excellent and entertaining *Story of Roadwater*, based not merely on documents but on the recollections of local people whose memories reached back well into the nineteenth century. To duplicate that information would be pointless.

This book attempts, rather, to recreate something of the life of Roadwater and its Leighland, Treborough, Golsoncott and Leigh Barton neighbours in their mid-nineteenth century heyday, and to recall some of the men and women, with their characteristics and occupations, who were living legends around the fireside when I was young. The story has been brought up to the present day by accounts of the people and activities of the various groups which even now help to keep the spirit of the community alive.

GLYN COURT, 2004

Village view, 2000. The scene is almost unchanged since 1900.

Pranketts, originally a monastic cell of Cleeve Abbey, with a 'holy well', as it was when Maria Milton, artist J.W. North's 'unofficial' wife, lived there in the late 1890s. Maria died in her early thirties of tuberculosis, but she bore North three sons and two daughters, all of whom survived. This photograph was probably taken by North, and was supplied by Steve Milton, a descendant.

The Incline, 1880s, taken from the north in one of Leigh Barton's fields, most likely Higher Broadfield. Quite a little masterpiece of photographic composition!

Acknowledgements

The Book of Roadwater has taken 40 years to prepare and less than half that number of weeks to write, and so it contains not half of all that could be told. We owe an inexpressible debt to all those friends of Roadwater, some of them now passed on, who kept alive by written word and speech the memories and traditions of a community in the days when it epitomised all that was typical of West Country village life. But more immediately, we are no less indebted to the many friends, whether here or elsewhere, whose contributions have made us feel a continual and growing interest which we hope will speak to you as you read. This has been a voyage of discovery with a favouring breeze, but even Captain Cook grounded once or twice, and so we hope to be forgiven if, in spite of all our care, one or two errors of fact, date or identity have crept in. If they have, we will express our regret and ask for your forbearance.

We are happy to record our particular gratitude to two professional novelists, Penelope Lively, for her appreciative recollections of her aunt, Miss Reckitt, and Nicholas Salaman, for writing so entertainingly of his childhood in Treborough. We would also like to thank Gill and Philip White for a lively account of their first winter at Leigh Barton; Mark Rattenbury for the photograph of Dr Maurice Hardman; the Golsoncott Trust for the photograph of Miss Reckitt; the editor of the *West Somerset Free Press,* County Museums Officer, Robert Dunning, general editor of the *Victoria County History of Somerset,* the staff of the County Record Office, and Mr David Bromwich and the staff of Somerset Studies for their ever willing assistance; David Gooding and John Nethercott for the use of their extensive collections of photographs, historical documents, press cuttings and old maps of Roadwater; Margaret Pocklington for her notes on the Nethercott enterprise; Mary Coles and Adam for help with publicity.

To the following we should like to express our thanks for the loan of photographs, written and printed material or for the generous gift of their time in recording their memories: Mr and Mrs J. Armson, Jennifer Asbridge, Beryl Baker, Douglas Bates, Gerald Beaver, Joan Beaver, Sylvia and Eddie Beaver, Hilary Binding, Sheila Bishop, Revd David Bolton, Joan Bosley, Gill Bowden, Sheena Bryant, M. Cadman, G.R. Cairns, Bert Calloway, Michael Chilcott, Mary Coles (Alcombe), Joan Collins, Elizabeth Constable, Joan Corfield (who sadly died during the production of this book), Dennis Corner, Jayne Cornish, Flo Croucher, Elizabeth Darke, Oliver Davies, Zara Davis, Alan and Beverley Dean, Debbie Dennis, Dianne Doran, Mavis Drew, Mr James Evers, Michael Figgis, Elizabeth Foster, John Fouracre, John Gliddon, Mr K. Grabham, Steve Guscott, Jennifer Hand, Gordon and Jack Harris, Marjorie and Gordon Hayes, Mavis and John Hill, Ivy Hoard (Topsy Takle), Harry Horrobin, Fred Hutchings, Michael Jones, Joan Kane, Joanne Knight, Veronica Lile, Brenda and Tad Mandziej, Eileen Mann, Rosemary Martin, Carol Matravers, Mr and Mrs P. Milton, Steve Milton, Marjorie Moir, Abby Morrill, Elaine Necchi, Jo Nethercott, Dennis Parsons, Donald Parsons, Glenda Patterson, Jim Patterson, Colonel Adrian Peck, Revd Peter Pengelley, Bill Poirrier, Andrew Priddy, Bob Reed, Mike Roberts, Bertha Routley, Charles Routley, Clement Salaman, Dr Myer Salaman, Pamela and Frank Scragg, Valerie Shopland, Mr Shopland (Doniford), Ruth Smith, Ian Sowden, Kevin Steer, Jane and Dennis Takle, Pat Taylor, Colin Tennant, Carol Tipper, Pam Thomas, Mike Twine, May Webber, Sally White, Mary Wickstead, Denise Yardley.

And to fix him firmly in the memory, our most lively gratitude to Val Hole. His constant and creative interest in the progress of the work, his initiative in seeking out items of interest from written and printed records, his vivid recollection and recording of the minutiae of village life 50 years ago, have been invaluable. His active memory has time and again rescued the characters in old photographs from their monochrome anonymity and restored them to their place in the history of the village. We are all deeply indebted to Val.

Lastly, thanks must go to Katy Charge and colleagues at Halsgrove for their co-operation and assistance in publishing this book. If we have omitted anyone from this list, please accept our apologies, and believe that 'our true intent is all for your delight'.

CLARE AND GLYN COURT

An early children's production by Mrs Salaman, possibly Peter Pan. *Included in the photograph are: Jean Bennett, Lily Furse, Frances Hole, Joyce Webber, Frances Furse, Olive Reed, Peter Taylor, Clifford Beaver, Joan Bond, Donald Coleman, Clifford Furse, Idris Beaver, Betty Coleman, Mary Bryant, Desmond Taylor, Peggy Lile, Gwen Taylor, Bubbles Beaver, Bill Sully, Charlie Hawke, Betty Beaver, Arthur Takel, Cyril Sully, Eddie Beaver.*

Right: *Rededication of Treborough church cross, 29 June 1927. The cross, which had been missing for over a century, was restored by Sir Walter Trevelyan.*

Chapel outing to Weston, August 1927.

Introduction

Bridge Cottage, probably built after 1850, as it stands on the line taken by the road before the bridge was made. The pretty porch over the front door was a feature of all the old cottages in this part of the village. Up the Luxborough road a corner of the old chapel can be seen with the beginning of the church path to Leighland.

Roadwater's remoteness from the main road has, until recently, saved it from major development, but the pleasure it offers does not come only from its setting in the very heart of a valley of exceptional charm. Visitors who take the time to explore on foot will find something of interest round every corner. Only a choice few of the dwellings are eye-catchingly picturesque, but this is more than made up for by the beauty of hillside, woodland, meadow and stream. Beyond that, its history, outstandingly varied in interest, tells of a time during Queen Victoria's reign when new industries came to stir the old village way of life and created a unique blend of old and new: traditional crafts and farming developed alongside engineering, quarrying and the wonders of the railway age, and brought many working people a modest prosperity which, although short-lived, gave them the means to broaden their horizons beyond the cares of every day. Such activity, recorded at the time in detail, which, for a small village, must be virtually unique, forms the substance of part of this book. Yet this volume brings the story of the locality that includes Roadwater, Leighland, Golsoncott, Treborough and Leigh Barton up to date and in doing so pays tribute to a unique and enduring community, and a very special place to call home.

Roadwater: a key to the text

1. Nethercott's foundry.
2. Roadwater Inn.
3. Garage.
4. Railway coach and bungalow.
5. Charlestown Cottages.
6. Island Cottage.
7. Broadie (Broadway), now The Crescent.
7A. Factory on site of allotments.
8. Manor Mill.
9. St Luke's Church.
10. Model House.
11. Day's Meadow (recreation-ground).
12. Village Hall.
12A. Post Office (from 1970s).
13. Fern Bank.
14. Roadwater Mill and House.
15. New Inn on Knap.
16. Methodist Church.
17. Gooding's Post Office and stores.
18. Tom Slade's house and smithy.
19. Burnett's Nurseries.
20. Mining company agent's house.
21. Bridge over stream.
22. Court's Post Office and stores.
23. Proud Street (Station Road).
24. Oatway House (1699).
25. Meeting of streams, railway bridge and level crossing.
26. Railway station (now a bungalow).
27. Harpers (in Nettlecombe parish).
27A. Coach road (in Nettlecombe parish).
28. Temperance Hall.
29. Leat (now dry) for blade mill, formerly on site of Temperance Hall.
30. Road Wood and Scrubbet.
31. Bible Christian Chapel (ruin).
32. Valiant Soldier (inn).
33. Vale House (formerly a mill).
34. Tacker Street.
35. Glasses Farm.

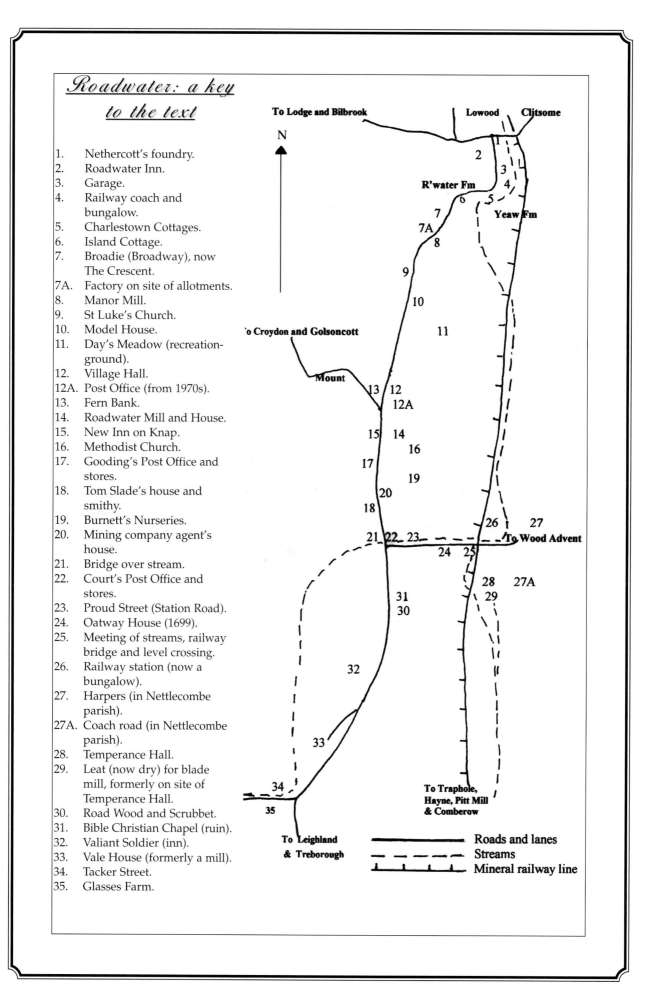

Chapter 1

The Roadwater Valley

The Roadwater valley from the top of the Incline, c.1935. The middle ground shows Leigh Woods, Pitt Wood is in the centre and on the far left is part of Erridge Wood. In the distance are Kingswood and the sea.

The Early Days

The parishes of Old Cleeve, Leighland and Treborough together make up a geographical unit of a small river system, with a wide, steep-sided vale containing two smaller valleys formed by streams which rise in the Brendon Hills near Luxborough and Treborough before flowing north to meet in Roadwater and then on through Washford to the sea at Watchet. Indeed, the area is physically so much of a piece, so self-contained, that early settlers chancing upon it might have felt compelled to organise it into a single unit of government. The early English knew better. Those who conceived and developed the idea of a parish decided that three-quarters of the valley and the escarpment of Brendon Hill should be taken up by the large parish of Old Cleeve (locally Cleeve for short), which rises from sea level at Blue Anchor to 1,250 feet on Brendon Hill, and that the good-grazing land to the south-west should go to the parishes of Treborough and Luxborough. The hill country to the south, up to a little short of the ridge line, 'a barren Mountain', according to a sixteenth-century lawyer, was allotted almost entirely to the parish of Old Cleeve or the estates from which it formed. The 'almost', however, is important, for the southern boundary stops a stone's throw short of the high line of the ridge, and the adjoining parishes of Clatworthy, Kingsbrompton and Withiel Florey protrude those few yards on the seaward side. (One may surmise that those early planners meant to make sure that that the three inland parishes took a share of responsibility for watching for danger from the sea in the days of the Vikings). Be that as it may, the result has been that although Old Cleeve reaches 1,237 feet at Brendon Hill Chapel, the highest points on the ridge (and incidentally the highest in the South or West of England, except for Dartmoor and Exmoor)

11

are in other parishes: 1,350 feet on Treborough Common, 1,274 at Leather Barrow and 1,390 feet at Lype Hill in Luxborough and Cutcombe. The western stream, for part of its length, separates Treborough from Withycombe, and the eastern, once it has come into the lowlands, forms the boundary between Old Cleeve and its eastern neighbour, Nettlecombe, so that it benefits both.

Roadwater and Leighland seem to have few monuments of pre-history apart from the Naked Boy stone (or perhaps the three remaining of the Four Naked Boys shown on a map of 1822) and the harepath forming the southern border of the parish. A flint scraper was found in Burnett's Nurseries near the old bed of the stream, but has been lost. Little else has yet come to light. Treborough parish has the tumulus of Leather Barrow (from the Celtic *lleithyr* meaning steep) and numerous ancient hedge-banks marking the boundaries of former estates (see Edward F. Williams' excellent *Survey of Treborough*, Taunton, 1990). In Langridge Wood a kist or stone-lined grave was uncovered in 1820 by men who were demolishing a cairn for road-metalling. (The skeleton in it was re-interred in Treborough church-yard.) The Bronze Age has yielded little in either parish, and apart from a necklace and other items from a smith's hoard found at Hayne (and now in the County Museum), we have few remains like those in which Exmoor abounds.

Our first written records come from the Domesday Book of 1088, which lists the agricultural holdings of the manors of Treborough, Leighland (under the name Legh, one of four in Somerset) and Brown. Both Legh and Brown had risen in value since 1066 – from 2s. to 6s. and from 20s. to 40s. respectively – perhaps because the agents of the Norman usurpers, having little compassion for the Saxons under them, were able to flog more work out of them. Brown was indeed a substantial holding; the Domesday survey lists 13 villagers, 3 smallholders, 2 slaves, 1 acre of meadow, 80 acres of pasture and 12 acres of woodland plus 2 cobs, 16 cattle, 23 pigs, 190 sheep and 42 goats.

Treborough (*Traberge*) had no such tale to tell; the Norman lord, Ralph, displaced English Edric and kept nearly all the land for himself (enough for five ploughs), except for 10 acres that remained the property of one smallholder. Not that the ploughs were much used, for the woodland was 30 acres and the pasture was '1 league long and as wide. Value 7s., and when he acquired it, as much; for it is laid waste.' This last is puzzling. There is no evidence that William the Conqueror's devastations in south Somerset stretched as far north as this. Perhaps it was merely a clerical error: *vastata* (meaning laid waste) instead of *vasta* (waste land), for Treborough was until recently 'purty vuzzy 'pon top'.

(Recent historians have suggested that a Saxon place-name does not prove a village's Saxon origin, but may be a new name for an older Saxon settlement; thus *Traberge* in the Domesday Book may have supplanted a Celtic *tre bwrw*: place of the waterfall, but there is no proof of this).

Whatever the difficulties, the work of clearing the forests and ploughing the land begun under the Saxons continued and, although we have no written evidence, the Saxon nature of many of the names and comparison with other districts prove that by the time the Normans arrived there were settlements at Golsoncott, Bilbrook ('the watercress brook'), Chidgley ('Cheddas leah or glade'), Rode ('clearing') or Road Water, Leighland, Hayne, Willeys (Willhays) and Comberow or Rowsend, as well as Wood (Advent) and Huish (Barton) in Nettlecombe. Whether Hook Hill and Dorniford had been established is more doubtful, but over in Luxborough, Langham and Old Stowey were definitely in existence.

The earliest document relating to Roadwater, or 'Rode', is as late as 1243 and refers to a mill, probably Manor Mill. By the end of the Middle Ages a small settlement had grown up near the bridge over the stream, and Oatway House must date from this time, although it was renovated in 1699–1700.

The settlement grew northward... to form Lower Roadwater. To the west of Roadwater, occupying high but sheltered positions on the northern edge of the Brendons, the later abbey grange of Croydon and the hamlet of Golsoncott were recorded by 1221, the first apparently as a habitation, the second suggesting in the last part of its name that it was a pre-Conquest farmstead. VICTORIA COUNTY HISTORY

Leighland, too, about this time, developed as a sheep farm attached to Cleeve Abbey, and around 1320 a chapel of ease was built there, to be served on alternate Sundays by a monk from the abbey or, later, the vicar of Old Cleeve. In 1563 Leighland officially contained 21 dwellings, but almost certainly many of these were in Roadwater, coming under the oversight of Leighland with its chapel of ease.

The Middle Ages have left us many buildings, mainly farms and mills, but all except a few – Manor Mill, Oatway House, Glasses Farm, Leigh Barton, Clitsome – have been transformed from their medieval aspect by later builders, beginning with the growth in national confidence in the later Elizabethan years. Treborough church is the one building that a fifteenth-century monk would recognise, for the simple chapel that he served at Leighland was demolished in the late 1850s and replaced by one with a certain Gothic rusticity.

Apart from that, however, nothing emerges from five centuries until the mid-sixteenth, when in 1569, under the threat of war with Spain and likely invasion and a return to the persecution and burning of Protestants rife under Queen Mary 12 years before, the parish authorities were required to draw up lists of men able to bear arms, or of women landowners who could provide them. In the list for this parish appear the names of John and Joan Glasse, who were called upon to provide armour, and whose family name became attached to a farm whose main dwelling shows every sign of dating from Elizabethan times. Not one of the other family names listed can be definitely assigned to Roadwater, so complete has been the change of local population since that time. Indeed, the names of residents changed almost entirely within 100 years, for by 1676 only one name, Hurford, remained from 1569. The new list of names included very many which have lingered in the locality, such as Berryman, Bindon, Burge, Burston, Blake, Burton, Chapman, Chilcott, Cucksley, Davis, Dyer, Evitt, Ford, How, Jerkins, Lewis, Nethercott, Norman, Norris, Pike, Poole, Prescott and Prowse.

The seventeenth-century records of the Quarter Sessions show plenty of petty crime and larceny, but they also offer interesting glimpses into the way in which certain public services were organised, particularly highways and bridges. When a length of road or a bridge had fallen into disrepair the tythingman of the parish would be cited before Quarter Sessions and ordered to see to the work or pay a heavy fine. Over the following quarter he would carry out the repairs and then report to the next sessions, whereupon a rate would be made upon the inhabitants of the

whole tithing in order to reimburse him. This happened to a John Glasse, perhaps a grandson of his namesake mentioned earlier, in April 1635. He was 'levied upon' for not repairing 'Road Bridge', but in July the sessions ordered that he should be repaid 'by a rate upon the inhabitants of the whole tything.'

If those were the worries of the 'responsible' members of society, it is not surprising that the irresponsible sometimes ran into trouble. The Quarter Sessions records tell of John Willis, who was 'committed, both for obstinate tipplings, contrary to commandment and warnings given him' (tippling in this context meant selling ale, not drinking it) and:

... setting forth of sundry unlawfull games, drawing therbie Disorderlie assemblies to the great and extra-ordinarie breking of his Ma'ties peace, wh' this whole p'ishe could hardlie support.

It is also recorded that Thomas Bindon was bound over for refusing to:

take an apprentice placed to him by the parish for as much as it is alledged by the said Bindon that the said apprentice hath beene accused for theft and to bee a person of lewd behaviour.

Bindon was freed from taking on the apprentice in return for 40s., which he was obliged to pay to the churchwardens and overseers.

In 1656, 20 years after the 'Road Bridge' case, our friend John Glasse made a deposition as follows:

He had lost a plough chain a year sithence [since], and a week sithence he passing by the house of Rice Davis in Roadwater saw a chain making fast a gate in his court which he challengeth to his goods. Rice Davis husbandman said that while deeking a ditch belonging to a ground called Lower Land belonging to Mr Nicholas Hartnell of Treborough he found the chain overgrown with brambles, and Hopkin Fluelly [another Welshman] was then present.

Another member of the Welsh contingent appeared in a case in 1663, when William Mattock of Williton lost a bale of cloth which had been in the charge of Mr Shutte, a dyer of Old Cleeve. The cloth was later bought of Lluelin Evans at Luxburrow. What verdict was delivered in these cases no one knows. Similarly, the outcome is not known on the theft of 20s. in gold when, it

View of Treborough, 1900.

was said, some of the accused 'spent two or three houres of this Saturday att one Jasper Nethercotts Alehouse in the said parish of Old Cleeve.'

We do not know whether any Roadwater men served during the Civil War of 1642–45 and 1647–51. If they did, they were probably not volunteers but were either enlisted in the troop of horsemen raised by George Trevelyan of Nettlecombe or they may have served in the infantry company of Thomas Luttrell of Dunster. No unmistakably Roadwater names appear in the lists of 'meighmed' (maimed) soldiers in the early days of the Commonwealth (1649 onward). Although Roadwater, unlike Nettlecombe and Dunster, had no manor-house to suffer attack and plunder, the village must have shared in the widespread misery, sickness, hunger and lawlessness of those years. The Civil War has so often been presented as a colourful struggle between dashing, daredevil Cavaliers and plodding, sanctimonious Parliament men, but this caricature hides the dreadful fact that the battles, sieges, wounds and fevers killed as many Englishmen in proportion to the populations, and devastated the lives of as many women, as the First World War.

These were terrible but stirring times, and the 20 or so square miles around Roadwater witnessed deeds of courage which have become legendary. These include General Robert Blake's siege of Dunster Castle, the capture of the Royalist ship at Watchet by Cornet Popham and his troop of cavalry, and Margaret Trevelyan's journey from Nettlecombe to London to save her husband's estate, which led to her tragic death.

Most tragic of all, however, is the story of Leigh Barton during this period. When Cleeve Abbey was closed down in 1538, Leighland ceased to be served by the monks, although it seems Roman Catholic worship took place in Leigh Barton (or perhaps was transferred there long after the Reformation). In the 1640s the resident Poyntz family even had a chaplain, Philip Powel. He was a Welshman, born in 1594 and trained in the college of Douai. After ordination Powel came to England and lived with the Poyntz family for 20 years. He had his own chapel but also preached without hindrance in the chapel at Leighland. When the Civil War broke out he decided to relieve the family of his presence and went to Cornwall to shelter with friends, one of whom was John Trevelyan, of the Nettlecombe family. When Cornwall was overrun by Parliament he embarked for Wales, either from a Cornish port or from Watchet (accounts differ). However, the ship was stopped and boarded, Powel was recognised and consequently arrested and accused of being 'one who had seduced people from churches.' He was taken to London, tried, found guilty of staying in the country contrary to law and being a monk, and on 16 June 1646 he was condemned to death. He was executed at Tyburn with the customary brutality, except that in

accordance with a petition of the Common Council of the City to Parliament his head and quarters were not set up on gate spikes. There is a story that they were brought back to Leigh Barton and immured in the south wall of his chapel. This prompted the legend that on the anniversary of his execution his ghost haunts the woods near Leigh waterfall (though why ghosts should be concerned to observe the calendar is never explained).

The Poyntz family and their successors, the Rowes, persevered with their 'old religion' and even during the reign of George III (1760–1820) the Rowes were reported for holding Catholic services at Leigh.

Whether legend has a rightful place in history or not, Powel's sad story has a tailpiece. In the mid-nineteenth century, on a fine, warm day in June, strange and disturbing noises were heard in Leigh Woods. A labourer was sent to investigate. When he emerged two days later, he could only stammer a few incoherent words. Whatever he had seen or experienced had shattered his reason in the dark depths of Leigh Woods.

As far as we know, nothing occurred for the next 200 years to stir the still pool of village life or break the unchanging round of the country year. If any men joined Monmouth's rebel army they went unrecorded (and unpunished), although some may have walked to Dunster or Minehead to watch the hangings that took place there. Similarly, it is unclear whether, in the early 1700s, local men served against the French with the Duke of Marlborough. However, as the Valiant Soldier inn was open by 1720 it appears that the village kept an interest in national affairs.

From the Napoleonic Wars comes the tale that a young man at the inn, as drunk as a three-bottle lord, took the King's shilling and drank his health, then, thinking wiser of it, went outside and chopped off his trigger-finger. The vast majority of men in a neighbourhood where agriculture and its ancillary trades were the only enterprise, would have worked from year to year and from cradle to grave, solely concerned for their livelihood and the survival of their families. Poverty-stricken though they were, they may not have suffered quite so acutely from the eighteenth-century Agrarian Revolution, enclosures and loss of common land as did their fellows up-country. It was in the years after Waterloo (1815), with poor harvests, devaluation, beggarly wages, housing often not fit for cattle, sickness and death for one child after another, that the worst suffering set in. The wonder of it is that for every man this period broke utterly, a dozen emerged strong, capable, stoical and enduring, if not without their eccentricities and foibles. These were men of 'character', whose womenfolk more than measured up to them.

Times of Change

The nineteenth century is the first whose people we

recognise as unmistakably akin to ourselves – partly because, among the ancestors of most people today, they are the first with whom we feel an immediate link. The generation of 1800 discovered that change was all around them and waiting to break in. Some would welcome it, some would resist, but in the end change had its will. While many moved away, those who remained kept the memories and some of the ways of the old times. Most discovered, however, that much of the change was for the better.

'I love Roadwater; I love everything in Roadwater, I love everything about Roadwater. Even if 'tis only an old sheepdog, I love it.' So cried one old stalwart, tough as leather breeches in all but his love for his home. No doubt there are a thousand other villages whose people might say the same of their home. But Roadwater stands alone. Down through the ages it has made a life of its own. Yet because Roadwater was not a parish in its own right, and had no resident landed gentry, the records for all that time, apart from one mention in 1254 and another in 1720, are little more than baptisms, marriages and burials, 'the short and simple annals of the poor.'

This may suggest that daily life for most of the people conformed to a routine throughout their lives that varied only by the changing of the seasons, church on Sundays and the two days' annual holiday of Christmas Day and the revel. However, life was not like that. Human nature could not be everlastingly ground down, and even in an apparently static society, over the centuries slow changes were at work. Change is the very nature of life and the physical world: the view we see from the top of Brendon Hill is not the one that greeted our eyes one minute before; it has changed in a million ways, a few of them visible, most of them infinitesimal. We are only conscious of this when the passage of time accumulates these changes in great enough measure for our senses to grasp. The first half of the nineteenth century in many rural areas of the west of England may present the picture of a static society, a powerful aristocracy or squirearchy, a dearth of freeholders and yeomen, and the vulnerability of a large class of landless labourers. But beneath this surface, in Roadwater, some remarkable changes were taking place, not only in the economic conditions but also in the very outlook and attitudes of many of the people themselves (see Chapter 8).

Agricultural labourers may outnumber other classes in many family trees, but even in a society totally absorbed in agriculture, farm labouring was not the only employment. Indeed, just as many men and women worked as shepherds or cowmen or carters or in ancillary crafts, as smiths, saddlers, grooms, thatchers, carpenters, wheelwrights and sawyers, or as lime burners, charcoal burners and quarrymen. And by virtue of the two streams which meet in the village, Roadwater possessed no fewer than five mills, three for flour, and one each for cloth-fulling and for making blades. There was a variety of occupations, but it existed in a unified common framework of daily life.

Four great estates surrounded Roadwater, each one centred on a mansion or large house – Dunster Castle, Nettlecombe Court, Chargot and Orchard Wyndham. In late-Georgian times the owners, by purchase or exchange of outlying properties, had consolidated their holdings, but it was only Nettlecombe that intruded into the heart of the valley and village. Sir John Trevelyan owned all the land beyond the eastern stream and a handful of properties in or near Proud Street, but all the dwellings on the west side of the main street, from the Valiant Soldier down to the bottom of the village, belonged either in freehold to the men or women who lived in them or to yeomen farmers. Although this may not have counted for much in the grand total of property, it must have meant much to them, in whom a sense of precarious but firm independence must have grown. It was this that enabled them to take up the challenges which the new century brought.

Some Roadwater folk accepted change, others dissented, but in fact, for 20 years in the mid-nineteenth century many, if not all, Roadwater people enjoyed a modest prosperity thanks to new industries. It was a hard-earned condition that was threatened when in 1876 agricultural depression set in. Roadwater and the hamlets represented a cohesive society whose members all knew one another and everyone did work essential to everyone else. Thus the humblest trades had their value, a fact that goes a long way to account for the dignity and composure of the men and women in the portraits created by the village photographer. Such characters form the subjects of the following pages. All are drawn from family recollections faithfully recorded by the generation passing away in the mid-twentieth century. If occasionally their lineaments seem veiled by idealism, I can only say that while the generation aforesaid might have relished a little present-day scandal they kept fairly quiet about the lapses of the heroes of their childhood past!

The mill in Leigh Woods (since disappeared), 1880.

Right: *Lowood, built or rebuilt by Sir John Trevelyan in 1822 and the home of the Sully family for 70 years.*

Left: *Riverside Cottage. The daughters of John Sully, the veterinary surgeon, who lived at Lowood are standing by the picturesque ford on the way to Clitsome, c.1890. The ford was not covered over until the 1950s.*

Ten years further on and the Lowood girls are young ladies.

Chapter 2

A Stroll Through Roadwater

This picture: *Clitsome Farm, c.1880; the farm cottage is on the right, with court and barns behind. The mineral railway is on the left.*

Below: *Cottage on the corner opposite Lowood, demolished c.1960 to make way for Clitsome View.*

Most village folk in West Somerset in the 'good old days' could, if they had been the complaining sort, have told you more about the bad side: grinding poverty, overcrowding, diphtheria, 'consumption', 'rheumatics', and the workhouse. However, for those with an eye for beauty, the landscape of the 1850s had attained perfection after centuries of maturing. In villages such as Roadwater the speculative builder had not arrived, gimcrack bungalows had not been dreamt of, and the farmhouses were still being built with local materials in a living local tradition. With the help of family memories and old maps, this chapter presents Roadwater as it appeared at that time – indeed, as it had appeared for perhaps 100 years, even though it stood on the threshold of change.

A visitor to Roadwater in 1850 may well have approached the village from Washford. At Lowood, at the entrance to the village, where the side road comes in from Slade and Clitsome, the open brook that flowed down from the fields below Golsoncott formed a ford with a footbridge. On the right of the road, set back in their gardens, were two thatched cottages (still standing in 1950 but gone by 2004), but the first substantial building to be seen was the Roadwater Inn. There was little else until Roadwater Farm behind its high wall. Off the road, a little way up the track to Golsoncott, was Daws Farm.

Across the stream on the left, Yeaw Farm looked as venerable in 1850 as it does in 2004. On the right, past Manor Mill (probably the oldest building in Roadwater) and round the corner were two cottages and a lime kiln. The left side of the road had no buildings until the two cottages near the foot of Mount Lane (almost on the site of the modern Village Hall). Day's Meadow stretched considerably further up the valley than the modern recreation-ground.

Off the road, at the first bend of Mount Lane, were two cottages which marked the edge of Roadwater in that direction. Past the mill cottages on the left stood Roadwater Mill, the leat for which was taken from the Luxborough stream a good way up. It flowed through gardens and out behind the village shop and here ran along the right-hand side of the road and then under it into the mill.

A lane led down beside the mill to the top of Day's Meadow, and up on Knap was the New Inn.

Just before the village shop on the right, but part of the same business, was the chandlery, which needed no notice to announce its business: the pungent odour of tallow was its own advertisement.

Just beyond here on the left, and opposite the smithy, stood the new house that the mining company built for their agent, Henry Court. A few yards further up, the road sloped down to a dipping- and watering-place where the stream widened into a small bay.

Above left: *Jim and Joan Beaver with visitor Edna* (left) *on the Mineral Line at Yeaw, c.1990.*

Above right: *Manor Mill weir. The two cottages, where the Brewer brothers lived, are thought to have been built by Elias Nethercott.*

Below: *Roadwater Farm.*

Above: *Manor Mill, probably the oldest building in Roadwater (a mill was mentioned in 1254). It was last worked as a mill by William Slade, who doubled or trebled as a builder and undertaker (evidence of which in the form of rough-sawn boards leaning against the wall of the mill, can be seen in this photograph). On the same premises, on the left, was Bob Smith's bakery. The allotments in the foreground fell out of use after 1945.*

Left: *Old cottages near the Village Hall, demolished in the 1930s; the Post Office stands on the site in 2004. Part of George Takle's garage can be seen on the left.*

Right: *Mill House, c.1900.*

Left: *Roadwater Mill area seen from Harpers.* Top left: *Road Barn;* middle left: *cottages and New Inn on Knap, and the mill;* centre: *skittle alley and mill cottages, the cottage where the modern Village Hall stands, once the site of a saw-pit;* right: *Fern Bank and Mount Lane.*

The station and centre of Roadwater seen from the top of Harpers, c.1890. The Mineral Line is still in use in this picture. There seems to be a leat or drainage channel running past the goods shed and the coalyard siding is in use. At the time of the picture there was no orchard for Oatway on the hillside and ruined barns on Scrubbet can be seen along with pretty gardens, since abandoned by the National Park to urban housing. The 'plume of smoke' in the centre of the picture is the road to Luxborough. Gooding's shop is visible (centre right) as is the New Inn on Knap.

Proud Street, alias Station Road, looking toward Wood Advent Lane, 1906. Christopher Mear and daughter are in the doorway, while the postmaster W.G. Court, is taking the air further along the road. Note the smart white summer boots in the window and the boulders alongside the houses to keep the hubs of cartwheels away from the walls.

Left: The interior of the Temperance Hall, with Lewis H. Court on the platform. The portrait over the door is of Sir Wilfred Lawson, MP.

The Temperance Hall, built by Sir Walter Trevelyan. It served for concerts, chapel and election meetings and, in the 1940s, as an 'overflow' school until 1950. This picture shows the opening in August 1878, with the band, complete with drum, on the right.

Glasses Farm, c.1890, pen and ink sketch by Lewis H. Court.
Glasses Farm must date back at least 400 years. Very remarkably it has kept the
name of the family who occupied it in Elizabethan days.

Traphole, 1920s.

Hayne, 1930s.

The road then turned sharp right and crossed the stream a yard or two up from the modern bridge, and then turned half-left to rejoin the line of the road. (The river was culverted here in the 1850s to create the area known as the Bridge, and subsequently Bridge Cottage was built partly on the return line of the old road.)

Here the road to Wood Advent branched off, running alongside an orchard. Along this stretch called Proud Street (later called Station Road, this street originally took its name from the landowning Prowse family) the only buildings on the left were cottages inhabited by road repairer John Slade on the corner, covered in a magnificent cotoneaster, and that of Nathaniel Edbrooke, which later became Bryant's bakery. His smithy faced it. Otherwise Oatway House had a fine uninterrupted view down the valley.

About 50 yards up Wood Advent Lane the coach road built by Sir John Trevelyan to drive around his Nettlecombe estate ran high along the hillside, and below it stood a blade mill powered by a leat coming down through the fields from Hayne. The mill was run by George Edbrooke who made edged tools and wrought iron. (His name remains stamped on the iron gates to the porch of Old Cleeve church. Thanks to him Roadwater tools had an enviable reputation in the neighbourhood.)

Returning to the street and moving toward Luxborough past a house and workshop (the site of Rose Villa) we would come to the Bible Christian chapel, where the church path to Leighland led off, although people were as likely to use the easier path up through the court of Oatway House. On Scrubbet the barns were still thatched and in use in 1850, and children no doubt played under a magnificent walnut tree 15 feet round, while on Hill Close there stood an ancient oak 6 feet through.

Beyond the Valiant Soldier lay the rackfield, where the cloth from the fulling mill at Vale used to be hung to dry – indeed, the number of mills in this valley was quite extraordinary, for the little stream, in its two branches, drove no fewer than 17.

There were only two other cottages down by the stream. The first stood on the near bank and on the right-hand side of the track to Rodhuish, while the second was on the other side of the stream and stood a few yards down. This pretty cottage was demolished later in the century and replaced by a two-storeyed house which still exists.

Slightly further up the hill lay Glasses Farm at the southern end of Roadwater village (about 1¼ miles from the starting point of this stroll). Both in 1850 and 2004 Roadwater remains the longest village in Somerset (1½ miles). It is actually a string of little hamlets, each defined by a bend in the road: Lowood–Roadwater Farm, Island Cottage–Manor Mill, Hayman's Cottages–Model House, and so on. Each has its own set of neighbours, all linked by satisfaction at being part of Roadwater.

This stroll has shown us at most 40 dwellings. Who would ever have thought that these few buildings would develop into a community that displays such variety in its characters and work, such a blend of agriculture, engineering, trade and industry, such creative movements in music, drama and religion, and so plentiful a record of past life? Such a heritage makes Roadwater a place not only unique in interest but one which lays hold on you and will never let you go.

Chapter 3

Three Men of Note

Sir Walter Trevelyan

The classic English village was ruled by a squire in the 'big house', abetted by the parson and churchwardens, with the farmers reluctantly paying the poor rate and watching eagle-eyed for malingerers. Roadwater had missed that pattern and never noticed the lack of it. As some saw, we positively gained. Our village enjoyed the diamond jubilee of 1897, but for every one who doffed their hat or dropped a mental curtsey to 'her gracious Majesty' there was another who pitched it no higher than 'th' ole 'ooman' or 'th' ole queen'. At any rate, resident squire and parson we had not, and as for their 'betters', the working folk respected them when respect was earned, but only then. Life was hard, the people had to bear with poor housing, ill health and poverty, but they escaped other servitude. The parson lived three miles away, and the principal landowners, two of them very benevolent, dwelt beyond the hills in Nettlecombe, Orchard Wyndham and Dunster. Better than that, in Sir Walter Calverley Trevelyan a part of the village had the benefit of a landlord who, though obliged to spend more time on his other estate in Northumberland, cared about the people down here.

In the 400 years since they had come up from Cornwall, the Trevelyans had mostly been careful, conscientious landowners, until a ne'er-do-well Sir George in the 1780s milked the estate for all the money he could. The estate was restored by his successors, mainly the Sir John who vigorously replanted trees and brought scattered properties together, so that at last he could travel nine unbroken miles on his own land and for that purpose built a coach road along the perimeter which can still be seen today.

Sir Walter Calverley Trevelyan (1797–1879).

Sir Walter had come into a good inheritance in 1846, and he was one of a new breed of landowner, as well as a formidable scholar in the new fields of geology and botany. (In 2004 the University of Newcastle set up a website of his collections and published work.) As a young man he visited the Faroe Islands and published accounts of his observations there, and he worked for many years producing three volumes of the family's papers from the years between 1360 and 1775. But despite all this

... the estates were greatly improved during his tenure, for he was a generous landlord and a public-spirited agriculturalist, much noted for his herd of short-horned cattle. DNB

And that was what mattered to the people over the hill in Roadwater. His tall, spare figure was not seen as often as some might have wished, but his presence nearby was generally felt to benefit them, and for clear proof they could point to the substantial, well-built sandstone houses he was having constructed for his workmen and their families.

Sir Walter had one peculiarity, however, which did not go down well with some of the men (although their wives and children probably appreciated it). He was not only an abstainer and President of the United Kingdom Alliance, he also encouraged the temperance friendly society, the Independent Order of Good Templars, instituted in Roadwater by shoemaker William Court in 1868 and to which, in a few years, nearly a third of the village belonged. The other two-thirds probably agreed with the labourer who attended a temperance meeting in Watchet, listened patiently to the lecturer expounding the advantages of staying away from strong drink, and finally delivered his judgement: 'You can say whatever you'm minded to, maister, but a bit o' bre' n' cheese an a drap o' zider dooes I a power o' gude!'

In recent years abstinence seems to have become less unacceptable to 'polite' society than it was, but it may still seem difficult to understand the immense popularity of the temperance movement in mid-Victorian England. Yet the reasons are simple enough. Although strong drink was cheap, it could take a good share of the working man's weekly wage of 8s.–10s. Furthermore, if he were harvesting, for instance, the abstainer could earn better wages than a man slowed by the cider that had been provided for workers in the fields, and that extra money could be spent on his family, and contribute to a happier and more comfortable home.

At the request of William Court, Sir Walter, just before he died, built the Good Templars a fine Temperance Hall to which, unlike the Victorian pub, a rural husband could take his family to a magic-lantern show, enjoy social conversation and hear a lecture or news from the outside world. Beyond this, he could feel proud of a growing, prosperous organi-sation with its codes of conduct and ceremonies, brass or flute and drum band, vigorous singing, public occasions and processions. It also helped families in times of great need. Above all, the organisation was run by officers from their own ranks. Rulings and decisions were not handed down from above. Naturally the members met opposition ranging from mockery to downright hostility and sometimes the threat of violence. A labourer faced a very real risk of dismissal and eviction from a tied cottage if the farmer disapproved of his involvement, and an active and outspoken tradesman could find himself boycotted at the farmer's command. The wonder is that so many counted the cost and stayed in.

Sir Walter's workmen were free from these dangers, and he was not known to dismiss a man merely because he enjoyed a drink. The estate was thrown open to meetings and rallies of several hundred people. Excursion trains with 300 people on board were run up the valley from Watchet through Roadwater to Comberow, and from there people climbed or rode in open trucks to the top and an open-air meeting with a tea party and sports. This enjoyed Sir Walter's support but he kept a look-out and some-times took a hand where he was not strictly entitled to.

Local lore tells of a sultry day – 'drouthy' in local speech – when two workmen employed in laying a hedge were seated in the shade, enjoying their 'nummet' with a small keg of cider. Along came Sir Walter and engaged them in friendly conversation. He had spotted the keg but to have remarked on it would have smacked of arrogance and he knew a subtler way. As he moved while speaking, his heel accidentally-o'-purpose came into contact with the keg, which tipped on to its side. The golden elixir seeped out, drop by precious thirst-relieving drop, but such was the defer-ence accorded to the landowner that the workmen sat gazing with thirsty eyes, never daring to utter a word in protest, nor perhaps even dreaming of it.

Revd Henry Gale

If the patrons of the Valiant Soldier, the light infantry imbibers, the moderate three-pint lancers or the two-gallon heavy dragoons came under observa-tion by Sir Walter, that was a mild hazard compared with the salvo of verbal grapeshot that thundered down from the rectory up on the hill. Sir Walter maintained a patrician detachment from heated argument, but the Revd Henry Gale, formerly of Trinity Hall, Cambridge, appeared to revel in it. He had started his career by being ejected from a Church Assembly for speaking in favour of total abstinence. A report in the national press came to Sir Walter's eye at a time when the living at Treborough, which was in his gift, was vacant. 'Aha', he thought, 'here is the very man!' He offered Gale the post; Gale accepted, moved in and opened the fight. Bishops and many of his colleagues, even those in sympathy with him, found him much too vociferous and uncompro-mising; but they recognised that speaking as he did carried the risk of reprisals and he was utterly fearless in the course he had taken.

For all that, he was no stump orator with a ready tongue to disguise poverty of ideas. When, for example, he sent a petition to the Prime Minister, Lord John Russell, for a ban on distilling, he obtained 'upwards of two thousand signatures of medical practitioners, among whom were the very elite of the profession': five Physicians to the Queen, the President of the Royal College of Physicians, the Physicians General to the Army and Navy, the Senior Physicians to Guy's and St Bartholomew's and many more. With naïve optimism he also outlined a reform of the tax system:

... a thorough revision and alteration of a system of taxation which has grown up to a state of inconsistency and inconvenience, as expensive and complicated as it is cruel and unjust.

'Sweep away all these taxes on raw materials and the necessaries of life which keep working men poor,' he said in effect, 'and put in their place a Property and Income tax, uniformly assessed according to the income and ability of every adult individual.' Similar to the attack launched by Sydney Smith, Anglican churchman, essayist and wit (1771–1845) he added:

Will posterity believe that at the very time of your government issuing sanitary recommendations during periods of epidemic diseases, it is penal to have fresh air in houses; penal to repair houses; penal to consume wholesome food; penal to wash and be clean; penal to be clothed; and finally, that it is penal to insure your property against the torch of the midnight incendiary?

He backed it all up with 50 pages of reasoned arguments, examples and statistics. One wonders what words he would find for a system which 150 years later still belabours the poor and leaves the well-heeled largely unscathed. Some critics reproached him with exaggeration when he called Roadwater 'the drunkenest little hole in the world'. About drunkenness, seen by other countries as a specifically English vice, he did not measure his words, and it was fortunate for his reputation that when he drove full tilt at the enemy his chariot, so to speak, was drawn by three steeds of equal strength: indignation, information and eloquence.

His 'likeness' taken by photographer Daniel Nethercott shows him in an uncharacteristically sedate posture, but he is booted as if about to spring to the saddle and gallop off to London and attack the legislators at Westminster for:

> ... their connivance in the liquor traffic and their part in the degradation of a whole class of society. The Temperance Enterprise arose from the working classes... The people have had nothing to do with legislation about drink, except to be victimised and to suffer incalculable wrong; their rulers have done it all.
> And yet what a credit it is to the poor, wronged, oppressed, plundered and enslaved as they are, that they are the first to reform themselves... The strong common sense of the working classes... has made them 'wiser than their teachers'.

Gale's name really had a milder meaning than its sound, but some of Gale's clerical brethren looked on him as a very ill wind, and as he admitted at one of the bishop's visitations:

> ... the propriety of my going sometimes into the parish of an unwilling Incumbent without his permission, and even speaking in chapels when no other place of meeting could be obtained, became a question for consideration.

The bishop heard all parties and allowed Gale 'all the liberty [he] could reasonably require, accompanied with a hope that Drunkenness, the great evil of our day, might be put down.' So Gale continued on his tempestuous way, and locally he had much success. When he came down from the heights to Roadwater everyone knew about it. They might admire him, they might loathe him; but ignore him they certainly could not.

Revd William Newton, Man of Mystery

Gentlemen parsons were plentiful enough around 1850, but the Church all too rarely allowed them an income to match, and the situation was made worse when clerics with family influence held a dozen parish livings, pocketed the tithes from them all and employed curates for a wage scarcely above the poverty line. Those underpaid curates in Trollope, with devoted wives struggling endlessly to make ends meet and bring up their children as young ladies and gentlemen, are not caricatures. One may ask why such men and women, educated and well-spoken, endured a lifetime of comparative poverty, but some felt a strong sense of vocation, and for others, unwilling to face the stress of business or teaching, it was parish work or starve.

The Church had not provided Roadwater with a building in which to worship, and the people had to walk to the chapel of ease in Leighland. As mentioned earlier, after Cleeve Abbey was closed in 1538 the duty of serving the chapel devolved upon the rectors of Old Cleeve, and this is how the Revd William Newton comes to add a scent of sulphur to the tale.

William Newton and his father James before him were rectors of Old Cleeve for nearly 70 years between them (1784–1802–1851), but it was the son who figured in the lore of the village, and old people in the 1870s remembered him passing through on Sundays not on horseback but sitting on a bale of hay in the cart generally used for collecting his tithes. That, to start with, was out of the ordinary.

One would not willingly traduce a long-dead clergyman, but evidently William Newton had some strange ways, and nobody could suggest why he should have veered away from the well-marked clerical track into a study of the occult. He was not alone in this, and we may be sure that gossip gathered around every scrap of evidence and magnified it. People who reminisced 20 years after his death claimed that he went beyond theory and practised the black art and warned his servants never to touch the books in his study. One Sunday, when he was preaching in church, a curious servant took a chance and opened one, and the study was 'instantly filled with little devils hopping about.' The parson knew it immediately. He broke off his sermon, hurried to the rectory and put his little demons, so to speak, back in the box; but nothing could stop the knowledge spreading abroad. Years later, one old woman averred that once, when Parson Newton was standing on the doorstep with his hands spread out, she heard him say 'Satan, Satan, Satan!', and she ran away terrified.

With this reputation, it is no wonder if Roadwater people eyed him with a wary respect. On the other hand, some of them reasoned that if 'passon' carried authority with Old Nick, he was best fitted to deal with a mystery which defied all their own resources and all rational powers. Newton's response to their invitation is recounted in Chapter 18 in the story of the stolen club chest. He did not let them down.

Pitt Mill, once home of George Matthews, seen here in 1960.

Far right: Tom Brewer (b.1855), quarryman, one of the young men who pooled their savings in 1878 to buy instruments for the brass band. He is clearly very proud of his cornet and smart pillbox hat.

Right: Frank Court (1855–1923), shoemaker, chosen as bandmaster of the brass band formed by the young men of Roadwater in the late 1870s; shown here as a young man wearing the insignia of the Order of Good Templars.

Roadwater Brass Band initiated by Charles Wingfield Figgis, c.1920, taken at his home, Vale House. Left to right, back row: Fred Taylor, Harry Vickery (from High Park), Harry Burnett, Charles Wingfield Figgis, Harry Nethercott, Walter Taylor, Harry Hemmett; front row: Edmund Burnett (from Hayne), Bill Ridler, Tom Ridler (father of Bill and Reg), Sidney Duck, Reg Ridler. Tom Ridler later served as bandmaster and eight of his sons played in the band.

Chapter 4

The Miller Musician and Music in the Valley

George Matthews

In the mid-nineteenth century our little stream, its flow harnessed by the skill and art of our forefathers, gave power to no fewer than 17 mills: Hydon, Chester and New Mills (Luxborough parish), Langridge (Carhampton), Vale, Leigh Woods, Pitt (Leighland), Edbrooke's blade mill (Nettlecombe), Roadwater Mill, Manor Mill and Nethercott's (Roadwater), Abbey Mill, Washford Mill and Gooding's (Washford) and Wansborough, Anchor Street and Manor Mill (Watchet). There may also have been one in the dell below Stamborough.

The 17 millers along the stream must have included one or two grist-adulterers and short-changers, but any ill fame of theirs has been happily swept over the weirs and out to sea. Two, in particular, left enviable reputations: the first, though he does not concern us here, founded the Watchet paper-mill which provided employment for 200 years; the second was George Matthews. Little is known of George's appearance, because he quit the stage before the photographer came on to it; but he is said to have been rather quick of temper and perhaps below average height. Nevertheless, he was certainly a man of mark.

His home was Pitt Mill, in the vale below Leighland, and hamlet and mill, then as now, were connected by a deep, steep, crooked lane only wide enough for a cart or putt, not a wagon, and used more at that time by packhorses. The mill consumed most of George's daylight hours six days of the week for much of the year, as the grinding of corn was not concentrated into the months after harvest but spread by the farmers to aid drying and to keep back enough for seed. From time to time the overshot wheel had to be kept in trim, the axle greased, the vanes mended and the leat cleaned.

All that kept George very busy, but it is said that his character of originality and strength came into its own on the seventh day of the week. For a start, he was the right-hand man and master of music to William Newton in the chapel of ease at Leighland; he led the band, and there was more to this than met the ear.

About 200 years earlier, after the Restoration, the church authorities had sought to improve church music, using whatever local instrumental and vocal talent could be found. Musicians' galleries were erected at the west end of the church and local singers and instrumentalists drawn in to form a 'quire' to encourage congregational singing, although the staid, four-square psalm tunes cannot have compared for appeal with the country dances. The innovation took root, techniques improved, performers became more proficient, the music evolved and became more varied and lively in style and metre. The quire – especially the players – became men of note in the neighbourhood, since they could perform for secular occasions as well.

Their reign lasted 200 years, and while their music and manner of performing changed considerably meanwhile, it reflected, perhaps surprisingly, not the modal and freely rhythmic tradition of the folk songs but the style of the recent past among professional musicians. As such, in the youth of George Matthews this was, so to speak, neo-Handelian. With this, in the late-eighteenth century, perhaps thanks to the Methodists with their love of congregational singing, their desire for refinement of thought and behaviour, and Charles Wesley's incomparable outpouring of religious poetry, a search for self-improvement in rural life, not least in music, became evident.

Matching this, new forms of hymn and carol tunes appeared: foot-tapping melodies, and anthems or extended hymn tunes with repeats and Hallelujahs. The musicians who crowded the west galleries took up the music of the Methodist meeting-houses and played it, when opportunity offered, with varying accuracy and delicacy but always with unbridled enthusiasm. Indeed, in *The Return of the Native* Thomas Hardy described cellist Yeobright:

... who had just warmed to his work, drove his bow into them strings that glorious grand that he e'en a'most

*sawed the bass viol into two pieces. Every winder in
the church rattled as it 'twere a thunderstorm.*

There was one season of the year when the players
cast aside all ecclesiastical decorum, for they revelled
in carols, not the type which have since become
popular, but part-songs with instrumental
'symphonies', melodic runs, strong rhythms and
fugal repeats, meant to be played and sung with
vigour and rejoicing: 'Awake, Awake! With angels
sing!' Many of these were written by village musicians, never published in printed form but handed on
from one choirmaster to another, eventually reaching
congregations in two or even three counties.

George was one of this select company: bandmaster, violist and composer. When his day's work
was done he would sit at his kitchen table with his
manuscript book before him and by the light of a
tallow candle write arrangements of popular songs
and dances, of anthems, psalms and carols – a technique known as 'pricking in the notes'. On the
seventh day he would make his way up to the little
church and lead his orchestra in the music he had
arranged or composed. The music and musicians
were well matched, for George had written specifically for his happy few: two clarionets, flute, key
bugle, trombone and the bass viol or the serpent
which he played himself. He wrote for whatever
instruments he had, and if the Leighland Union Band
did not match concert standards, no one was
disposed to cavil.

The bandsmen could not claim their duties
burdened them. At the start of the sermon they
would slip out of the gallery and down the steps to a
little 'tib shop' across the way, kept by a widow, and
only return – more or less steadily – when the sermon
was drawing to a close, having been warned of the
close of the sermon by a little 'tacker' who had
perhaps been paid a penny to keep watch.

The band would also be called out for jollifica-
tions during the year, for example in mid-September
to play for the dancers at the revel. Here again
George's skill came into play, for they performed not
only George's arrangement of the Welsh melody 'The
Rising of the Lark' and 'Rule Britannia' but also his
own compositions. Indeed, the band book still
shows, in his own writing, the 'Somerset Waltz', the
'Roadwater Quick Step' and other pieces 'Composed
by George Matthews, Pitt Mill'. Whatever the
players' degree of skill, George would not let them
disgrace him, and on summer evenings he would
train them by lining them up in a field on the hillside
above the mill and conducting them from the opposite slope. If all went well his face would light up
with pleasure, but let there be a false note or entry
and he would career down the slope and course up
the other side like a 'long-dog', and the culprit would
feel the rough edge of George's tongue.

With all this activity the crown of the years was
still Christmas, almost the only weekday holiday for
working men and women. The singers would sing
and the players play the grand old carols proper to
the neighbourhood or, in a manner naturalised from
foreign parts; music, as noted earlier, springing
from the great revival of the previous century,
sonorous baroque anthems that carried participants
irresistibly along. Such tunes were performed all
over England and their radiance was captured by
Thomas Hardy even as it was fading away. It is
worth turning to his pages to recall, however dimly,
the feeling of those days of simple, artless art, with
the 'ancient and time-worn hymns, embodying a
quaint Christianity in words orally transmitted from
father to son through several generations.'

With George Matthews and his generation a
tradition of two centuries of music-making came to
an end, yet it ended not at sunset but in the golden
light of a late summer afternoon, when the sound of
the music rang true with the nature of the men who
played it. The parts, like the players, were unpol-
ished and sometimes at variance with one another
but they spoke of feelings seldom to be expressed in
words: good music of fairly good men. With the new
age they had to go. The High Church parsons of the
1850s who imposed new ritual and ceremonial,
found this rustic music making to be vulgar and they
banished it together with the bandsmen. Thus began
the estrangement of so many countrymen from the
Church which has continued to the present day. In
1858 George's church was closed, razed to the
ground, and replaced with a large Gothic building,
bringing up the stone by the new railway that passed
George's door. He died, aged 80, two years later, but
in point of fact, music-making did not die with him –
what happened to it is told in the section on village
blacksmiths.

Some tunes have survived in a hymnal compiled
by Thomas Hawkes, land surveyor of Williton, and
printed and published in 1838 in Watchet. The book
contains over 600 tunes, and remarkably, nearly
200 of these were by local musicians such as Joel
Thorne, William Besley, Thomas (?) Gill, William
Jones and George Matthews. More than 80 of the
west gallery carols (words and music) have been
published in Glyn Court's *Carols of the Westcountry*
(Halsgrove, 1996).

The Brass Bands

One by one George Matthews' bandsmen died, but
the memory lived on, and in due course evoked a new
and enterprising band. The excitement aroused by the
advent of the brass band in the mid-1870s was keenly
felt by Lewis Court, whose account is given below:

*Among the most vivid recollections of my childhood is
that of the coming of the brass band. The 1870s were
the prosperous times for our countryside, for then the*

great mining industry of the Brendon Hills was in full swing, and the money paid out in wages filtered through all classes of our society. Farmers and tradesmen found a ready sale for their goods and even the cottagers in the valleys around could turn their garden produce into money among the miners who lived on the less productive hills. The result was that the young working-class men of Roadwater generally had a few spare shillings to spend. The days of the bicycle were yet to come and there were no cheap excursions to town, so that the young souls of our neighbourhood had to be content with such recreations as their own quiet countryside afforded them; the long winter evenings and the rest days between shifts in the mines dragged rather wearily and so some of the steady youngsters began to moot the subject of a brass band. They knew the local tradition of music and were anxious to revive it. There was also quite an influx of the Celtic stock from North Wales and Cornwall – men with their wives and families who had recently settled on Exmoor because of the mining industry – and these with their passionate love for music set our hills and valleys ringing with song. I remember how sometimes in our valley when the wind was in the right direction we used to hear the music of those fine male voice parties floating down the evening breezes from the hills where they were wont to sing after their day's work was done... and the natives caught the enthusiasm.

About a dozen of our men formed a club and paid in their spare shillings every week until the fund was assured. Then a secretary was appointed and the great catalogues from leading houses were sent for and estimates obtained. I was but a little child when this enterprise was launched but I can remember the eager spirits of these would-be bandsmen, and the light of enthusiasm that shone in their eyes, for they held their meetings in the home of my childhood, and since the drum was always my favourite toy as a lad, I too became enamoured of their great idea.

After much anxious consideration the order was given to the house of Butler, Haymarket, London. How these words stamped themselves on my boyhood memory! I hope the honourable firm had due appreciation of the favour we had done them – we at any rate were very conscious of it, for with a man's average wage of 14s. a week, a £100 order was a tall one for us. Once, 30 years after, when in London, the memory of it all came back so vividly that I tramped a good journey to see that shop in the Haymarket. I am afraid the firm's reputation suffered in my esteem, for while I saw many records of noble patronage ('patronised by Royalty', etc) there was no mention of its supply of instruments to the Roadwater Brass Band.

William Gooding, grocer and general dealer, the first of his name in the village. He was the trombonist in Tom Slade's band. His son Arthur and grandson Harold were both organists at St Luke's.

It was not long before there landed outside the shoemaker's shop the bulkiest case that had ever aroused the curiosity of the village. One by one brass instruments were drawn out: cornets with mouthpieces of polished nickel, euphoneums, a trombone and the big bass fellow that wreathed its coils of brass about the body of the young Laocoon who was told off to struggle with it. Then came the drum and the kettledrum and a supply of little music holders to attach to the instruments.

Our village puffed itself out like a strutting turkey-cock at the thought of the figure our band would cut at the coming club-walks of the surrounding villages. How green with envy would Treborough and Withycombe folk be! News of the arrival of the instruments spread like wildfire and our men lost no time in getting home from work that evening. They came bounding in from mine and field and forge to claim their respective 'piece' and what followed that eventful day baffles description. Up and down the valley, morning, noon and night could be heard rising and falling scales, which reminded one of a tipsy man trying in vain to get upstairs, climbing a step at a time so cautiously and succeeding as far as the fourth or fifth step, only to fall again to the bottom one.

It was a nerve-racking business for the villagers for the first few weeks, and as yet there was little promise of those brilliant conquests of which we had proudly dreamt. Then came the simple exercises, a slight improvement on the scales which did afford us some relief... Some would shut themselves up in the garret, fondly dreaming that closed doors and windows would obviate the nuisance. Others would slink off like guilty creatures to some quiet haunt beyond the village, there to wrestle with the mischievous imp, which seemed to baffle their every attempt to master the medium. The hollow of our vale was as a whispering gallery to carry the sound of those brazen instruments and so we had to grin and bear it.

Within a month we heard the strain of 'Bluebells of Scotland' ring out over our valley – with some degree of hesitation. Then the 'Last Rose of Summer' began to bloom rather shyly and within three months the 'Men of Harlech' had invaded our village and were challenging us to all sorts of daring exploits under command of Jim Perkins and his cornet. When Frank Court could play 'Yankee Doodle' with confidence we knew we were getting on. Our main trouble was with the bombardon and the trombone. The rustic mind couldn't follow them, couldn't see what they were driving at. There was no tune at all in them, but just a monotonous bom-pom-pom, bom-pom-pom, ping-pom-ping. Later we learnt how admirably this fitted into the general harmony.

29

Opposite page: *The band on an outing to Cheddar, June 1925. Charles Wingfield Figgis and Tom Ridler are in the front seat.*

Above: The Magic Cup *operetta by Maurice Johnston, performed by members of the choir, teachers and scholars of the mission church Sunday school, 1898.* Soloists, left to right: *Thomas Willis (Mr Fidfad, agitator), Herbert Brewer (Captain Courage), Alice Tuckfield (Fairy Queen), Arthur Gooding (King of Caribee), Alice Sully (Princess Mabel), Frank Risdon (astrologer holding wand). The chorus consisted of soldiers, lifeboatmen and conspirators – quite enterprising for a small village!*

Above: *Leighland carol: a manuscript written by Walter Lile.*

Carol singers, 18 December 1976. Picture includes: *Glyn Court, Harry Horrobin, Douglas Stevens, Mark Court, Torquil Cosgrove, Clare Court, Vivian Gee, Sonia Baker, Elizabeth Cosgrove, Nicola Baker, June King, Philippa Court, Andy King, Derrick Lile, Mr Browning.*

Once some individual proficiency had been reached, arrangements were made for a collective effort and the services of the Minehead bandmaster were requisitioned. By the autumn we had our first band parade. It was not however a show affair but a preliminary canter. The public were not invited, and the scene selected was the brow of one of our steep fields some half a mile up from the village. A simple march movement had been learnt which the band could render with tolerable accuracy, but that was confined to the practice room. Whether they could march to the tune they played, that was as yet an untried experiment, hence the discipline of the open air and the distant field. So to and fro they marched, their instruments flashing in the light of the setting sun and the big drum beating time to the steps. It was a proud moment in the history of the band, a great step forward in the life of our village community. To think that never before since the morning stars sang together had such music wakened the echoes of our solitude! We were indeed making history and many would hear tell of it.

By the following spring the band was literally and metaphorically on its feet; they played at their first public engagement – a temperance fête in Withycombe. As the day drew near the men began to feel they had let themselves in for something. Pride of the smart appearance they hoped to make was tempered with a fear lest their performance should not come up to the required standard. They gave themselves to the practice of their limited repertoire with great assiduity. Evening after evening they paraded on the brow of that field above the village and rehearsals with uniforms were a sight for the gods. The day arrived and our folk assembled to see the march past and give the boys a send off. It was a proud day and the sun shone gloriously. They assembled on the bridge, as smart a band of young hopefuls as ever graced a country scene, and there they gave us the first fruits of their genius, 'Will You Meet Me At The Fountain'. On the third verse they formed fours and quick marched in the direction of the fête. Many admirers followed them, others remained and listened until the strains died away.

It had been agreed that as they came in sight of Withycombe they should strike up a measure and march right onto the scene of action. The idea was to make an immediate impression suited to their dignity. But no one seemed to have remembered that marching right on meant negotiating the ford at the entrance to the village, and by the time they had turned the bend in the road which brought them right upon it, confusion spread. Some broke rank and took in file the narrow footbridge by the side of the ford. Others, led by the bandmaster, pluckily took to the water as if sublimely unconscious of such trifles as running brooks and sloppy feet. This breach of discipline was

vexatious to the diehard section of the band, whose show of bravery did more credit to their courage than to their common sense, and it came perilously near to a discord in more sense than one. After a sharp passage the band re-formed and, on the whole, the first day was a success.

For a considerable period things went well with the band, and they filled many engagements with credit to themselves and Roadwater folk in general; but on the closing down of the mines our countryside became seriously depleted and our young men especially were obliged to seek a livelihood elsewhere. Most of them crossed the Severn to the Welsh coalfields, some migrated to the north of England and others made off to the colonies. Depression settled down on our village life and those who remained had to adapt themselves to the changed circumstances and suffered much impoverishment. To maintain the band was no longer possible; Roadwater Brass Band was a glory departed. A few of the instruments were preserved in our cottage homes; but they cannot give the faintest conception of the romance, the sensation, the glory which the coming of the band brought into the lives of a generation of Roadwater lads. The pageantry of a score of brass instruments, gold braided caps, and the great drum with its many-coloured device heading a procession of garlands and banners borne by the old club-men or Sunday school boys and girls off for their annual treat – that is a pageantry of the past. No more does it move down our Exmoor ways; but memory sees it still, back there in the halcyon days of our lost youth... so much comes back to me with that memory: the pageantry of shady woodland bowers and sunny meadowlands, the light of the setting sun upon those Brendon uplands, the thatched cottages nestled in the valley where swallows came home to nest, and the old familiar faces of those early years with their look of pride as they listened to the music of the band.

After that, Roadwater heard no band music for another 40 years apart from the little groups of itinerant German musicians who showed up from time to time before the First World War and played on the bridge. Then, in 1922 Charles Wingfield Figgis came to live in Vale House. He soon set about reviving the dormant tradition, and with the help of Tom Ridler, the gardener at Treborough Lodge, and a dozen other Roadwater men, created a band that, for smartness of appearance as well as musical ability, probably outclassed any of its predecessors.

Mr Figgis left Roadwater in the early 1930s but the band, led by Tom Ridler, continued with success until 1939. Legend has it that Tom taught each of his ten sons a musical instrument and eight of them played in his band.

Right: Bill for shoe repairs by Thomas Ettery (1819–21) dated just before the one on page 35. Note how customers went on avoiding payment of debts to tradesmen for years at a time. This lasted until at least the 1960s, when supermarkets took over and demanded payment on the nail.

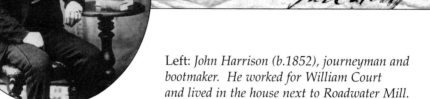

Left: John Harrison (b.1852), journeyman and bootmaker. He worked for William Court and lived in the house next to Roadwater Mill.

George Grinslade (1815–1911) in his forties, c.1860. (PHOTOGRAPH BY JAMES DATE, WATCHET)

Henry Court and sisters, 1855.

Chapter 5

Working Roadwater

Shoemaker Thomas Calloway and his wife Lavinia at the door of their shop, 25 August 1885.

'Working' is the right word, for in the years just before the decline of the 1880s the agricultural and industrial businesses of Roadwater, Leighland, Chidgley, Treborough and Brendon Hill employed 12 farmers and their families (3,500 acres), 80 farm labourers, 3 carters and 3 shepherds; 64 iron-ore miners, 30 slate quarrymen, sawyers, cutters and planers, 6 stonemasons, 2 stationmasters, 9 railwaymen and 6 fitters or drivers of stationary engines. In addition, there were 14 carpenters and a wheelwright, 8 blacksmiths, 5 bootmakers; timber sawyers, lime burners, charcoal burners, 2 road contractors and their men, 4 shopkeepers (drapers and grocers) and 4 publicans. With that, 15 women were dressmakers, 5 were laundresses and 4 schoolmistresses or teachers.

Add to those the minister, rector, banker, slate merchant, landowner, domestic servants, 3 gamekeepers, groom, veterinary surgeon, sculptor, photographer, postmen, licensed hawker, general dealer, stone cracker, baker, butcher, gardener, herbalist, saddlers, tailor and a hotel keeper, the domestic servants and all the busy housewives and children, and you have a mosaic of a society organised to keep the world moving round. The picture does not show the whole truth: it ignores the unemployment and suffering of some farm workers in the dead season. Apart from that, however, it is a society in which nine people out of ten work – and work hard. They have to, in order to stay alive.

To delineate the methods and techniques of the trades and crafts is beyond the scope of this book, and the author has chosen instead to present the work of a few craftsmen whose characters and skill gave them importance in the life of the village: cordwainers and their henchmen, blacksmiths, animal doctors and the photographer – and for good measure, those 'immigrant workers' among us, the artists.

The Cordwainers: Henry (1802-61) and William Court (1847-1929)

The cordwainer in his native plumage was a rare bird in these parts, a worker in kid or goat leather, the best of which reputedly came from Córdoba, so that he made fine footwear, jerkins and such. But even Somerset had cast off leathern upper garments by the nineteenth century, and cordwainers were obliged to concentrate on footwear alone. That

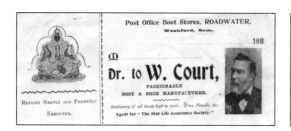

A selection of billheads, 1890–1931.

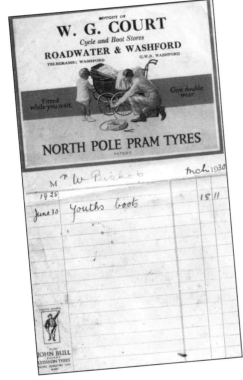

demanded enough variety of workmanship to keep boredom at bay.

If his keeping an old name suggested some slight regret for a lost skill and status, there was nothing backward-looking about Henry Court. His father and grandfather had been bootmakers in Stogumber and Chidgley, but he set his sights on something which would take him out of the old rut and not into a new one. He found a place in gentleman's service, travelled with the family to London and remained there three years, witnessing such wonders as gas light in the streets and the opening of London Bridge. He did indeed go into shoemaking as an 'improver', a workman in employ but also learning the trade; but he soon found that the streets paved with gold had less charm than the green fields of Somerset; at last the longing proved too strong, and he returned home.

By this time in his mid-twenties, he set up in business and soon afterward married his boyhood sweetheart Elizabeth (Eliza) Burge, and settled back into village life. He and Eliza were well matched, with different and complementary personalities, he dignified and rather earnest, Eliza vivacious, with a sunny countenance, sparkling eyes and jet black hair. George Matthews, the miller musician, found them a cottage, and they settled to work.

In a poverty-stricken area orders for new footwear did not crop up every hour, and shoe-makers had more practice in repairing, cobbling and tapping than at their proper trade, as is indicated by a typical annual account sent out by Thomas Ettery, Henry's predecessor, a few years earlier:

1821	*James Langdon, dr* [debtor] *to Thos Ettery*
Mar 12	*Mending Shoes your self – 0s.9d.*
	Mending 3 Shoes for Mary – 1s.2d.
	Hill Taping [sic] *Mending Ss for Ann – 1s.0d.*
Mar 26	*Pair Shoes your Self – 9s.0d.*
June 25	*Pair Shoes for Mary – 6s.3d.*
Aug 20	*Pair Shoes your Wife – 6s.0d.*
Sep 3	*Taping, Mending Shoes yr GranSon – 0s.11d.*
Oct 22	*Pair Shoes for Ann – 6s.0d.*
29	*Taping. Mending your Boy – 1s.3d.*
Nov 3	*Taping Pair Shoes your Self – 2s.8d.*
3	*Pair Shoes your Self – 9s.0d.*

	Thos Ettery
Jun 4	*Settell this Bill – £1.5s.10d.**
	£3.15s.3d.
Apr 22	*Mend S for Mary – 0s.3d.*
	£3.15s.6d.
Apr 30	*Paid £2.10s.0d. Due £1.5s.6d.*

(* Thomas was 27 at this time, and presumably well launched in his work, but this debt had started in 1819 and had been outstanding since 1820.)

It may seem extraordinary that a poor craftsman struggling to make ends meet should allow his customers' debts to pile up for more than a year without 'rendering an account', but he simply knew his customers and knew likewise that to write more often was wasting paper and ink. There was a well-established tradition among the less scrupulous aristocracy and landowners of obtaining goods from tradesmen on credit with manifestly no intention of paying until the tradesman took legal steps. They then settled, but in a huff, abusing the tradesman for his insolence and announcing that all patronage was being withdrawn. This practice among the leaders of society naturally seeped down and contaminated those on the way up, who may have adopted it as a sign that they too had 'arrived'. On the other hand, there is a more charitable explanation – that this was the country, where everyone knew everyone else's business and Tom knew that Jim was having as bad a year as himself and would not be decamping in a hurry; and if enough other customers paid on the nail, he could make do for the time being. (It is worth pointing out, however, that this annual rendering of accounts and failure to settle up was still in full flower or fury in the footwear business in the similarly depressed 1920s and '30s.)

That was the unpromising financial climate in which Henry set up shop, but from his travels and other experience he had acquired certain advantages which fitted him for the extra-vocational role that shoemakers often played in their community. As a class they enjoyed in nineteenth-century village life a reputation to be admired or deplored according to one's view of the world and how it wagged. They were often the central figures of whatever intellectual activity the village enjoyed, the counterparts of the cracker-barrel philosophers of the American small town – but operating, of course, in a society in which democracy on the American scale was unknown. Unlike the labourer and ploughman in the lonely fields, the shoemaker could keep in touch with the current of social life, sluggishly though it may have flowed, and his work gave him time to reflect on news of the outside world that some of his customers brought. His shop became the debating chamber of the village and he himself gained a reputation which made him gravely suspect to the establishment: they deemed him a radical, an atheist or, worst of all, and only to be spelt out in hushed tones, a D-i-s-s-e-n-t-e-r! Henry, in fact, never broke with the Anglican Church in which he had been reared, but he approved of the work of the Bible Christian missioners and their successors, which led to the growth of literacy and the decrease in drunkenness and coarse language.

Two decades after his death his contemporaries recalled him as a credit to his stock. They remem-bered him as a tall man of commanding presence and philosophic turn of mind. He subscribed – the only man in the village to do so – to a 6d. weekly news-paper and collected it from the stagecoach post at Hungerford, and discussed the news with the village witan on Saturday evenings. They did not lack for topics. As each week in the 1820s and '30s added some detail to the catalogue of tyranny abroad and injustice at home, Henry's generous spirit rose in indignation. Despite his interest in politics and world affairs – or perhaps because of it – he was a welcome visitor to the homes of the farmers and landlords around, for no one could suspect him of demagogy. When the mining company laid its railway up through the valley and made Roadwater the railhead, it appointed Henry (who was, by this time, an elected parish constable) as their agent, gave him charge of the station and coal yard and built him a house.

Everyone needed the shoemaker, but that does not mean that his work was enviable. Crouching forward for nine or ten hours a day, six days a week for years on end, bent his back, and when he straightened up to pull the threads, it was not to the full extent, so that after a time he found it difficult to stand erect at the end of a day's work. However, if he reflected on his gathering infirmity, he was probably thankful to have a dry shirt to his back and a roof over his head while the ploughman, whose boots he made, was trudging along the furrows up to 16 or 18 miles a day with only an old sack thrown over his shoulders against the driving rain.

Henry, as a man of enterprise, did not remain long in this rheumatic rut. By dint of dependable work he made a name for himself. Then he went into the adjoining parishes to seek custom, established a clientele and was able at times to employ eight to ten men in his shop, and as his children came into their teens he brought them into the business, his son as an improver and a daughter as a boot-binder. He did his share of the work, too, checked and superintended it, but after his years in the wider world he could not stay chained to the bench. The business, in capable hands, remained buoyant even in these hard times, for footwear was the one item nobody could do without. People may have been ill-fed and ill-housed, wearing the same patched and threadbare work clothes for 20 years, but they must be shod; indeed, it was not unknown for a more compassionate farmer to buy a pair for his ploughman at Christmas. The cordwainer might have to wait for payment, but it was generally settled in the end, and money kept its value in the meantime.

If Henry had learnt 'fancy' work in London, he had little scope for it here. Plain, good and hard-wearing – that was how the labourers and their families wanted their boots, and if the trading families looked for a finer leather for their Sunday footwear, the qualities required were still the same. Some of the leather was produced locally, at Linton, near Old Cleeve, and Porlock, but other consignments came by sea from Bristol to Watchet and were then brought home in a dog-cart drawn by a huge mastiff. Every boot or shoe was made to measure. The customer set his foot on a piece of brown paper, the shoemaker drew round it and then took another piece of paper and moulded the shape of the vamp and instep, taking care to allow for erratic bumps and bunions. His real skill came later when cutting the upper and sole from bends of leather with as little waste as possible, shaping the pliable leather of the upper and calculating the extra amount needed for sewing it to the sole. With this came the test of his dependable workmanship, for the boot had to be made watertight – at least, proof against ground water – without the use of any of the modern man-made materials.

The late 1850s, with the iron ore mines and railway, brought the outside world, new interests and opportunities into the valley. Henry died a victim of pneumonia without being able to profit from them, but the way in which the next generation, as represented by his son William, responded to them has an interest which goes far beyond the individual. Some, recognising that the opportunities, though welcome, would not lead to wealth or fame in this rural district, chose to move to a city or overseas: the Thomas brothers of Woolston, Bicknoller, became wealthy clothiers in Bristol; William Vickery from Stogumber, became known in Canada as 'the Poet of the Prairies'; and Martin Langdon, from Roadwater, became a Member of the State Parliament and Minister for Agriculture in South Australia. Others, however, judging that whatever else they might find, Somerset was too good to lose, stayed on here and found outlets for their energy in engineering, as did the Nethercotts, in estate management and legal work, as with the Risdons from Golsoncott, or as with William Court, who created for himself a judicious arrangement of work to give him a modest income and the time for involvement in a number of causes which concerned him greatly.

His elder brother moved to Wales when their father died, and William, aged 13, the youngest child, had to support his mother and a nephew. He had already interested the mining company by trying to stop a runaway truck (see page 54), and they took him on as a fitter in their works in Ebbw Vale. He moved there with his mother but she pined for Somerset, so after 18 months he brought her home and re-established the business. In a very few years it was sound enough for him to put his energy into other fields. At 16 he became a local or lay preacher with the Bible

William Court with his pony, Dapper, on Dapper's 30th birthday.

Christians and continued with them for 65 years, riding Sunday by Sunday over Brendon Hill and Exmoor as far as Bury, Dulverton and Luckwell Bridge on a succession of white ponies, all called Dapper. For 35 of those years he managed the finances of the circuit and travelled widely for conferences.

At the age of 20 he founded a lodge of a temperance association, the Good Templars, organised and led meetings, lectures and entertainments, and persuaded Sir Walter Trevelyan to build them a hall which remained in constant use for meetings, concerts and social gatherings for 70 years. For some events 200 or more people would crowd in, by no means all of them abstainers, for the enjoyment to be had was known throughout the valley.

Change and opportunity were nowhere more evident than in political life. At the time of the Reform Bill of 1832 the few Roadwater householders with the vote had used it pretty solidly for the more progressive of the candidates, but for 30 years more very few of the men – and none of the women – had a say in the matter. Then 1860 brought a change. Early in the decade William, with millions of other Britons, had revelled in the heroic romance of Garibaldi and the liberation of Italy, and they thrilled to the knowledge that the Great Liberator was a man of the people, not an aristocrat by birth. Now, with the passage of the (Electoral) Reform Act in 1867, all could see that a 'new political age had dawned' and young men threw themselves into the struggle for yet more reform until the Election Act of 1883 gave the vote to farm workers and completed the process – at least for adult males.

Election times found William chairing meetings in a crowded Temperance Hall or canvassing farms where his own Liberal views met with equally determined Conservative opposition. One dark night, he rode out on Dapper to try his eloquence on Farmer Widden (not his real name). He tethered Dapper in the court and went in for a chat or wrestle, whichever it might be. As half expected, Widden would not budge an inch, but just as William rose to go, the farmer's sons clattered in, grinning broadly and guffawing 'fit to bust'. William forbore to ask the joke, but left, mounted Dapper and rode home. Then, as he lit the lantern to give the pony a rub down, the joke became clear. In an effort to turn Dapper into a true Tory pony, the boys had daubed him all over with a blue-bag from head to hoof.

Maintaining the line, William's son William George also became a lay preacher and speaker on Liberal platforms, but he adapted to change – first a skilled and ingenious carpenter and then a postmaster and storekeeper who provided the young men and women with the bicycle which widened their horizons and outlook on the world. His son, author of this book, lacked most of his father's manual skill, but also became a lay preacher, specialised in music and modern languages and

became the first Liberal member and committee chairman on Somerset County Council.

The Cobbler: Robert Ettery

Even the best-made and hardest-wearing boots come to a time when the soles cry out for attention, refurbishment or repair, and that was Bob Ettery's work. Hardship and labour had crippled his body, but had left his spirit untouched. He was 'a little round-faced, merry-looking man who had been so long bent over his lapstone that the back of him was bent hopelessly'; but he had a claim to dignity and a modest local celebrity, for he played first violin in George Matthews' Leighland band. In the 1880s he was the only one of the players remaining. Lewis Court recalled that:

> ... he had outlived most of his generation and his voice was hoarse and his legs tottered under him, but poverty kept him at work till nearly the very end. Yet even in old age he would sing in his husky, jerky voice the ditties he had learnt in his youth.

Sometimes in the evening the lads could hear him 'scraping away at his old violin which was as jerky as its master's voice.' His songs sprang up out of a happy, bubbling spirit that poverty, decrepitude, old age even, could not keep down; it seems he sang at his bench because he found genuine pleasure in his work. And why not? For some minds, creating is the supreme pleasure, but not everyone aims so high, and without pressing it too far, one may see an analogy between the artisan team of cordwainer and cobbler and that of composer and the instrumentalist who interprets and recreates. All make something new, and take delight in the making.

So it would have been with Bob Ettery. Work filled most of the hours of daylight, but that was normal, and he was happier than millions a century later in that as long as his skill and sight held out he need not fear unemployment. Besides that, he was spared the dreadful sense of futility imposed by the unending repetitions of the production line, for no two pairs of shoes or boots that came to him were worn down in the same way. All needed inspection and thought before he could set them to rights.

If they only lacked a few hobnails, the trick was soon done, but to re-sole took care and preparation, and for a thorough job the heel was removed and the whole sole restored. The author remembers from his youth in his father's workshop, all that was removed and replaced was the front as far back as the instep. The stages were as follows:

Cut out a pattern of the sole in cardboard; use it to cut out a new sole as economically as possible – economy guided the eye, not only because generations of craftsmen counselled economy, and the word 'waste' had 'wicked' nailed in front of it. Soak the new sole in water for 30 minutes. While waiting, cut off the old one, and finish off other work. Take out the new sole, bevel the straight end under the instep, lay the sole face down on the slightly concave lapstone and hammer it out to the curve of the foot. Place the boot on the last and tack on the sole with sprigs or, for an especially stout repair, sow with thread coated in beeswax. Nail on the tips and hobnails and replace the cues. Trim the edges with a knife and rasp, dye them and smooth and burnish them with a heated shaping iron. Apply dubbin to all the joins, and the boot is good for another year.

It may sound a humdrum business when repeated year in year out, but within its limits it gave the reward of endless variety for a man with skill.

The Shoemaker's Apprentice: Jim Thresher

On the other hand, a number of people had caught on quite early to the idea that while hard work might bring success, equally it might not and should be kept in its place. The world held greater pleasures than punishing leather, and a life that was all work would turn every man into the dullest of dull dogs. That is not to say that they scamped their work, but when it was over for the day the 'prentice boys would enjoy their cakes and ale.

They were, by all accounts, a lively crew. One of them, Jim Thresher, was a keen, resourceful lad well up in all kinds of larks, the riskier the better. A born leader, he took the others into many scrapes and then safely out again, and for some years they kept night life from growing stagnant, and in the morning the old folk, shaking their heads, would say, 'Ah! they shoemaking chaps have bin at it agen.' The pranks sometimes amused and sometimes annoyed them, but they agreed that the mischief was never destructive nor held the slightest touch of malice. Besides, Jim and his mates worked in complete silence, so that no one knew of their carryings-on until they were, so to speak, carried.

Farmer Henry Coles lived at Glasses Farm and John Hill at Roadwater Farm, three-quarters of a mile away, and they met only occasionally. However, one morning Coles came down to find that his heavy five-bar farmyard gate had been exchanged for one from Roadwater Farm, and Hill found his gate was that of Glasses Farm, yet the exchange had been made without a soul in the village being aware of it. Sometimes, too, the farm tools left for repair in the yard of the smithy were moved far away, but again so quietly that the culprits were never caught.

Another morning, when the apprentices' master came down to open up, he found a load of turnips had been carted from a field and unloaded against his door, and once a neighbour opened his door to find a row of pea-sticks blocking the entrance.

The lads used their brains. One year, not long before Christmas, another of the apprentices, Ted, was sent at the end of the day's work to deliver a sack of boots to Chapel Cleeve. He objected, but orders were orders and he set off, in no mood for a stumble in the dark and saying to himself, 'I know a lark worth two of this'. In a field near the bottom of the village an old horse was quietly grazing. Ted found a halter behind the gate, placed it on the horse, rode to Chapel Cleeve, delivered the boots and rode back again. But on his return, instead of putting the horse back into the field he rode to the farmhouse and knocked on the door. The farmer came out. 'Oh Mr Langdon', said Ted, all innocence, 'is this your 'oss? I found un strayin' on the highway, 'sknow, so I reckoned I'd best bring en in an' see if he were your 'oss or not.' 'Oh aye, he's mine, for sure', said the farmer, 'an' 'tis very good of 'ee to bring en back, boy. Zo come on een an' have a drop o' zider, wull 'e?'

Strangely enough, it was on an errand to the same destination at the same time of year that Jim was sent with another apprentice. Passing along the park drive they came across a flock of turkeys plump for the Christmas market. Without thinking – unusual for him – Jim aimed his walking-stick at the flock and knocked one of the gobblers to the ground, where it lay, apparently lifeless. 'My, we'll be for it now, Jim', said his friend and, scared by what he had done, they put the bird in the bag and went on up to the manor-house. Having delivered the boots they were waiting in the porch for the customary glass of cider when the turkey, which had only been stunned, came round and gobbled lustily at his imprisonment. Shades of the prison-house began to close about the apprentices. In desperation Jim thrust his hand into the bag and strangled the bird, but his face as he drank the cider was unusually pale. In due course they shared out the turkey with the others, but no one was so impolite or unwise as to ask where it had come from.

The Blacksmiths

Thomas Slade and Nathanael and George Edbrooke

All we thought was, that for us old ancient singers to be choked off quiet at no time in particular, as now, in the Sundays after Easter, would seem rather mean in the eyes of other parishes, sir. But if we fell glorious with a bit of a flourish at Christmas, we should have a respectable end, and not dwindle away in some nameless paltry second-Sunday-after or Sunday-next-before-something, that's got no name of its own.

It was not much that tranter Dewy asked from Mr Maybold for the quire, but it was the most they were likely to be allowed, and no one knows in how many vicarages the same unhappy scene was played out before the old quire was banished from the west gallery and the 'box o' whistles' set up in its place. From a narrowly aesthetic point of view the vicar may have been right, but as a man supposedly with a care for the happiness of his parishioners he was woefully wrong.

As we have seen, bandmaster George Matthews did not long survive the dispersal of his players, for it must have seemed to him that real, manly, full-blooded music had passed away. However, a resurrection of that music was at hand, led by a man whose skill as an instrumental player and leader, if not as a composer, was equal to George Matthews' own.

Tom Slade was born in the village in 1831 as the eldest of possibly ten children. His father, John Slade, was a farm labourer, but the rheumatics that crippled those men exposed to all weathers with no water-proof clothing had attacked him early and he was forced to apply for parish assis-tance. The overseers of the poor set him to sitting by the roadside – still in all weathers and virtually unprotected – to crack a yard of stone for road metalling for little more than 1s. a day. (Some of those cracking-bays can be seen even now – for example on the A39 at Halscombe between Washford and Dragon Cross. A line of bricks in the wall shows the height to which a 'yard of stone' was piled for cracking). It was an occupation for which the skill, though elusive at first, was quickly learnt and became automatic, so that the employment offered neither hope nor exercise for the mind. (Readers may remember how Richard Hannay, in *The Thirty-Nine Steps*, takes over the roadmender's work to deceive his pursuers, tries to think as the roadmender would, and finds that his mind is dead to thought.)

When a travelling preacher arrived he spoke to John Slade and he lifted his eyes from the dark cave of his toil to the hills of hope. Slade opened his house to the preacher for services – the first in the

Fred Blackwell (b.1853), blacksmith, and his wife Mary (b.1856) lived at Sellick's Green.

village to do so – and gradually, as his sons came of working age, the fortunes of the family improved and he was able to have some of them bound as apprentices.

Young Tom was probably about ten when the blacksmith took him on, and he had to look forward to seven years of work and learning, twelve hours a day, six days a week, but any trade or craft which offered the chance of a wage to match with the skill and hard work was seen as a rung up the ladder. All that the lad learnt to start with was to sweep the floor of the forge, fetch water from the stream, work the bellows to create a good body of heat first thing in the morning, and avoid a beating when he could. Then after a few months he was given a thin strip of metal and set to his first real task: making dozens of brads, the long, flat, round-headed nails used in all country timber work and always made locally.

After rigorous, if informal, training he became a master of his craft and forged his masterpiece – it may have been a church gate, or perhaps a harrow, but no one asked him in later years. He was a journeyman, free to work by the day and keep his earnings. But Tom had further ambitions – indeed, he intended to marry, save his money, and learn a musical instrument; he accomplished all three.

In the Slades there ran a vein of music, and although it may not have surfaced before, it ran strongly in Tom and his brother William, in Tom's son, Jim, an able organist, violinist, conductor and concert arranger, and has continued to the present day. Both Tom and his brother set their hearts on the instrument which formed the backbone of the church orchestra, the bass viol, or cello, the 'queen' of instruments because it would play both melody and harmony. So Tom put together enough from his meagre earnings,

The forge is open for business, but Tom Slade is taking his ease, hands in pockets, with his wife Eliza, son Jim, and shoemaker Tom Calloway from over the road.

Tom Slade (1831–1907), blacksmith, cellist, band- and choir master in the Bible Christian chapel.

set off early one morning and walked the 20 hilly miles to Taunton, bought the cello, strapped it, in its case, on his back, walked home again in the same afternoon and put in two or three hours in the forge to show his scorn for weariness.

This must have been about the time that the church band was dismissed. Tom may not have played in it, but he was determined not to let its music die away. He got the musicians together, and under their new leader the old tradition of the 'waits' continued long after it had lapsed nearly everywhere else. In the previous decade the Bible Christian chapel had twice been enlarged to take increasing congregations, and now a gallery had been added. Tom transferred his players there, they played for the Sunday services and the boys down below watched eagerly to see the slides of the two trombones thrust out and drawn back for all the world like the pistons of the locomotives on the mineral railway at the end of Station Road.

His son's best friend looked back, 40 years on, and remembered Tom in the prime of life:

He was a man of medium height and strong build, with a good head and pleasing features. His eyes were some-what soft and dreamy, but capable of a fierce glance under strong moods. His ears were finely shaped, and so set as to be on the qui vive *for harmonious sounds. His mouth bespoke firmness and a natural refinement. He had, as becomes a smith, good muscular arms, 'strong as iron bands', but with hands quite the reverse, hands beautifully shaped, with finely-tapered fingers – such hands as could have done credit to any gentleman of quality. They were more in keeping with the slender neck of his cello than with the sledgehammer and the forge. And here, in this strange combination of physical parts, was a true index to the man's temperamental complexity. Strength and weakness, storm and calm, had got mixed up in him. His finer sensibilities were at war with the elemental passions of his nature. He could soar and swoop; flare at you and as quickly forgive; so there was a petulance in his make-up which trivial faults would set on fire. But however ruffled he might be, all that was untamed in him would capitulate in a moment to the strains of music.*

To him music was indeed Queen of all the Arts: he worshipped her; and she, in turn, cast a golden spell upon his otherwise arduous and unromantic life. It was great reward for his devotion that he was able, in his later years, to sit in his own little village parlour and listen to the choicest themes of the great masters being worthily interpreted by his own son, who became a gifted musician.

It must be noted, however, that while Tom Slade and his musicians kept up the old tradition of music making with instruments from all the families (string, brass or woodwind), others, who were perhaps spurred to emulate him but wary of his unpredictable

moods, were caught up in the spreading brass band movement; their story can be found in Chapter 4.

Thomas was rightly proud of his band, and as determined as George Matthews had been for the men to achieve the best of which they were capable. He was not a humourless man, but his upbringing had given him a vein of sternness and he was something of a disciplinarian with his musicians. He prized the traditions of Christmas and the old carols above everything else. As the season approached he rehearsed them, and year by year, late on Christmas Eve, a little before midnight, when the village had retired to rest, the band would come along the street with its instruments and enter the warmth of the parlour at Tom's smithy for cordials and cakes. The band would then set off in a happy group for the first call, the Elizabethan farmhouse half a mile up the valley. Talk and laughter drove away the cold, but as the men neared the farm Tom called for silence. He knew how precious a part of great music is silence, but beyond that, as a man of deep emotion, he felt – though he could not have put it into words – that while speech was man's distinctive attribute, music was divine and the music to usher in the day of days must be accorded full reverence and honour. He believed the sleepers must be awakened not by idle laughter, like the crackling of thorns under a pot but by a noble harmony, a 'concord of sweet sounds'. So they gathered around the door, Tom counted four beats, the instruments sounded the great G major chord and in measured stentorian tones he announced the first carol: 'Mortals – awake! – Rejoice and sing, The glories – of your heav'nly – King.' The notes rang out and presently a candle glimmered in a bedroom window, and as the carol ended the door opened and the farmer's wife invited them in for refreshment, mulled cider or hot peppermint or ginger ale and cakes. Then they would go to the next farm or mill and repeat the performance with 'Angels from the realms of glory' or 'Hark! Hear what news the angels bring!' or 'Awake, your grateful voices raise!'.

They would continue like this until three o'clock in the morning, when they returned to the bridge in the middle of the village to play in the holy day with: 'Behold! once more the day is come, The great and glorious morn!, Let every tongue on earth rejoice, For Christ the Lord is born.'

'And what could ever be more entrancing', wrote Lewis Court, who heard it every year as a boy:

... than to be awakened by the strains of Christmas music stealing in upon one through the silence of the night, or on the clean air of a frosty morning! The deep, full tones of the bass viol, the celestial notes of the clarinet, the suave, appealing plaint of the flute, and the blend of good human voices.

In the morning the musicians played again at the village chapel, but after Old Christmas Day, 6

January, no more carols were heard until the season came round again. This was because Tom, along with many village musicians, held firmly that everything had its due season, and a Christmas carol out of its proper time was an overturning of the universal order that they could not abide. It therefore seems strangely fitting that Tom Slade died on Boxing Day 1907, in that season whose tradition of music he had done more than anyone to preserve.

The three blacksmiths lived and worked within sound of one another; Tom Slade in the main street 20 yards below the bridge, Nathanael Edbrooke the same distance down Station Road, and his brother George on the other side of the railway and the river, in the adjoining parish but still in the village. A third brother, Richard Edbrooke, was also a blacksmith but lived two miles away on the eastern edge of the parish and so does not come into this story.

The Edbrookes had originated as a family in a farm of that name overlooking the Exe valley about three or four hours' walk away, but they had been resident in this neighbourhood for several generations. Nathanael's portrait, taken in his early fifties, shows him as a man of impressive presence, tall and well-built, with only the slightest detectable stoop from his long hours over the anvil in the forge. The picture reveals a large head with unusually long features, high brow, clear, level eyes, strong nose, firm but kindly mouth above a round chin, the face framed in a ruff of white whiskers and the whole crowned with a shock of iron-grey hair parted on the left and neatly brushed – all of which suggests a man of firm will but contented mind and ready to give service when called on. Besides that, the expressions and dresses of his wife and daughters, and the gold watch and chain in his waistcoat pocket, speak of loved and loving husband and father, generous with what he earned.

If a blacksmith did not learn to be ingenious and inventive, he would not last long. If he could not make an effective new device to order, his customer would go elsewhere. Farriery and shoeing would have formed the backbone of Nathanael's business, but he had to be able to make any of the hundred tools in daily use on the farm or in the garden, such as ploughshares, coulters, prongs, rakes, mattocks, bizgies and two-bills, spades, forks and grubbers, hooks, boot irons, potato planters, slate knives and cleavers for the quarry, iron gates and railings, hapses and door hinge-bands for churches or great houses. From time to time a man would come in with an order for a specific implement for a particular job – in which case the smith would have to summon up his ingenuity and produce a nameless tool, never seen before but for which the customer would cry aloud 'Why, 'tis the very thing!'

Even with this variety it is doubtful whether Nathanael ever received a stranger request than one made by 'animal doctor', John Bond, around 1870.

During 20 years in the neighbourhood Bond had built up a considerable practice which took him to beyond Taunton (20 miles) in one direction and on to Exmoor in the other. This involved long days, tiring riding or walking, and probably nights away from home. It is possible that he saw the solution to his problem either in the weekly newspaper or in the recently founded *West Somerset Free Press;* indeed, one imagines that he came into the smithy holding a piece of paper and enquiring, 'Do 'ee think you could make me one o' these machines, Natty?' whereupon, no doubt 'Natty' pursed his lips, said 'I'll must think about it. Leave the paper'. A short time later John Bond pedalled away on his Roadwater-made bicycle. Here was progress unmistakable, with John Bond at the head, for it was only as recently as 1867, when pedals were attached to the front wheel of a velocipede, that the cycling 'craze' had begun.

Such contraptions were commonly called 'boneshakers' but John Bond's was a solid, dependable affair, the product of our rural society, able to endure hardness and offering no concessions to the weak of spirit or body. The frame, a one-inch tubular S-bar, carried a projecting horn for the saddle and a simple step. The front forks were of hammered iron, and their shaft passed through a straight handlebar and was secured by a heavy bolt. The handlebar was gently tapered at both ends. The front wheel was moderately high – about 4 feet 6 inches – with the hub and spokes made of oak and felloes of ash, all bound and kept firm by a half-inch iron tyre shrunk onto the wheel. All the wooden parts, including handlegrips and pedals, were almost certainly the work of the wheelwright, Thomas Popham. The 12-inch rear wheel was more sophisticated and bound with a grooved rim which probably carried a wooden tyre. And what of brakes? No need for those if the rider had a stout pair of hobnail boots to hold against the tyre.

Nathanael Edbrooke
with wife and daughters, 1875.

Besides, it had been found that applying a 'spoon' brake to the front wheel sent the rider over the handlebars like a cannon-ball. The keynote of the machine was simplicity. As for response to handling and ease of control, the plan took no account of such namby-pamberies – that was the rider's responsibility, not the smith's!

One casual employment of a village smith demanded no training, no specialised knowledge, no particular skill in technique, simply a steady hand and an iron nerve. He was a dental surgeon.

The incidents and treatments related to the author and repeated here may sound more like rural myths than true accounts of what actually happened, but knowing the utter truthfulness of his informants, the author believes that any exaggeration was involuntary and slight. The treatments showed, in the operator, a brutal directness having more in common with the Middle Ages than with Victorian England and in his patient a desperate stoicism, attributes both quite alien to us today.

Since 1945 the coming of the National Health Service and many improvements in the technique of dental surgery have, for most people, removed much of the anxiety with which they used to anticipate a visit to the dentist. However, within living memory, it was a service, or luxury, that millions of people either could not afford or simply could not face until the toothache or neuralgia became completely unbearable. At that stage, very many people, when offered the choice between a filling and an extraction, often chose the latter, and when false teeth became readily available, they had a full set in their twenties.

In the Victorian village none of these improvements were available. It is commonly thought that rampant tooth decay is a particularly modern condition arising from too much sugar and too little cleaning, but that is far from the truth. The results of a bad diet and neglect – bad teeth, inflamed gums and pyorrhoea – were probably even more prevalent 150 years ago than now. Toothbrushes and toothpaste were unknown in cottage homes; at best the children were made to clean their teeth with a hazel twig, more often nothing was done. If a cottager's teeth decayed in childhood or adolescence, he or she had to go through life with an ugly mouth. (Perhaps the rather grim expressions with which family groups faced the camera came from some of them having bad teeth which they did not want to reveal to posterity.) Be that as it may, a cottager – call him Old Bob – with a tooth at the end of its tether and not a spare half-crown to his name, did not trudge to town, he went to the forge. The smith, sizing him up and the tooth likewise, either let him choose one of three painful methods or none at all.

The first method, the practical one, involved thrusting – 'ramming' might be a better word – Bob down on to a stool, clamping his head with one arm and holding down his jaw with powerful fingers, taking a firm grip of the tooth with pliers and trying a sudden, powerful yank. If that did not work, the smith would just pull until the tooth came out. No anaesthetics, no half-bottle of whisky, not even a mallet on the head. (What happened if the tooth merely broke off it is as well not to consider.)

The second method, the artistic or wily one, does not seem to have been used in Roadwater but was vouched for by a farmer in the hill country, so with some reservation it is recorded here. In brief, the smith would tie one end of a length of cord around his patient's tooth and the other end to a door handle and slam the door. (How a cord could be fastened around a rotten tooth was not explained – presumably thin wire was used at that point.)

Roadwater favoured the third method, the psychological and co-operative. The smith fastened the cord around the tooth and the door handle or something else firm, so that it was taut. Then, without warning, he took a red-hot iron from the fire and thrust it within a few inches of Old Bob's face. Bob sprang back horror-struck, but his bad tooth was out; he had, in a fashion, pulled it out himself.

With such examples, it is not difficult to visualise how the smith and a cold chisel at Cutcombe got rid of incipient gangrene in a patient's finger.

The third forge, that of George Edbrooke, stood just beyond the eastern stream, a few yards above the confluence. It had disappeared by the 1870s before anyone had the leisure or inclination to sketch it, but at mid-century it was operating in a special way, under the title of blade mill. George, as a bladesmith, specialised in the making of edged tools – scythes, sickles, staff hooks, billhooks, dung knives, cleavers, axes, hatchets, choppers, adzes, spokeshaves, chisels, and heavier items such as ploughshares, mould boards and coulters.

To some extent the smiths duplicated one another's work. George, for instance, made a splendid pair of wrought-iron gates for the Parish Church which bear his name to this day. However, the edged tools won him his reputation. It seems their excellence came from superior mild steel or from the higher temperatures achieved before tempering, for George had a mechanical aid equal to another pair of hands. His forge had water-power from a leat drawn off the stream nearly a mile up the valley – its course can still be traced – and it turned a wheel which drove a trip-hammer and probably a fan to create a miniature blast-furnace effect. Any of the tools, if well honed and kept free from rust, would outlast a workman and his children's children. Many of them, stamped clearly with his name in bold capitals, were still being used in the district for generations after his death. Indeed, when clearing out a woodshed in the 1960s the author found a sickle stamped 'GEORGE EDBROOKE'. It had been used regularly for a good 100 years and still carried a good edge, fit for heavy work or light.

Most of the edged tools were sharpened by the

Above: *By 1917 so many men had been killed in the fields of Northern France that Portuguese forestry workers were brought in to work at Drucombe. The foreman (hatless, three from the right) is the artist J. Carruthers Gould.*

Frank Williams, saddler and harness maker, chats with a neighbour outside his cottage on the bridge, while Mrs Williams holds the baby. Reins and bridles, horse collars and hames are displayed, all the skill of the harness-maker's craft.

Above: *In Venn Wood, 1919. Sawing with the old cross-cut. Left to right: Portuguese woodman, J. Carruthers Gould, William Burgess.*

Below: *Frank Williams, his son and the policeman from Washford, c.1900. The fourth character is probably Henry Voss.*

Below: *The butcher's boy from Williton stops to breathe his horse outside the saddlery.*

workmen with an emery stone or on a grinding-wheel, but a few, such as the coulter or the ploughshare, when dented by repeated collision with rocks under the soil, had to be brought back to the mill for re-working. That requirement lay at the root of a strange and tragic happening which took place a little earlier than George Edbrooke's time, but the superstition – a firm belief in the physical existence of the Devil – which drove a man to violent crime still burdened the minds of many men, women and children until much later.

Local lore has it that at early twilight or 'dimpsy' three young ploughboys from Rodhuish – more properly 'Roddish' or 'Urdish' – were at the smithy. Their names have not been preserved but with Tom, Bob and Billy we shall not go far wrong for the purposes of the story. Two of them were having their horses shod, while the other had brought a coulter to be lined and sharpened. There was no light in the smithy other than the blacksmith's fire, and it cast an eerie glow on the four faces and dim, distorted shadows on the grimy walls around. As the evening closed in, Tom and Bob began to play on the younger one's superstitious mind:

Have 'ee heard the Devil's out on Urdish 'Ill? Aye, er is, you, horns an' hooves an' all. He'll be on the look-out fer 'ee, Billy boy. Mind thee dissn' let en get 'is claws in 'ee. 'Tis a wisht poor time o' night fer goin' up dru dhick 'ood, 'snow, wi' Ole Nick layin' fer 'ee. Best watch out, or he'll 'have 'ee, bwoy.

They rode off, leaving Billy to start his homeward trek in no happy state of mind. Presently the other two separated, Bob to his place of work, Tom to a cart-linhay where he had seen a bullock's hide hanging up to dry. He picked it up and carried it to a gateway on the path through which Billy was bound to pass. Then he put the hide over his head with the horns facing upward and outward, and sat on the gate facing his victim's approach.

Billy's nerves had had a hard time of it in the wood. The path in the lower part led alongside a deep ravine, and a false step in the deepening gloom would have sent him tumbling 20 feet. He was literally not out of the wood yet, and though he hummed a song to keep his spirits up his heart beat faster as the unearthly figure on the gate loomed before him. He stepped back, grasped the coulter firmly with both hands and challenged the figure: 'Be 'ee the Devil or bean't 'ee?' Only a groan came as an answer. Again he cried, 'Be 'ee the Devil or bean't 'ee?' Again only a groan or a growl came in reply. Billy took a pace forward, raised the coulter above his head, and yelled his question in desperation, but the 'Devil', his face hidden inside the skin, could not see the imminent danger. Billy brought the coulter down on the 'Devil's' skull and split it asunder, causing him to fall backwards off the gate, stone dead.

Billy fled down through the woods back to the smithy where he sobbed out the tale of his encounter with the Devil. Records show that in due course he was tried for manslaughter, but it seems that his extreme simplicity and conviction at the time of the deed saved him from the 'extreme penalty of the law'. No doubt it was well for his peace of mind that right up to the end of his 98-year life, despite all the evidence, he believed that he really had killed the Devil on Roddish Hill.

The Animal Doctors

William, John and Fred Inkerman Bond

Even the best families can gain from an infusion of new blood, and so can the best of counties. Both Devon and Somerset have been enriched by cross-border marriages, and at some time in the 1840s Roadwater gained a character whose originality and enterprise gained him a lasting fame. William Andrews Bond was born in Axminster in 1809 and was in the prime of vigour when he came to Somerset. In the census of 1851 and in the Bible Christian register of the baptisms of his sons he is variously described as 'doctor', 'herb doctor' and 'medicine vendor'. None of these descriptions quite fits the bill, because he not only worked as a veterinary surgeon, he also made and dispensed his own remedies, and wrote down some of the 'receipts' for the benefit of the sons who would follow him in the profession.

William's eldest son John (b.1851) was looking for work in the 1860s. There was no question of his taking over the animal doctoring while his father was still active, so to give him a second string to his bow he was apprenticed to a carpenter. In time, however, William retired and John took over. Around 1870 the blacksmith made John a bicycle to order, a majestic machine and the very first of its kind in the neighbourhood. This put John Bond in the forefront of progress and with this ultra-modern mount new horizons opened up before him. The radius of 15 or 20 miles possible by pony could be doubled; he toured all over the district, including Taunton and beyond. He even made periodical visits to Devon and Cornwall. Now he was widely accepted as 'Dr' Bond, and a resplendent top hat made his status clear to all. He travelled everywhere in this headgear and frock coat administering herbal remedies to man and beast. When it was not being used professionally, his boys kept the bicycle wheels turning merrily and it remained much more than a nine-day wonder.

Dr Bond's nephew recounted one such incident:

I can mind father telling me about a time they were up Mount Lane [a steep hill with a hairpin bend]. There were three of them up on the old penny-farthing: father on the seat, another boy on the step behind him, and another sat on the handlebars playing a concertina.

They came down the hill fine and picked up speed, but it was a rough old lane in they days, and at the bottom the front wheel hit against a great stone. I can tell you they got off a sight faster than they got on!

Both Dr John Bond and, surprisingly, his father before him appreciated the developing craft of publicity. They realised that if you want your trumpet to draw a crowd, you had best compose a rousing fanfare, so when William went on his rounds he sent in advance a leaflet adorned with the royal coat of arms and headed: 'CONSOLATION TO THE AFFLICTED'. He told his public that 'these HERB MEDICINES are acknowledged to do all that is required to conquer disease and PRESERVE HEALTH!' and that:

Mr Wm A. Bond, Licensed Vendor of Medicines, from ROADWATER, begs leave to apprise the afflicted, that he continues to devote his attention to the cure of the diseases to which the human frame is susceptible. No person need fear taking these medicines, as they are entirely free from mercury, being prepared from herbs, nuts, oils and barks, from which preparation the patient is not liable to take cold...

He reinforced the claim by a lofty claim:

The herb bloometh in obscurity, withereth, dyeth and is forgotten, but for thee, O Man!, was it created, and flourished for thy service.

Fine words for the Bonds and their like, but such sentiments were wasted on hard-headed Somerset farmers who ate their parsnips unbuttered. For them William Bond tried the confidential approach:

You say Bond's Oils are very good,
In strength and virtue too:
And here we candidly admit
We quite agree with you!

To avoid the disbelief that always greets self-praise, he claimed the patronage of a score of JPs, landowners and farmers from as far afield as Nailsbourne, nearly 20 miles east, and Clayhanger, almost as far south. He certainly would not have dared this if the manifold:

... inflammations or Bruises of Ewes in Lamming, Swelled Udders... Blows from a Stick or Whip in a Horse's or Bullock's eyes... Broken Knees, Stubs in

Horses' feet in Racing or Hunting... Inflammation, or Navel gall, in Lambs, shortly after dropping...

had defied the curative powers of Bond & Sons' Universal Somerset Oils. William also warned his public against:

... bold, ignorant and unprincipled Quacks, travelling through the Country with Oils of no merit, representing them to be the same as Bond & Son's... but cheaper. This insidious and unseemly practice, is intended to entice the unwary into their treacherous Nets; but Bond & Son feel assured that from the extensive knowledge they have of the Spirit of the Gentry and Agriculturalists of West Somerset and part Devon, that they will not allow themselves to be entrapped by these Purloiners of other Men's Rights. Nor will they be Parties to support a Practice so base and dishonourable.

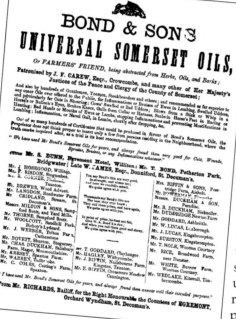

Whatever the scourge, Bond & Sons had the cure: for nervous and bilious complaints ('ask Mrs Thorn, of Taunton') or for rheumatism, as certified by Mr Joseph Court, of Exford, who had been 'unable to walk without crutches but, by using only two bottles and one box of pills, has been cured in a fortnight and can now walk without a crutch or stick.' The oils were evidently meant for external use and other medicines for internal use or for use on cattle. However, some of the hill-country farmers used the products on their animals rather warily. They might be persuaded to buy a bottle at 2s.6d., 3s.6d., 5s. or even 10s. as advertised; they might risk their money, but not their cattle. They waited until the missus or another of the womenfolk was 'took' with a 'dizzy spell or sudden qualms, faintness or fit' and then administered the dose with grave attention. If no harm came of it, they could safely use it for the beasts in the stall.

It pointed to a change in the rural scene when Dr Bond senr, who had earned a living by combining traditional country lore, intelligence, initiative and energy, realised that this would no longer do for the coming age; something official and certificated was required. The old herbalists would retire into obscurity, and so he made sure that at least two of his sons, John (b.1851) and Fred Inkerman (b.1855) also learnt a craft (they both became carpenters). As well as working as a doctor, John worked on the nearby Nettlecombe estate for 40 years, reared a family and lived to see a great-granddaughter born. Fred carried on with the veterinary business for some years and then became a builder foreman. He eventually acquired his father's 'receipt' book, added recipes and prescriptions of his own. Below are three of his or his father's well-tried prescriptions:

A Receipt for a Bad Leg: One pennyworth of Olive Oil, One pennyworth of White Wax, One pennyworth of red Precipitate. Scrape the Wax and dissolve it in the Oil – When nearly cold, mix(ed) the ingredients, and apply on Lint – Night and Morning.

For Bronchitis Remeddy One Pound of Treacle and two Ounces of best Ground Ginger well mixed together, take teaspoon full has often has you like.

He also used the book to note down events that had imprinted themselves on his memory. This has proved to be a valuable record, as it reveals some little and otherwise unremembered things which make up the mosaic of past village life:

1887 Was the Jubilee Year of Queen Victoria of England when the great Celebration was carried on all over the land and the date of the year that I was married in and also on the Evening of that Day, there was a Man and Woman Killed by the Bursting of a Gun through bad judgement Over on Withicombe Hill Bringing a Day's enjoyment to a very sad end. That was a day well to be remembered, there was to be a great Bonfire lighted up at a given time upon every Becon on high Hills throughout the Land.

June 26, 1902, King Edward 7th Coronation was held at Roadwater. Subscriptions collected and a Dinner given to all in the Parish. Games and Sports to the great enjoyment of all. Tent up at Lower Mills, and held in a Field called Broadie. Lovely weather – there was no Band to be got for Money, so they Hired a Street Organ from London.

The book also includes many details of happenings to village people: for instance, '26 of February 1904, When Thomas Bryant (miller) of this Village died, Burried March 2nd Aged 54 Gone to Heaven. He worked hard for it'.

The Photographer: Daniel Nethercott (1831-1918)

To claim a photographer in mid-Victorian days must mark a village as unusual. Daniel (or Dan'l) Nethercott was an unusual man with vision and enterprise but free from self-centred ambition.

The name of the farmhouse in which he was born in 1831, Drucombe (meaning 'narrow valley'), reflects the almost alpine nature of its surroundings. Until recently the valley was dominated by forestry plantations of fir and larch, but in Daniel's childhood the lower part was covered with a forest of broad-leaved trees, probably oaks. About 1,000 years

before, wise men in this part of the world had so drawn the boundaries that livestock could always reach fresh water without straying on to neighbours' land. This generally meant designating the middle of the stream as a boundary or, as at Pitt, where Nettlecombe parish came to the stream, negotiating a tongue of land to lead to a drinking-place and ford.

That tells us something about Daniel's inheritance. Drucombe occupied the most remote corner of Carhampton (and later Withycombe) parish and the Dunster Castle estate. It had no direct connection with the nearest hamlet, Rodhuish, and it was six miles by a roundabout hill road from Dunster. Whoever was granted the tenancy of a farm so situated must be a man on whom the landowner could completely rely.

Such a man was Daniel Nethercott senr, entrusted with the farm and the office of gamekeeper, which demanded a share of two-o'clock-in-the-morning courage. A keeper needed mastery of woodcraft, courage for encounters with poachers and indifference to unpopularity, and for these he received, by the standards of those days, good reward.

Daniel junr was the youngest of ten sons, but when the time came for him to earn his keep at about the age of ten, his father's circumstances saved him from having to stumble along beside a plough or scare birds in the cold and rain for 6d. a week. He was apprenticed to a mason, but his active mind was also reaching out for other work. By going on errands for a penny or a ha'penny he gradually built up the capital to buy a donkey, and then a little cart, and he established himself as a carrier up and down the valley and out over the Brendon Hills. Travelling around the farms and noting the isolation of the people, he hit on the idea of a 'raree show'. He painted a backcloth, rigged it up in his cart and put on shows at a penny a time. From that he moved to a new interest. This would have been the time of the Great Exhibition, and he heard of the amazing new art by which the likeness of a man or woman, a building or a tree, could be captured by sunlight on prepared glass. It set his imagination on fire and he resolved to master it.

None of these new artists had arrived in Taunton as yet, so off he went to London, with a £5 note from his father, to see a photographer. On arriving in the city he aimed to buy a camera and something like the following exchange took place.

'Sir' said Daniel to the proprietor, 'would it cost much to learn to take likenesses?' The proprietor looked this determined but rustic youth up and down.

'Rather more than you can afford, I expect, young man.'

'More 'n that?' queried Daniel, triumphantly, spreading his £5 note on the counter.

The photographer was amused. 'Well, I think we could manage something for that, but...' He paused and looked more closely: 'but I'm afraid I don't know that bank. I can't accept that note.'

The photographer refused his money as it had been issued by a Somerset bank – sound and respected at home, but unknown in the wilds of the metropolis. Crestfallen for a moment, Daniel went outside and considered what to do. He had relatives in London, but did not know how to get to them, so asked the first policeman he saw and, to his amazement, was answered in the friendly tones of West Somerset. His friend in need escorted him back to the shop and vouched for the honour of Fox & Fowler, whereupon the photographer took charge of Daniel and taught him the elements of his craft.

Equipped with camera, plates and chemicals, Daniel returned home and set up in business. He built a little studio in the woods near his home, with a few pieces of furniture and a backcloth, and over the next 50 years there came to him men and women of almost every calling that made rural England: the labourer, the thatcher and his family, the quarryman, the parson, the farmer, the smith and countless others.

In West Somerset, where the little wealth was held in very few hands, Daniel could not earn a living from photography alone, so he also advertised as a mason and sculptor. When he retired he built himself and his wife and family a 'model house' overlooking the meadow which was the children's playground. Here he lived into a green old age, photographing every aspect of local life – farming, milling, quarrying, mining, the railway – and growing more patriarchal in appearance with the years.

We who look back across the abyss of a century may at first find a humorous incongruity in the stolid labourers posed stiffly against a Renaissance balustrade or Italianate arches, but these photographs reveal them not as simple or quaint figures from the past but as men and women endowed with a dignity which we in our century have lost. They do not, as we do, perch uneasily on the front of a chair; they sit enthroned in their chairs with their feet planted firmly. Poverty-stricken and oppressed though they often were, they knew their place in God's world, a place moreover that only they could fill, with a task that their brain and hands alone could carry through. These were the first of their race to transmit the memory of their faces to posterity; a landowner might have been able to contemplate the painted portrait of ten generations of his ancestors, but the face and gestures of a ploughman would formerly not have survived beyond the memory of his grandchildren. With the photographic age that was changed for ever. Even a labourer could hope to be not wholly forgotten, and Richard Jefferies' lament that 'the faces fade as the flowers, and there is no consolation' would lose a little of its poignancy. These people approached the taking of a 'likeness' with deliberation and solemnity. 'Well, Sarah', one of them was heard to say, 'if I do die fust, thee shall have

the likeness, an' if thee dost die, I shall have un.'

They no longer be numbered with those 'who have no memorial' and we cannot value too highly what was done by Daniel Nethercott and others of his art to raise the dignity and self-respect of a whole class of men and women who could, for the first time, be sure that their memory would live on in quiet places such as Roadwater.

When Daniel died in 1918, those who cleared out his house gave orders not merely to throw out the hundreds of glass plates recording half a century of life in the neighbourhood but also to smash them, an order shamefully obeyed. A few were saved, just enough to give a hint of the treasure lost.

The Artists

Sir Hubert von Herkomer and John W. North

Four late-Victorian artists, then of national repute – Frederick Walker, Robert Walker Macbeth, John William North and Sir Hubert Herkomer – were drawn to our district by its beauty. Last to come was Herkomer, but he will serve, if illogically, to introduce the little colony.

Herkomer arrived in the spring of 1892 after a bout of illness and took up residence at Lodge – and very heavy weather he made of it. By his measurement they were six miles from a butcher, four from a baker and three from a grocer, and 'as for a doctor, he was immeasurably far from us.' His health suffered:

The air, instead of helping me, seemed to take the last fragment of the little bodily strength left in me. The loneliness of the place, the un-get-at-ableness of anything and everything, was appalling. A ramshackle old gig, and a weak-kneed old nag, hired from a neighbouring farm, was our only form of locomotion beyond our own legs.

The note of rather querulous discontent with Somerset may put some people out of humour with Sir Hubert, but the matter is not so simple. Herkomer was a man of wide vision and experience, enterprising and generally adaptable. West Somerset in the early-twentieth century was not an earthly paradise; agricultural depression had taken its toll.

The son of a gifted Bavarian woodcarver who came to this country in the mid-nineteenth century, Hubert Herkomer – the name itself means 'immigrant' – belongs to that cohort of foreign artists, intellectuals, patriots and democratic politicians who found in England a home and freedom, and by their activity and that of their children made a lasting contribution to the heritage of their new country. He rapidly established a reputation for portraiture which rendered the true character of his subjects, and his work combined accuracy of draughtsmanship with sobriety of tone.

Drucombe.

Right: *Daniel Nethercott in old age (at Model House).*

Left: *William Jewell (b.1847, Wiveliscombe), farm bailiff at Torre and farmer, possibly at Comberow. He was photographed by Daniel Nethercott, 25 March 1883.*

Below: Sweet Water Meadows of the West *by J.W. North. This could well be the valley just below Roughmoor, where a steep cart track leads up to the road.*

Right: *John William North, a watercolour artist of national reputation, lived at numerous places in the district: Woolston, Bilbrook, Withycombe, Beggearnhuish and Stamborough. He was also a defender of the people's interest in challenging the closure of footpaths.*

Herkomer was as inventive and resourceful as he was energetic, and in his 50-year long career (he died at Budleigh Salterton in 1914) he worked as a painter, musician, actor, sculptor, metal worker, film producer and, for 40 years of that 50, he ran an art colony at his home in Bushey, Hertfordshire.

Maria Milton, J.W. North's 'unofficial' wife.

He was clearly not a man to yield to difficulties, and he soon adapted to the rigours of rural life and explored the countryside, particularly between Bilbrook and Luxborough, in search of subjects. He rigged up a portable studio, a canvas hut on wheels, and rattled around in all weathers, sketching and painting in the open air as opportunity offered. His initial displeasure soon gave way to praise as he found matter for art even in the run down appearance of many farmhouses at that time:

But what a country for the artist! The rich red soil, the undulating country, the apple trees tumbling about in their eccentric untouched shapes, the dilapidated farm-steads: all a treasure ground for painter and poet. In spring, the fast budding of leafage, like jewels set in the deep purple tonality given by the massing of tree branches not yet in leaf; the offset of the strong green masses of ivy growths that have taken overwhelming possession of the stems to which they are attached, give a witchery to this corner of England unsurpassed, I should say, in any part of the world.

One may ask, however, why an artist of national fame should have come to this corner of England? Why not to Newquay or St Ives, where other artists lived? In fact, Herkomer came here at the invitation of a fellow artist, J.W. North, whom he greatly admired and who lived in the neighbourhood. No one, for sure, can still recall Herkomer in person, but a few will keep a corner of their memory for North, who resided here for half a century until his death in 1925.

John William North was born in London, but in the late 1860s, early in his career he found subjects congenial to his taste as a landscape painter in the scenery of West Somerset, and in the late 1860s, at the invitation of Frederick Walker, he took up resi-dence at Halsway, and made this neighbourhood his home ever after.

After Walker died in 1875, North moved from Halsway to Woolston Moor; then, having married Selina Weetch, a farmer's daughter from Upcott, Bicknoller, he lived from 1884–94 in Beggearnhuish House. Here eight of his children were born, and after his wife's death he resided for a time at Bilbrook – probably in Dragon House – near his friend, the distinguished engraver and photographer Robert Macbeth, who lived in Bilbrook House and had come here on North's recommendation.

After Bilbrook North spent a busy decade at Withycombe in a large house on a high bank over-looking the church. He was the first occupant, for it had been built on the site of the old King's Arms Inn, which had been destroyed by fire. His last home, from about 1914, was at Stamborough. He did not subside into disconsolate widowhood; he had an 'unofficial wife' called Maria Milton, a labourer's daughter of singular beauty, who bore him several children, the last of whom died in 1999. North was buried not at Leighland, but with his wife in the new cemetery at Nettlecombe, the parish of their Beggearnhuish home.

In his Withycombe days he ran a four-wheel carriage, with A. Stevens as driver (probably Alfred from Bilbrook) which took him to a studio at Langridge Mills and to another at Roadwater. (He had a third at the top of the orchard high above his home.) When he lived at Beggearnhuish he was driven by Joe Duddridge, who had come from Lawford and was landlord of the White Horse, Washford. Joe's son Ernest, when nearly 100 years old, remembered North well. As a boy he lived in the cottage on the corner facing Lowood, and often trav-elled up and down the valley with the painter, who took an interest in the boy and treated him with considerable kindness. He remembered:

He put me in a painting once. It was a scene near Drucombe and it showed the river, a rustic bridge and sheep in a field – and he put me in as a shepherd boy. [This sounds like *Sweet Water Meadows of the West*, although the scene looks rather more like the river valley between Roughmoor and Pranketts, but artists have their licence.]

J.W. North's venerable appearance with long white beard, at least in his later years, earned him the name of Father Christmas among his friends, though only a rash fellow would have presumed to address him in that style. No doubt he had his weaknesses, but he had a strong personality and did not brook presump-tion or injustice from landowners or anyone else – particularly not from landowners. Physically a small man, he was nevertheless a sound, fearless Radical and, in those days of subservience and oppression, he gave courage to others.

He was also a devoted friend of Richard Jefferies – a recommendation in itself – and he almost certainly entertained him at his Beggearnhuish residence when Jefferies was writing *Red Deer* in 1883. When Jefferies died four years later, tragically young, North organised a fund for his widow and son with generous expenditure of his own time and effort, and lodged them for a time in his home.

More detail is provided about this excellent painter, this adopted son of Somerset, in the account by the late Berta Lawrence in the *Exmoor Review*, 1983. She describes him:

Little Mr North effervesced with energy. Very warmly clad in a wool comforter knitted by a female relative, sealskin cap, dark overcoat, wash leather leggings and thick shooting boots from Bond Street, he was met at times carrying a large canvas on his head, holding in one hand his favourite brushes and palette, in the other, a workman's rush basket containing colours, brushes, bottles, razors.

Interlude: Georgie

Most villages had a Georgie, or someone like him. Today we disguise his condition by some such phrase as 'slow learner', but then they were more direct. They had to put up with his ways, and when they lectured him it went mostly over his head, and after a cuff over the ear, a howl, a cupful of tears and a recuperating snivel, Georgie was his exasperating self again. Still, the mere fact that he was always 'Georgie', not plain George, suggests that people felt tolerant, even protective, toward him.

Georgie lived at Hayne and was the second son of a hard-working and respected thatcher, but it became obvious early on that he would never have the skill for such a craft; but Georgie was not burdened by his weakness, for he had a cheerful mind and was shrewd enough where his own interests were concerned. Unlike most of us he usually spoke the first thought that came into his head, and as some of his thoughts were strange and irrational, his sayings amused people and nurtured an unexpected affection in their hearts. He was erratic and unpredictable, mischievous and given to odd imaginings, but there was no malice, which counted for a great deal.

One day he was sent to the stream to fetch water in two earthenware pitchers. As he lumbered down the path one of his braces buttons came loose and to do it up he held both pitchers in one hand. They jolted together and at each step gave a dull clunk which offended his fastidious ear. He paused and told them to be quiet and, as long as he stood still, they of course obeyed. Off he went again and the pitchers resumed their argument. Again he stopped and warned them. Same result. The third time exhausted his patience. Taking a pitcher in each hand he held them apart and admonished them 'Now then, you devils, you bin quar'lin' long 'nough, now you shall have fair play an' fight it out!'; and dashing them together he broke them into smithereens. He paid with a thrashing, of course, but justified himself with 'Wull, they 'ouldn' stop quar'lin', so I maade em fight it out.

Georgie's brother Jim, two years his senior, had a brace of pet pigeons of which he was very proud. When both boys were still young, Jim had to go away for the day but made Georgie promise to see that the birds came to no harm. When Jim returned in the evening the birds were gone and Georgie could not or would not say what had become of them. Little Jim's face puckered up and the tears began to flow. This was too much for Georgie. 'What d' ee want to cry vor?' he said. 'Bain't goin' to cry, art? They pigeons be safe 'nough, Jim. Come 'long o' me an' I'll zhow 'ee where they be to'. Down in the garden, in a little cave or recess he had hollowed out, lay the pigeons, safe from all further harm. Georgie had made doubly sure by putting one in each pocket, where they had stifled. 'There they be', said Georgie as his brother sobbed, 'they be safe 'nough, heads, eyes, toes an' toenails, all to 'em, zo what do ee want to blubber zo vor?'

The sympathy that these children of Nature are supposed to have with the animal creation seemed to have given Georgie a miss. One bird was much the same as another, all were stubborn, obtuse and – not to put too fine a point on it – bird-brained. Down in the village, in the dame-school next door to the Valiant Soldier, perched a talking parrot. Its vocabulary was limited to one word, 'Uncle', but it gave Georgie ideas. 'What one vuele of a bird can do, another vuele can.' So off he scampered up to his home, took one of the pigeons out of its cage and began Lesson 1. The pigeon eyed him with that beady-eyed contempt that the tribe display for us humans and declined to utter even a whisper of a word. His teacher soon lost his scanty patience. Angrily cuffing the pigeon over the head he exclaimed again and again, 'Say 'Uncle', wull 'ee? Darn 'ee, say 'Uncle'.'

One year, as the revel drew near, Georgie begged to be allowed to go and enjoy the fun, but the farmer had some fine ricks to be thatched as soon as Georgie's father could manage it, and he insisted on Georgie carrying the reed for him. Georgie, to start with, was sulky and resentful. But on the morning of the revel he changed his tune, trotted along with his father and worked like two Trojans, carrying the bundles of reed up the ladder at such a rate that soon there was enough on the rick to last the whole day. Then clambering down he pulled the ladder away and shouted up to the old man, 'There now, you bide up there an' finish the job. I be off to the revel'. As the rick was in an outfield, hours went by before the father could attract anyone's attention and get down from his perch. It was evening before he ran Georgie to ground at the revel, but when he did his ash stick made contact with the seat of Georgie's breeches and sped him tearfully on his homeward way.

It seems Georgie did not enjoy long life, but in his way he enjoyed what he had of it, and this 'mentally disadvantaged' boy left a mark which one might envy a little. He played his tricks and said his quaint sayings in the 1860s and '70s, but nearly 80 years later they were still remembered; in the 1950s people in the village were still quoting, 'What be goin' to cry vor?', Bain't goin' to cry, art?' and 'Darn ee! Say 'Uncle'.'

Modern Village Occupations:

Roadwater Fishery: By Ben and Penny Hanson

In 1970 we were looking for a suitable site to start a business rearing trout. The requirements were a clean river water-supply, a mild climate and land suitable for ponds. The field above Tacker Street seemed ideal, and was of little agricultural use providing summer grazing only. In late 1970 we negotiated a lease for the land known locally as the Moors, and in May 1971 moved from Bibury in Gloucestershire to Roadwater.

We started work excavating six ponds and building a hatchery and tool shed. In 1972 the farm was completed with eight more ponds. In 1974–75 we built our house and expanded further, building ponds on the Mineral Line for small brown trout. The year 1983 saw the construction of circular ponds at Torre fishery. Roadwater fishery is one of the few fish farms still using earth ponds. They require more maintenance but produce the high quality fish for which Roadwater is renowned. The trout are sold live to stock rivers and reservoirs all over the country.

Blacksmithing: Harry Horrobin

Harry is a native of Dudley where the tradition of ironworking is in the blood. He joined the RAF at the age of 16, and served his apprenticeship as an armourer. After 26 years in the RAF, Harry and Betty settled in Bridgetown near Dulverton, where Harry took over the local blacksmith's shop. By 1964 he had outgrown the premises and moved to Roadwater, taking over the workshop formerly owned by Slades, builders at Manor Mill. Harry worked to commission and took on apprentices, among them, Bill Poirrier. Harry also taught Rachel Reckitt, who went on to create many works in wrought iron, which can still be seen in the village. Harry's son Jim and grandson Ben have carried on the family tradition and won many awards for their work.

In 1984 Harry's doctor advised him to give up blacksmithing. A self-taught player and lover of classical music, he conducted regular evenings playing quartets with a group of friends. He had always enjoyed making violins as a hobby, and this became a full-time occupation, until failing sight prevented him from working.

Two Rivers Paper: Jim Patterson

In 1973 Jim Patterson was made redundant from the paper-mill in Watchet. After a spell living and working in Hertfordshire he bought Pitt Mill on the Mineral Line, and set up his own papermaking business in the 1980s. He has restored the leat and waterwheel and produces hand-made paper using traditional methods but taking advantage of modern technology. He sends his paper all over the world.

Ben and Penny Hanson, Roadwater fishery.

Roadwater blacksmiths, left to right: *Bill Poirrier, Harry Horrobin, Jim Horrobin, Ben Horrobin.*

Left: *Bill Poirrier at work in his forge at Riverden, 1980s. Bill came to West Somerset in the 1960s. He worked part time with Harry Horrobin before setting up his own business as an artist blacksmith.*

Right: *Millwright Malcolm Cooper* (left) *and Jim Patterson celebrate the reinstallation of the mill wheel, 2000.*

Left: *Jim Patterson in his workplace, 2003.*

Left: Roadwater Mineral Line station, c.1890. Dicky James, stationmaster, is on the platform.

Below left: The first locomotive on the Mineral Line was a 'box' engine delivered from Neilson of Glasgow in 1856. Here it is driven by Tom Stevens, with his son Charlie as fireman, c.1888.

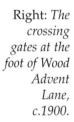

Right: The crossing gates at the foot of Wood Advent Lane, c.1900.

Reopening the mines and Mineral Line. The first engine can be seen arriving at the station, July 1907.

Chapter 6

Men and Machines

The Mineral Line

The water of the Brendon brooks had fuelled our village industries for perhaps 500 years, but the new age of steam broke in on a day in April 1857. William Court, 70 years later, recalled the occasion:

Well I remember the day when the first railway locomotive this side of Taunton came puffing and snorting up the valley, until we could see its smoking funnel peeping up towards the station. Soon several of us lads went down the line to inspect this wonderful iron horse.

It is said that others ran away terror-stricken, shouting, 'the Devil is here!' Either way, it was unquestionably a great and exciting day for Roadwater.

The surge of excitement must have ebbed a few feet when people realised that for the time being the trains would only carry goods, and passengers would have to wait their turn. Nevertheless the village had already gained from the coming of the railway, and the population knew it; for three subsequent generations it was boasted, 'We had the railway long before Minehead'.

Roadwater was the railhead to which the carts laden with ore came down Treborough Lane and past the Valiant Soldier – or more likely a stop for emergency repairs to man and beast – crossed the stream

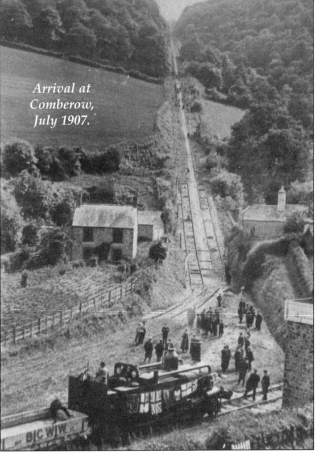

Arrival at Comberow, July 1907.

and turned right into the station yard. In 1857 they were already bringing down 30 tons a day and the bridge, as shown on the tithe map, was only one cart wide and probably unfit for heavy traffic. Although the history of the railway gives no mention of a bridge, it seems certain that the Ebbw Vale Company undertook covering over the river to make what we, in 2004, refer to as the Bridge. No other competent authority would have had any interest in the work, and it proved to be a great gain for Roadwater.

The company took eight further years to provide a regular passenger service, but with Watchet only 25 minutes away by train, instead of the old 75 on foot via Washford, Washford Cross and Five Bells, it would not have said much for youthful enterprise if young folk had not hopped on an ore train while the engine driver stared ahead. Older residents also gained because even though the trains did not run on their only free day, Sunday, the track made a pleasant hour's walk without any hills – unusual hereabouts – between meadows and woods, past the ruined abbey and alongside the rippling stream. On work days the miners and railwaymen who lodged in the village were taken up the line by the early morning train and brought back by the last train at night. Very occasionally special trains ran up to Comberow, with a further ride to the top of the Incline 'at own risk', for meetings and rallies

53

of the Lodge of the Order of Mountain Hope, with performances by the Brendon Hill Teetotal Fife and Drum Band and Brendon Hill Choir.

The Ebbw Vale Company had not at first meant to provide a public transport system; but in doing so they won more good will than they could have expected; and even after the mines closed down in 1883 the terms of their charter obliged them to go on operating the train for another 15 years.

To have a station with a uniformed stationmaster boosted the status of the village, at least in its own eyes, and Richard (Dicky) James in the 1880s maintained a suitable dignity of office, although relaxed enough to shout, when he espied a stranger on the train, 'Roadwater Junction! Roadwater Junction! All change here for Egypt and Greenland!'

There is no cause to go over the story of the Mineral Line outside our part of the valley, and we may hope that before long a new account of the whole enterprise will supply the want of Roger Sellick's book, at the time of writing out of print for 30 years. Still, three snippets of verbal lore should be jotted down and not lost: the first, that when the new church at Leighland was built in 1858 the stone was brought probably from Torre to Pitt by train and from there up the lane by horse and cart. The second concerns Nicholas Redd, who drove the 'Pontypool'

Above: *Halfway up the Incline, 1862.*

Front view, with truck.

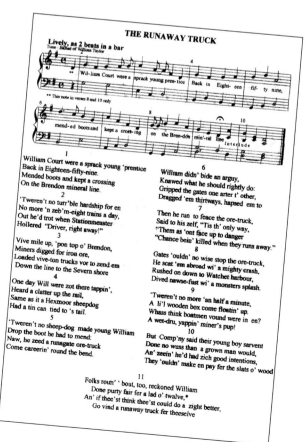

Right: *'The Runaway Truck'.*
Words and music by Glyn Court, 1999.

54

Railway bridge with postman.

Left: *Jim Hoyle in the winding house. He made a working model of one of the pumping engines and used it to drive his wife's sewing machine.*

Right: *Jim Hoyle's model.*

The first truck arriving at the top of the Incline, July 1907.

Viaduct at Clippers Pool.

The Incline at Colton.

Light railway, Colton–Raleighs Cross.

Ore bins at Colton.

Left: *John Greet, foreman of mine buildings.*

Right: *Mr and Mrs Morgan Morgans, c.1890.*

Iron ore bunker and bin, Colton, 1908.

The Pontypool, c.1890.

engine on the line for many years and was always signalled to go ahead by the stationmaster's 'Right away, Nicol!' A hundred years after Nicol's heyday a lady exclaimed, 'Why! We still say that!'. The third is the incident of the the the runaway truck at Oatway or Harpers Crossing, the story of which is told in the song printed on page 54.

The Nethercotts
By Margaret Pocklington

The visible power of steam in the railway did not inspire our pocket industrialists, the millers and blacksmiths, to change over from water-power. That would have been economic madness. Yet it came at precisely the right time, for it accustomed the farmers to the new ways and new power which, whether they wished it or not, would largely supplant the muscle power they had relied on ever since farming began.

Two men – Nathanael Edbrooke and Elias Nethercott – have been differently credited with bringing in Roadwater's first road traction engine in the early 1860s, and Nathanael, having moved from smithing, is described in the census of 1881 as 'Engine Driver Fitter in Slate Works'. However, it was the family of Elias that seemed to flourish, so – with many thanks to Margaret Pocklington for her research – the life of Elias is discussed below.

Elias (b.1826) gave his place of birth variously as Old Cleeve and St Decuman's (Watchet), and the latter most probably refers to the detached parcel of land which includes Hayne. In 1841 George and Ann Nethercott and their sons Elias and Henry were living in Leighland, but by 1851 they were in Roadwater. A lingering idea that the Nethercotts came here from the north seems rather far-fetched, except that a Henry

Nethercott four years younger than Elias and living in Durham gave his place of birth as Williton, which was also in St Decuman's parish. Perhaps some connection existed and Elias had served an apprenticeship, seen for himself the wonders of the industrial revolution and come home to try them out at a promising time for himself – with the coming of the mineral railway to his home village!

This represented a tremendous opportunity for Elias as he was subcontracted to make railway keys and 'trunnels'. A railway key was a block of wood that retained the rail in the chair, the chair being the iron socket with a deep notch that secured the rail to the sleeper. The chair was fixed to the sleeper by two trunnels. Elias used the word trunnel on his billheads but they are more commonly known as trenails, this word being derived from tree nails, large oaken pegs.

Key and trunnel making was only a small part of the developing business. Elias was one of the first men in the district to own a steam engine. Such engines supplied the power for work in the woods, powered the sawmill and drove the threshing machines. Elias built farm wagons, made gates and fences, designed and built his own rack saw bench for planks and posts, cast brass bearings, repaired farm machinery, made wheels, dressed millstones, kept local mills in working order, did blacksmith work and built several houses that still stand in Roadwater (the block known as Sellick's Green and the three cottages of unequal height on the bend between the foundry and Roadwater Farm).

Right: *Elias Nethercott.*

Wallace and Lily Nethercott, with ? Bowden (centre).

Harry senr and Wallace Nethercott.

Above: *A trial of engineering ingenuity – William Slade's traction engine has overturned on Cutcombe Hill. Harry junr (centre), Wallace (right) and Will Slade are working out their next move. As always, pulleys, levers and wire ropes – with feminine encouragement up on the hill – did the trick.*

Above: *Harry Nethercott's threshing machine at Paul Gliddon's Bridge Farm in Williton, c.1975. Left to right: Walter Guppy, Alan Wilson, John Dunn and John Putt.*

Harry junr on his Field Marshall KYB763.

Touch and go in the timber trade!

Harry junr (right) and Wallace in the foundry, 1970s. The drive shaft from the water-wheel is above Harry's head.

In 1863 Elias paid £92 for a piece of land opposite Roadwater Inn from the Orchard Wyndham estate. The ground stretched up to Clitsome Lane behind Riverside Cottage and included a small parcel behind Lowood. He built Foundry House, in which he lived until his death on 6 April 1900. During his dinner hour one day in 1864 he moulded a plaster bust of himself on the front flank wall in the apex of the gable. He is shown wearing a double-breasted suit with three rows of buttons. The bust is plainly visible today and Foundry House has been a Grade II listed building since 1985.

Elias' eldest son, Harry, was running the business for a few years before his father's death and he proved to be an excellent businessman. The sawmill, thrashing, casting, and other facets of the company continued in much the same way but the number of clients increased and the business expanded. With the profits Harry Nethercott bought land, woods and houses. He married Lucy Hearne at the end of the nineteenth century and they had 11 children. All the children were brought up in Foundry House. Harry junr was the eighth child, born in 1911.

In 1916 Harry Nethercott went to collect his new Model T Ford car from Salisbury accompanied by his daughter Mabel who was aged 13. The journey home was delayed by military traffic on Salisbury Plain and they decided to sleep in the car as the lights were inadequate for night driving. The Model T offered virtually no protection against the weather for although a canvas hood could be pulled over the top it was open-sided. Poor Mabel suffered from a chill which developed into pneumonia and she died shortly after the trip.

The first car that Harry had owned was a second-hand 1902 Darracq. It had bright red upholstery and green bodywork. There was a 'dickey' seat at the back for extra passengers. The Model T that he owned later lasted for many years and the body of the car was taken off eventually and put on the chassis of a Seer, which had been bought for scrap. The one-door Seer was the first self-starter automobile.

In the early 1930s Mr Bissell of Home Farm, St Audries, decided to use some of his land as a holiday camp. Such camps were quite recent innovations and had proved popular. Harry senr and his sons were involved in the construction of the camp; the original chalets, the staff quarters and rest room, the dining-room tables and the long drive into the site. The first task was to get shingle up from the beach to use in the foundations. The cliffs around St Audries vary in height (60–80 feet), and the only way down to the beach was by way of a steep and narrow path. The Nethercotts used narrow-gauge rails at a point where the gradient was flatter and levelled the track up with sleepers. The rails went over a guiding drum at the highest point on the cliff face. This drum was a couple of feet wide with flanges to guide the wire rope which was attached to a dram or trolley. The other end of the wire rope was fixed to the winch on a steam engine which provided the power. Down on the beach the men dug out the shingle and loaded it onto the dram. As the tide came in the hole dug by the men would fill up with shingle again. Harry junr would ride on top of the shingle in the dram as it was winched up the cliff face. When level ground at the top was reached, Harry would knock out the linchpin and tip the dram sideways. It seems a remarkable feat when looking at the steepness of the cliff today.

The 100 or so chalets were built of pitch pine and each completed one, including furnishings, cost £11. The staff quarters were built with corrugated asbestos sheets fixed to an oak frame. The camp opened in 1933 and the inclusive charge for a week was two and a half guineas rising to three guineas in July and August. During the Second World War the camp was closed and taken over by the Army; troops from the United States were billeted there too before the Normandy invasion.

The Somerset Mineral Syndicate reopened the Brendon Hill mines in 1907 and repaired the railway but the venture failed through lack of funds. The track was sold at auction on 8 August 1924 when Harry senr bought Lots 20, 21 and 24. Lot 20 was the track from the south gates at Clitsome level crossing as far as the south quoin of the bridge where the river crosses Yea Farm together with a garden plot. Lot 21 was a small section of ground at the end of the three cottages near Manor Mill and Lot 24 ran from the south gate of Roadwater crossing near Oatway to the north corner of Comberow Farmhouse. This long section was made up so that timber could be brought down from Leigh Woods by steam wagon. The gates near Oatway were padlocked but the lock was frequently broken.

In the 1930s the Nethercotts tried to reopen part of the mines and drove a trial adit into the hillside above

Comberow near the waterfall. Harry Nethercott senr had become friendly with two men who had come to Watchet when the HMS *Fox* was anchored in the harbour. It was believed that it was a viable proposition to mine ore again and if the adit was driven in at a slight incline the problem of flooding would be overcome. The three men put up £1,000 each and a dozen men were employed working two shifts. However, the veins were patchy and the venture proved uneconomic and was abandoned.

After 1945 the foundry work was largely run down, but the firm continued to thrive with timber-felling and hauling and agricultural contracting in the hands of Harry senr's sons Wallace and Harry, who were not only directors but did their full share of the heavy manual work. They moved on from the steam age to the diesel and their threshing machines and balers were familiar sights all over the district. Wallace worked in the Leighland and Treborough area and Harry in the lowland.

Wallace and his wife lived in Riverside Cottage and Harry and his wife in a converted railway carriage on the Mineral Line. Both were picturesque dwellings in their different ways, although Harry was raised above the worst of the watery ills to which Roadwater was so long heir.

Wallace's son Joe inherited an enthusiasm for engineering which he took into the wartime RAF. He rose to the respected and highly responsible rank of Warrant Officer I (equivalent to RSM). He did not return to the firm, but took a degree and made a career in civil engineering. He now lives in Newport, Gwent.

Margaret Pocklington concluded her research by recalling that Harry Nethercott:

... could be cantankerous and argumentative and managed to fall out with most residents at one time or another but never showed me anything but kindness. He was a good man who helped many villagers who came knocking quietly on his door in times of need and the church owes much to his generosity.

At his funeral in Leighland nearly all the countryside seemed to be there.

George Grinslade, 1815–1911

George Grinslade did not come to Roadwater until he was aged 70, and by that time he had more than 60 years of work behind him as an apprentice and then master shoemaker in his birthplace, Watchet. He embodied perfectly the legendary characteristics of the shoemaker, assiduity, tenacity and an open and enquiring mind – and Watchet, with its seafaring population and visiting seamen from far away, supplied an ample diet for him to digest.

He was born in 1815, the year of Waterloo. He was the son of a sea captain and smallholder, but this gave no defence against the dire poverty of those years, and he was sent to work with an uncle, a shoemaker, at the age of seven. He was afflicted with a club foot and weak chest, but enjoyed a buoyant spirit. When the doctors gave him only six months to live he bought a Culpeper's herbal, gathered the herbs, made infusions, cured himself and lived to be 95.

With this background he was, it almost goes without saying, a strong Christian of the 'born again' type, but this, far from leading him into abstraction, quickened his interest in the wonders of the natural world. He bought books on astronomy and geography, as well as two globes, terrestrial and celestial, and tried to explain to his grandchildren the unimaginable distances of light years.

All this, though, was theory, and his hands, busy earning their bread ten hours a day six days a week, needed a task where they could work with his brain and create a tool of precision, and in middle life George found it.

In 1851 the Great Exhibition in the Crystal Palace kindled enthusiasm even down here in West Somerset. The 20 miles to Taunton station would have been heavy going for a club foot, but somehow he got there, and to London, and the universal display held him enthralled. One object in particular captivated him: one of the first American sewing machines. 'My!' he thought, 'wouldn't one o' they be just the thing for my boots and shoes', but an enquiry as to the price soon knocked that on the head. George took careful note of the dimensions and principles, observed the wonderful synchronisation of all the moving parts, came home – and built one. It took 18 months of his spare time, but he succeeded, incorporating an improvement in the form of a cam for lifting the foot. He used the machine in his workshop for over 30 years; and even a century later, massive though it is, it still runs easy and smooth. With the experience, he made two more for his son-in-law and his nephew, both shoemakers, as well as a wood lathe, but these have disappeared.

Why, the critic may ask, did such men as the Nethercotts and George Grinslade in an era of development and change, not follow the Stephensons, the Watts and the Armstrongs and seize the opportunities for advancement and fortune? The truest answer is simply that the canker of ambition had left them alone, and having been born and bred in West Somerset they thought the place too good to lose.

Right: The *Post Office, c.1905. Postmaster William Court enjoying the summer sun.*

Below: *A large stock of shoes are displayed and a store room and letter-sorting office have been built out over the stream. Where the girl is standing (left of the shops), steps lead down to a dipping-place. Harold Bryant's bakery is next along the street; Mrs Lily Murrell is standing by the wall of Rose Villa.*

Roadwater Post Office in the 1960s.

Chapter 7

Postmasters and Shopkeepers

William Gooding

Up to the 1850s Roadwater had been pretty well self-sufficient, catering for most of the simple daily needs of food and clothing, with the few luxuries and items for occasional use supplied by pedlars or bought at the stalls set up at the September revel. But when the opening of the mines and the railway led to a growth in population, more cash circulating and glimpses into the outside world, there came a new type of general dealer, the entrepreneur. William Gooding, 33 years old, had run a grocery and general retail business four miles away in Stogumber, where the population of 1,000 boasted a physician, a solicitor, a magnificent church, a handsome Baptist chapel and a celebrated brewery. However, Stogumber was situated just a little too far from the main highways, and no new industry came.

Roadwater and its valley offered just that opportunity, and Gooding moved in, set up a grocer's and draper's shop in the main street and obtained the concession for a Post Office. Following the introduction of the penny letter post in 1840 the number of letters sent daily had increased tenfold and went on rising, but it is very doubtful that correspondence, even at a penny a time, caught on with countryfolk; by and large they had no one to write to, except sons and daughters who had migrated to 'better themselves'. The very poor could not always afford a penny for the stamp.

William's personal appearance did not promise a man of enterprise. He seemed withdrawn and as if brooding over a secret misdeed. He played trombone in the church orchestra, and his love of music passed to one of his sons who, in his twenties, was elected leader of the new brass band formed by the lads of the village. Introspective or not, William Gooding made his enterprise a success. A village Post Office was no gold mine, for the postmaster had to provide rent-free premises, furnishings and an endless supply of pens, ink and paper for the public. His or her stipend was no more than a postman's and he had to run a supplementary business to make ends meet: Gooding dealt in provisions, and the author's father,

when he took over, in footwear and bicycles.

Still, in the 1860s and long after, the Post Office was worth having, for the incomers, the miners and railwaymen, and the navvies for a time, earned higher wages than the farm workers. Until a mining settlement was built on the hills they lived as bachelors, but the married men who wished to send home some of their wages to Cornwall or Wales could now use the Post Office Money Order service and be sure that the few pence commission would keep their remittance out of the hands of that ogre of industrial working-class lore, the middleman. They received their week's pay on Saturday evening, and a couple of hours later they crowded the shop for their postal business and to buy groceries. Years after, Gooding remembered that:

... waiting people thronged as far as the bridge and the shop was so full that baskets of goods, with change, were handed out on crooked sticks over the heads of the customers by shopmen standing on the counters.

His range of groceries was small and basic as there was no need for refinements. Nothing was prepacked; dried fruit and flour came in barrels, and vinegar in a cask to be drawn off as bottles were presented for a refill at 2d. a pint. Sugar came in the proverbial sugar-loaf and was chipped or clipped off with specially designed pincers and handed over in purple or blue paper bags. Tea was sold by the ounce (at 2¼d.) or two ounces (at 4½d.), and as for coffee, very few people drank it. Not many items would have yielded more than a few pence profit. All in all, the business needed a quick turnover for the small individual returns – but those small profits added up to a tidy sum week after week.

The trade must have dropped off when a rival store opened up on the hills, and too many of his customers must have been as short of cash as the widow whose weekly bill rarely went over 4s., payment for which had often to be postponed. However, with over 300 customers the business yielded a comfortable living. Over the years William added another enterprise, providing tents and sideshows for the revel and club day, and weathered the economic depression until the new century.

For a while he also kept a chandlery where tallow dips or candles were made, the only domestic lighting for really poor folk until oil-lamps were introduced. They were produced by dipping a number of cotton wicks on a frame into a vessel filled with melted tallow. The cotton was dealt out in skeins to women of the village who cut it into the right lengths for dipping. The candles were known as 'eights' or 'twelves', signifying the number needed to make a pound in weight. Long after oil-lamps had superseded them in cottage homes, these 'dips' were used by the iron-ore miners, who fixed them to their felt hats with a daub of clay, giving the dim light by which they delved deep down into the earth.

By 1900 the shop had become something of an institution, trading steadily year after year, yielding a good income, and William's son Arthur felt able to give up the postal side, which William Court took on at the bridge end of Station Road. In spite of the agricultural depression Roadwater still offered enough variety of business and social life to satisfy most of its people, and Arthur kept on the other business until his death in 1938. (By then he had completed 50 years' service as organist at St Luke's.)

William Court & Selina Mear

The postal service continued at the Bridge under William Court, who combined it with the sale of footwear and bicycles until 1920, when he handed over the office to his sister, Selina Mear. He then moved to Washford, married, built himself a house and shop at the top of the Ramp and carried on the same business there. A simple arrangement assured Roadwater people of their everyday boots within hours. Tom Evans, say, would come in about midday and ask,

'Have ee got a pair of eleven wellingtons, missis?' Missis would ring Washford 1: 'Send up a pair of eleven Wellingtons,' and come two o'clock the boots would arrive by the afternoon post and Tom would walk home as sprucely shod as the Duke himself.

This line of business suffered when buses began running twice a week to Minehead for 10d. return, although people would still pop in for small items: 'Oh, I've just bought some new shoes in Minehead and forgot the laces. Have ee got any?'

The lack of ready money continually made itself felt by both shopkeeper and customer. Few men earned more than £2 a week, and throughout this period a farm worker's basic wage was 28s., which left little free for luxuries. Many wanted a bicycle, which would save them several miles walking and thus give them more time at home, but £3.17s.6d. for a Hercules was a massive outlay, so they paid half-a-crown a week for 15 weeks. They bought boots and shoes for their families on the same principle, and payment was known to drag on for years and finally fade from sight, but both parties to the bargain agreed that 'you can't let the kiddies go barefoot, can you?' Most people paid as and when they could, though some of those who could best afford to felt no scruple at leaving their bills unpaid for three years or even more.

Telephones were a luxury, and throughout the 1930s the number of them in Washford, Roadwater, Leighland, Luxborough and Withycombe combined, hovered around 50. The Post Office had Roadwater's only public telephone, and whereas in the twenty-first century one can direct-dial anywhere in the world, at that time each call had to go through the exchange. The postmistress had to find the number, put the call through, enquire the charge, collect it from the caller and enter all the details in a register – and for this the Post Office paid her, on average, a halfpenny a time.

Proud Street or Station Road, three feet deep in water in October 1960. People found it impossible to clean up afterwards – mud discoloured the walls and worked into the furniture and could not be wholly removed.

Left: *Island Cottage – no need to ask why.*

Below: *Walter Lile cleaning up the Post Office after the flood with David Taylor – but the mud and the memories stayed much longer.*

Above: *Looking up past Taylor's garage, Harry Nethercott's railway carriage is out of harm's way.*

Above: *Water buffalo?*

Inset, above: *Clitsome Corner and Riverside Cottage.*

Right: *The term 'water garden' took on a new meaning in the court by the old smithy.*

The Liles

When Mrs Mear reached 80 years of age in 1953 she handed over the business to her son-in-law and her daughter, Walter and Kathleen (Kathie) Lile, who ran it until Walter died in 1963. The postal service was then moved back to its original site and eventually to the shop by the Village Hall, where it operates in 2004. The floods which every few years engulfed Roadwater were never accepted by the GPO as sufficient reason for shutting up shop. In 1960 Walter Lile had to hire the Village Hall, without repayment, and carry on postal business from there. The GPO replaced stamps and postal orders ruined by the flood, but that was their only concession.

Val Hole has this to add:

The Post Office in the 1950s when I was young was in the shop on the bridge, run by Mrs Mear and Mr and Mrs Lile. As there was a public telephone in the Post Office a message could be left there for someone living in the village or at Leighland, Golsoncott or Hook Hill. Mr Lile would write down the message on a telegram form and take it to the person who was supposed to receive it. If there was any of us village boys around, he would get one of us to go instead. Sometimes you might have to wait to find out if there was an answer. On returning to the Post Office you would be given 6d. I have taken telegrams up the Mineral Line, when

it was just a track full of potholes. It got very muddy in winter. Telegrams were withdrawn in 1986.

All the post for Roadwater came up from Watchet at 6.30a.m. and was sorted into three rounds (Treborough, Croydon and Leighland/Roadwater). The postbox on the wall of the Post Office would be emptied and if any of the mail was local it would be stamped with a Roadwater postmark (something which does not happen in 2004). In the late 1940s the Treborough round started at the Valiant Soldier and cottages, then progressed to Vale House, Glasses Farm, Tacker Street, Treborough Lodge and Treborough Lodge House. It would then follow the footpath up through the woods to Quarry House, then to Treborough, down to Chapmans and farm and up through the fields to Cold Harbour. It then went back down to Windwhistle, Longcliff and Leigh Barton. If there was no post for the cottage down in Leigh Woods, the postman took the path for Comberow, from there up to Timwood and on to Hook Hill before going down to Old House and Pitt Mill and back down the Mineral Line to the village. I remember Fred Beaver walking this round and his wife walked the Croydon round. He lived in Mill Cottage which, along with a garage, was pulled down in the 1960s to make way for the shop that stands in 2004.

Mr Beaver's wife at this time did the Croydon round. Leaving the Post Office she would start up at Golsoncott, then on up to the Bungalow, then the

John Lyddon, probably delivering at Chargot, c.1910.

John (Jack) Marlow at home, Higher Hayne.

lodge of Golsoncott House (the home of the Reckitt family). She then went on to Croydon Hall (the home of Captain Bridges who gave the recreation-ground) and the cottages around, then on to Hyde Park Cottage, along the track to Culverwell, back down to Greenland, then back to the Post Office.

Postmen: Our Men of Letters

The postmen of the 1930s whom the author knew at Washford earned praise, for he remembers them coming back to the office from their rounds in winter with faces and hands blue with cold, and stories of struggling through driving rain and howling storms, wading thigh-deep through snow-drifts or even walking on top of the hedges to deliver to the Brendon Hill farms.

Roadwater 'letter-carriers' of old have traditionally been sturdy men, able to read, write and tell the time by a watch, fit to endure all weathers and tramp 16 or more miles every day – and 16 miles in this district can involve a climb of 1,000 feet and several smaller ascents. A ploughman may have trudged just as far in his daily work, at every step wrenching his boots out of the 'clitchy' clay, but the postman's 12s. wage represented a rise in the world. Besides, he might, if ingenious enough, fit in other work on his travels, as did shoemaker Henry Court's son, Lewis, in the 1880s. His round took him four miles up the Mineral Line with a long climbing detour to Leighland, Leigh Barton and probably Treborough, and brought him in the late morning to the top of the Incline. There the GPO allowed him – compelled him, rather – to wait three hours in a platelayers' hut, and he used the time to repair shoes for delivery on his way home and to teach himself Latin.

The mail was brought twice a day to Roadwater by postmen from Washford whom older readers may remember: Silas Locke, Jim Leigh, Tommy Atkins, Will Bellamy and others. There were two Roadwater postmen of the same vintage who made too deep an impression to be passed over. First was John (Jack) Marlow, who lived at Higher Hayne. He was an ex-sergeant-major who took his martial bearing, strict discipline and Old Bill moustache into his civilian career.

John (Jack) Lyddon, on the other hand, exemplified an old type of countryman: trustworthy, independent, salty of speech, and down to earth but not to be

Charley Routley delivering mail as an auxiliary postman in Leighland. During the war Charley spent four years in a prison camp in Poland, including a spell in a coal mine, and survived a forced march across East Germany.

trampled on. When he retired after 35 years of 16 miles a day – the equivalent of walking nearly seven times round the globe – a tribute was paid to his devotion to duty and his strict adherence to regulations. Nevertheless he spoke his mind and feared no man or woman. A public servant Jack may have been, but servile and mealy-mouthed he certainly was not.

This was back in the days of King 'Teddy' and George V – that is important. Jack was never sure whether the Major ordered his daily newspaper by post to make certain of getting one or simply to annoy and aggravate the postman, but he believed the latter. When, one warm, 'drouthy' day in summer, he toiled up the long drive with the Major's penny-worth of Fleet Street blue, he was in no mood to put up with brusque orders or peremptory commands. The Major, however, knew no other way. He came out holding a letter.

'Here, my man', stick a stamp on this for me,' he barked.

'I bain't your man, for one thing, maister,' Jack growled, 'I be me own; an' for another, I bain't goin' to lick the king's backzide for ee, thee'st can lick en theezelf.'

Inevitably the Major complained, but Jack, interviewed by the postmaster, denied meaning to offend. 'I didn' say nort out o' place, you. A stamp have got a front zide an' a back zide to un, hab'm er? Whatever's thik feller gettin' upzot about? Can't zee it mezelf.'

In those days freshly shot rabbits could be sent by post, unwrapped, simply with a label tied round their necks. Not surprisingly, the goods could be messy. Generally the dispatcher, not the deliverer, was to blame, but a particular lady receiving a rabbit seemed not to realise this. 'Oh, postman, that rabbit you brought yesterday was in a terrible state. He must have been a long time in the post and he bled all over the place.'

'Very sorry to hear that, ma'am,' said Jack peaceably, 'I'll zee what I can do nex' time.'

When the second rabbit duly arrived, Jack kept his word. He rang the bell and the lady came to the door.

'Yere's another rabbut fer 'ee, ma'am, an' I've a-putt stickin' plaaster awver the nawse an' eyes o' en an' stuck a cork up 'is aass 'ole. You 'on't 'ave no trouble wi' he.'

Never could 'sweet-scented manuscript' close on more fragrant a note.

The chapel built in Scrubbet, in its heyday.

Ruin of the Scrubbet chapel, 2003.

Laying the foundation-stone of the new Bible Christian chapel on a bitterly cold day in January 1907. Note the flags and the patriotic banner.

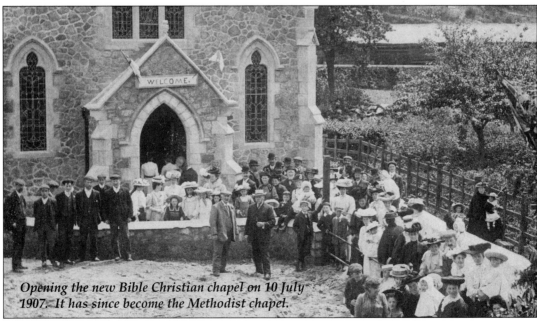

Opening the new Bible Christian chapel on 10 July 1907. It has since become the Methodist chapel.

Chapter 8

Worship

The Heralds of Change

The memoirs of some English writers born in the nineteenth century tell of their childhood apparently overshadowed by the gloom of moral lectures by the 'pater', family prayers morning, noon (possibly) and night, and three church services on Sunday, each one including a 60-minute sermon. The reality was far less dismal, and the experience of those writers, who came mainly from the middle classes, was by no means typical of the whole population.

In 1851 the Government held a religious census, and the results showed that the English were far from being the church-going nation that they were formerly believed to be. Over half had no contact with any church at all. In the working-class districts of some cities fewer than a quarter of the people ever went to church. The national average of 40 per cent was made up by country areas where more people went regularly to church than not.

Although it has been suggested that many people only went to church in rural areas because squire was watching, clearly quite as many did have a genuine faith and going to church was simply the natural outcome of that faith.

Roadwater and Washford people were typical of many villages in their mixture of the committed and the detached, but in one important respect they were very unusual – neither had a church. Washford people walked a mile over the hill to Old Cleeve, while Roadwater residents took the church path to Leighland, both places being served by the rector of Cleeve. Around 1800, however, Wesleyan churches began to spring up along the coast, but very little of this activity touched Roadwater until the 1820s when a young woman arrived from Devon.

In the summer of 1815, when England was drawing breath after Waterloo, a Cornish farmer named William O'Bryan left home to try to evangelise North Devon and founded a new church at Shebbear with 22 members. In a year membership swelled to 1,100 and they became known as 'Bible Christians'.

Right from the start, with a largeness of mind most unusual for those days, O'Bryan engaged women as missioners on virtually the same terms as men; they went everywhere on foot and were paid £14 a year, no more than the labourers they served. One of these young women, Mary Mason, came to Somerset in 1821, and the following year she and William Mason (not related) travelled all over the district, encountering much hostility and sometimes ill-treatment. They nevertheless persevered, finding receptive minds here and there, and sometimes a place to meet. On coming to Roadwater one of them stopped to speak to a roadside stone cracker, John Slade. Whatever was said struck a chord in John's heart and he made the preachers and congregations welcome in his cottage home (which later became the Post Office by the Bridge). Numbers grew, and after some years they were able to obtain enough land on which to build a chapel in a steep bank in Scrubbet. The bank had to be shovelled away before even the foundations could be dug, but the chapel was built and opened in 1841. For 50 years it was a place in which the lives of working men and women were transformed. That needs clarifying. The experience of conversion or spiritual rebirth may not have radically changed a man's or woman's character, but it certainly changed the way they thought of God, the 'unseen world', the way they looked at the natural world, the way they behaved and the way they thought of themselves.

As outlined in Chapter 1, the mid-1800s was a particularly difficult period for the agricultural class in rural England. Some were former smallholders, yeomen or tenant farmers forced off their land, and many who had enjoyed commoners' rights had been cheated of them by enclosures. After Waterloo, they all existed on wages barely sufficient to support family life. To stand erect and free with untugged forelock was out of the question for them, and perhaps beyond the imagining of most. Although it was not recorded what the missioner said to Slade, one may happily hazard a guess. It was pointless to preach a political revolution or promise any swift release from painful toil, but it was possible to give the roadmender a sense that he was not forgotten, that he mattered to God as much as King George himself, and that one day, if not in his earthly life, he would be richly rewarded in a heaven of joy. Parsons might talk abstractly, but for the labourers:

> ... it was a world of concrete realities that made up the objective of their faith and spiritual endeavour – 'sweet fields beyond the crystal flood' and 'golden harps, and thrones of gold' – and the poetry of it all appealed to them, as poetry always does appeal to the elemental instincts of the human spirit.

They came to believe that their poverty and trials in life would make them richer once in heaven; this re-birth gave them something for which to live.

To gear our minds to those of the re-born labourers taxes the imagination, but it is worth trying. From before daybreak on Monday until beyond sunset on Saturday we have been working for a pittance, we come home wet through and have nowhere to dry our clothes, our wives and children are hungry and 'starved' with the cold, the feeble fire is smoking, the thatch is letting in the rain and the bed is damp. Worst of all, we have our cottage only on sufferance, and at the end of it all, unless our children get on in the world, all we can look forward to is the shame of the poorhouse. Then, after half a lifetime of this, we are made to understand that by an act of belief, and of constancy in believing, we can find joy and 'holy, spiritual delight' here and now, and in the other life a heightened form of that joy in the presence of God, where we shall be princes, with crowns of stars infinitely superior to those worn by kings on earth. 'Sorrow and sighing shall be no more, neither shall there be any more pain.'

Many converts felt an impulse to tell the rest of the world about their new-found happiness and recommend them to take the same road. Life had taught these impromptu orators that everything had to be worked and paid for; the gift of salvation was earned by right living and by warning others of the penalties for sinning and failing to repent. If the new life gave them certainty and a quiet joy, it was also a solemn charge which made some of them over-censorious of harmless but worldly pleasures. However, this can be understood in the light of their emergence from a coarse stratum of society which was often brutal; they simply wished to save their neighbours from what they saw as the eternal consequences.

Besides that, it was peculiarly fitting that for some of them the new birth – the transforming moment – did not 'etherealise' them but heightened their vision of the beauty of the natural world. They had never read the English poets nor even heard of most of them, but in that one moment they recaptured something of the angel-infancy of Vaughan and the time when for Wordsworth all nature seemed apparelled in celestial light. One such Bible Christian, Lewis Court, recognised the transforming experience of Masefield's converted poacher as his own:

> O glory of the lighted mind.
> How dead I'd been, how dumb, how blind.
> The station brook, to my new eyes,
> Was babbling out of Paradise...
> The narrow station-wall's brick ledge,
> The wild hop withering in the hedge...
> Were God's eternal garden flowers.
> I stood in bliss at this for hours.

Such men and women, newly conscious of the dignity of their worth, became acutely aware of their illiteracy, their ignorance of grammar and 'correct' speech. To be worthy of their new calling they felt compelled to learn, to seek out or make for themselves the opportunities denied them in childhood. The Bible Christian Sunday school lending library was meant to serve this purpose. With this new learning came the acquisition of skills such as public reading and speech, and many, after an informal apprenticeship, were enrolled as local preachers. In the Roadwater membership of 88 and congregation of perhaps 150 there were seven or eight such men and women, who walked great distances, often up to 20 miles, six or seven Sundays in a quarter, to 'preach the word' in places as far apart as Watchet, Timberscombe, Bury, or Luckwell Bridge. Few could afford a pony, and some of these rugged individuals have left a memory in the hill country even after 100 years.

Of the characters who made something of a stir in the life of Roadwater many, including the animal doctors, the photographer, the cordwainers and bootmakers, the band leaders and at least three of their bandsmen, the wheelwright, the blacksmiths, the postmasters, the postmistress, the Vale miller and others, were all Bible Christians and proud to be such.

The Growth of Village Methodism

Methodism in Roadwater and the hill country dates back to the coming of the Bible Christians in 1821, and between 1870 and 1900 Roadwater, with more than 60 members, figured as numerically one of the three largest churches in the Kingsbrompton Circuit. More than double that number of people, however, were adherents who did not join the church or society but attended the simple, ritual-free services; the little chapel in the bank of Scrubbet must have been uncomfortably crowded, even after a gallery had been added.

In 1892 one of the ministers bought Fern Bank for the circuit and it remained the circuit manse for nearly 20 years. Shortly after the new century dawned, and encouraged by a succession of vigorous

Quarterly meeting, 1914. Left to right, back row: *Percy J. Bryant, Sidney Lile, John Coles, ?, Frank Hayes, Robert Chidgey, ?, George Westcott or Robert Burnett, ?, W.G. Court, Bob Melhuish;* front row: *Jack Quick, ?, Sammy Coles, Revd Morley Huxtable, William Court, Revd W. Arthur (?), Robert Melhuish, Jim Slade, ? Priscott.*

ministers (Albert Knight, Henry Down, Reuben Green and T.C. Jacob), the members turned their thoughts to building a new and more spacious chapel, one fit to be the head of the circuit; and as most of them were working folk on a low wage, or tradesmen only a little better off, the problem of raising the funds loomed very large. They were not to be put off, however, and one summer evening in 1906 a dozen members met to see what they could do. They found that if they contributed their savings they could put together £120 (or £10,000 in modern money). Thus encouraged, they went ahead. An old Roadwater boy, Revd Lewis H. Court, gave his architectural services, the blacksmith Tom Slade gave the site, they appointed Hine & Co. of Dunster as builders, Jim Slade as secretary and William G. Court as their representative on site. In January 1907, a bitterly cold day, the stone-laying took place.

In five months the work was complete, and on 10 July, a glorious summer day, the opening ceremony was held. Luncheon for 300 was provided in a large shed at Vale House and Captain A.F. Luttrell, of Dunster Castle, a gentleman greatly loved in the district, presided and 'expressed his pleasure at all he had seen and heard.'

It may have been more than a coincidence that the week the chapel was opened, the mines and railway reopened too, although perhaps both resulted from an upsurge of national confidence following the general election of 1906 and its promise of social change. The old chapel continued in use as a Sunday school and meeting room for 30 years until a builder, commissioned to 'tidy up the roof', knocked it in.

In 1950 the members again dug into their savings to build a manse in Mount Lane. It was opened on Whit Monday 1951 but was lost again 20 years later, together with the resident

Right: *A congregation came from far and wide for the opening service and lunch at Vale House, 10 July 1907.*

A sponsored walk of 32 miles was completed by Revd David Bolton to raise funds for the renovation of the Methodist chapel in May 2003. **Left to right:** *Jennifer Hand, John Staniland, David Bolton, Karen Bolton, Mark Court, Carol Tipper and Clare Court.*

*Jim Slade,
(1870–1923),
chapel organist
for 45 years.*

Right: *Christmas
Entertainment,
Boxing Day 1924 –
plenty of home-
grown talent!*

**United Methodist Church,
Roadwater.**

CHRISTMAS ENTERTAINMENT,

IN THE SCHOOLROOM.

Boxing Day, Dec. 26, 1924 at 7 p.m.

∴ **Programme** ∴

SONG .... A Christmas Greeting
RECITATIONS .. . M. Willis, B. Ridler, T. Ridler and W. Beaver.
SONG .... Some folks like to sigh.
RECITATIONS .... M. Taylor, M. Reed and E. Taylor.
SOLO .... Marion Murrell
RECITATION .... Miss Bourne.
DIALOGUE .... By six little girls.
A DEVONSHIRE DIALECT READING .... Rev. S. Arthur.
A SKETCH .... The Seasons.
SOLO .... Henry Shattock
RECITATION .... Mrs. Arthur.
DIALOGUE .... Daphne Bailey and Doris Ridler
SOLO .... Mr. S. Lile.
RECITATIONS .. U. Bennett, D. Warren, N. Bennett and M. Murrell
DIALOGUE .... Daisy Beaver and Edith Warren.
A SKETCH .... Her One Proposal.
CHRISTMAS SONG .... The Girls.

Price 2d.

Here's wishing you a **HAPPY CHRISTMAS**

*Walter Lile
(1898–1963),
chapel organist
for 40 years.*

Right: *Centenary booklet
for Beulah chapel, 1961.*

Below: *Beulah chapel, in the
corner of the Taunton–Bampton and
Taunton–Wheddon Cross roads, was built by
Bible Christians in 1861 for use by iron-ore
miners, many of whom came from Cornwall.
It fell into disrepair when the mines closed
but was restored in 1908–10 and serves a
widespread farming community in 2004.*

BRENDON HILL
"BEULAH" CHAPEL

KINGSBROMPTON METHODIST CIRCUIT
ORIGINALLY "BIBLE CHRISTIAN"

" Beulah "

Centenary Celebrations
1861-1961

Left: *John Cording of Roadwater Mill. He was largely responsible for having the mission room built.*

Below: *Miss Dorothea Shaw laying the foundation-stone of the church room, 1906. Her father, Revd Charles Shaw (with umbrella) is giving support.*

Church fête at Vale House, 1948.

Below: *The choir and guests, 1950. Left to right, back row: ?, ? Smith, Peter Lynes, Harry Nethercott, Sid Duck, Tom Reed, Geoff Carpenter, Percy Poole; middle row: Tom Webber, ?, ?, ?, ?, David Reed, ?, ?, Richard Burge, Mrs Lynes, John Tomkins; front row: Mrs Vi Burge, Mrs Amy Burnett, Barbara Nethercott, Revd Dr Beazeley, Revd G.V. Yonge?, Mr Gooding, Jennifer Ford, Mrs F. Carpenter, Mrs H. Gooding.*

Right: *Stone-laying ceremony for the manse, Whit Monday 1951. Revd J Martin, author of the best selling* Uncle *books for children, and William G. Court* (far right) *can be seen in this picture.*

minister, when Roadwater was absorbed in the new West Somerset Circuit. However, through two great wars the chapel, unlike the mines, and despite a heavy cost in maintenance, has gone on and never closed.

In 2004 the members take pride in the history of their church and in maintaining it in good working order, but they are no less concerned to look ahead. At the time of writing, plans are well advanced to make the interior suitable and attractive for a variety of purposes as well as Sunday worship, with a kitchen, access for disabled people, comfortable chairs and more space – for art and history exhibitions, coffee mornings, carol concerts and the like. (For further reading on Methodism in this area, see Lewis H. Court's *The Romance of a Country Circuit* and A.G. Pointon's *Methodists in West Somerset*.)

So many men and women have served the cause it is impossible to name them all here, but two men who earned a special tribute were the organists, Jim Slade and Walter Lile, who between them gave 85 years of unpaid service. Indeed, the renovated two-manual organ is worthy of them, with few rivals in village chapels for sweetness of tone combined with power when needed.

The Mission Church: St Luke's

For hundreds of years Roadwater had no Anglican church, but in 1841 the Bible Christians built their chapel on a small parcel of ground dug out of the hillside of Scrubbet. Those were times of mutual suspicion between the churches, and the conventional churchfolk of Roadwater, with the chapel before their eyes, must have been sore vexed at still having to tramp to Leighland every Sunday, rain or shine. This went on for over 30 years until about 1874, when they

The Sunday school, Easter Day, 1961. The picture includes: *Annette Ford, Diane Chidgey, Mr H. Gooding, Wendy Burge, Veronica Routley, Marlene Beaver, Marian Coles, Valerie Beaver, Marion Pugsley, Joan Case, Chris Priddy, Susan Nethercott, Jackie Lile, Shirley Nethercott, Geraldine Lile, Penny Porch, Angela Ford, Sheila Pugsley, Molly Routley, Susan Halliday, Tim Stollery, Andrew Priddy, Brian Routley, Philip Routley, George Case, John Nethercott, Shauna Taylor, Gill Priddy, Pat Beaver, Sally Chidgey, Mary Case.*

Presentation to church members Mrs Lynes and son Peter on their leaving Roadwater for Weston, 1950s. Left to right: Revd Dr Beazeley, Harold Gooding, Mrs Lynes, Peter Lynes, ?.

Coffee morning, 1991. Left to right, back row: Josephine Marshall, Chas Collins, Yvonne Evans, Vi Burge, Peter Pengelley, Nell Blythe, ?, ?, Vera Collins, Desmond Post; front row: May Webber, Flo Croucher, Evan Evans.

experimented with services in the 'large room' of the Valiant Soldier. Good numbers came, but they still felt the need of somewhere more regular, in both senses. A few of the more prosperous parishioners took it in hand, and with the cooperation of Revd W. Sweet Escott of Hartrow, who gave the site, G.F. Luttrell, who gave the stone from Lodge, Benjamin Nurcombe & Co. from Watchet for the masonry, and John and James Nethercott for the carpentry – all well-known, dependable names – the building was completed in four months for £350. It opened on 18 October 1876; being St Luke's Day in the Church calendar, he was taken on as their patron.

From the outset the trustees, Revd W.W. Herringham of Old Cleeve, Thomas Stone of Clitsome, John Cording of Roadwater Mill, John Risdon of Golsoncott, John Howse of Stamborough and William Gooding the postmaster, saw the building not as a substitute for Old Cleeve church or Leighland but as a mission room. The report of the opening ceremony read:

A small portion, about eight feet, is used for a communion, and is fitted with an altar, rails, etc... Services will be held on Sunday evenings, but occasionally in the morning... On week-days it is intended to hold an infant school in the room.

How long the school continued is not known, but it was still running seven years later with 35 children under the charge of Miss Henrietta Cock.

William Gooding's 20-year-old son, Arthur, took the post of organist – or harmoniumist – and in 1928 he and the church celebrated their golden jubilee together. In the meantime the harmonium had given place to a two-manual organ, and in the establishment's 30th year, perhaps when the kindly old rector retired and a High Churchman replaced him, the mission room became a regular church.

By 1906 a new church room, given anonymously but almost certainly by Cyril Tubbs of Croydon Hall,

had been added. The foundation-stone was laid by Miss Dorothea Shaw, the daughter of the newly-arrived vicar of Leighland, and in the years that followed she won universal affection for her work in the parish and beyond, particularly as a leader of the Scouts and Guides. Only two years later Mr Tubbs also gave two stained-glass windows as an offering of thanks for the recovery of his daughters Thelma and Dorothy from a serious illness.

In 1926 Harold Gooding succeeded his father as organist and served for 25 years – but this service was only one of the many benefits he conferred on his native village. After 1945 St Luke's, like churches throughout the country, was deserted by the children of its faithful supporters, and with the burden of repairs to the bell tower, its future seemed to hang in the balance. But as so often, the dark hour heralded relief. New residents attended and took active parts, a Sunday school was established and the organist, Charles Browning, formed a choir. Local artists Rachel Reckitt and Harry Horrobin created imaginative works of art, Major George Drew carved a Virgin and Child, and over a few years the interior of the church was remodelled, redecorated and given air, brightness and light. A visit to see the artefacts and memorials, including a bust of a former parishioner, John Brown, is better than any amount of description. Revd Peter Pengelley provides an overview:

It doesn't look like a church from the outside except for its bell cote and the notice-boards. However, on entering you find a well-appointed ecclesiastical interior with a sacred atmosphere. The church consists of nave, choir and sanctuary with two altars and is open for private prayer daily.

Adjoining the church building is the well-appointed church room, used regularly for both church and secular functions. As a 'daughter' to Old Cleeve Parish Church, St Luke's is a valuable asset to Roadwater, and our community would be impoverished if it ever became redundant through lack of support.

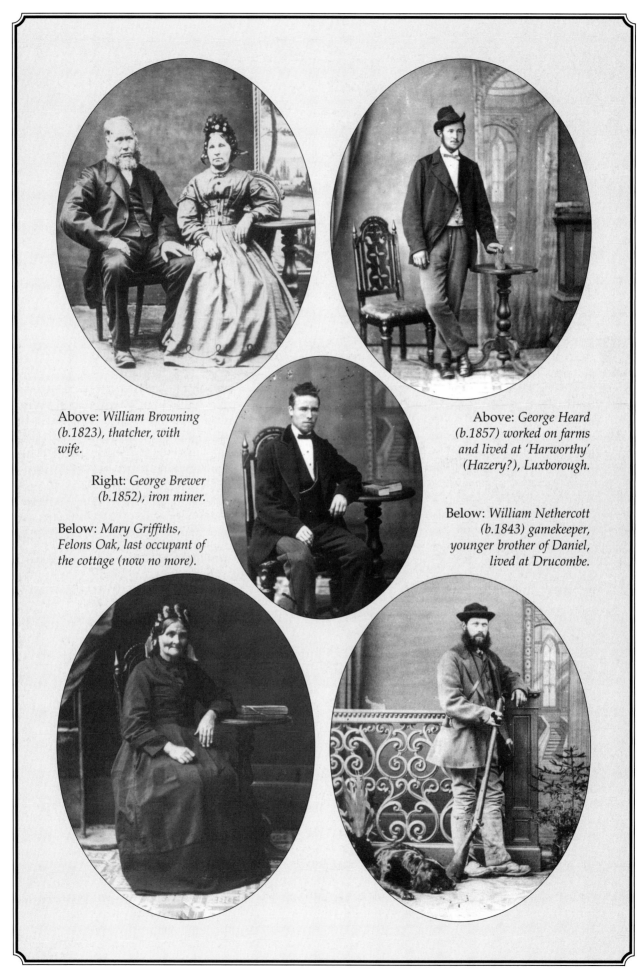

Above: *William Browning (b.1823), thatcher, with wife.*

Right: *George Brewer (b.1852), iron miner.*

Below: *Mary Griffiths, Felons Oak, last occupant of the cottage (now no more).*

Above: *George Heard (b.1857) worked on farms and lived at 'Harworthy' (Hazery?), Luxborough.*

Below: *William Nethercott (b.1843) gamekeeper, younger brother of Daniel, lived at Drucombe.*

Clockwise from top:
Avis, wife of William Nethercott, Drucombe; Keeper Hole from Luxborough; Abraham Reed (b.1815), lived at Lodge Rocks, spent all his working life on Escott Farm, his son George became a farmer, first at Broadwood, then at Sandhill; William Reed (b.1833?), great-grandfather of Bob Reed; Hugh Risdon, farm servant; Harry Nethercott.

Left: *Robert Rowe (1831–1904), thatcher, lived at Hayne.*

Right: *Lizzie Stone (née Court) of Golsoncott, wife of Thomas Stone, c.1890.*

Left: *George Shopland (b.1841), a packer on the railway line who lived at Pranketts.*

Right: *George Sully, farmer, of Lowood.*

Left: *William Welsher (b.1840), farm worker, lived at Hayne. His son Edward, a Bible Christian minister, won the Military Cross and the Belgian Croix de Guerre in the First World War.*

Right: *William Warren (b.1851) lived at Greenland and worked in Treborough quarry.*

Right: *Frank Court (1855–1923), nephew of William, with family. He was a master shoemaker and bandmaster of Roadwater's brass band in the 1870s. He moved to Nether Stowey and retired to Clitsome. Left to right: Alice (later Kemp), Wallace, Mrs Court, Katie (Morrill), Frank, Emily (Burnett), Lottie (Burnett).*

Left: *Lewis Court (1870–1960), minister, author, poet, historian, architect, woodcarver. He entered the Bible Christian ministry from Roadwater in 1893 and served in Cornwall, Devon and South Wales. A tall and powerful walker, even in his eighties he would walk from Washford to Luxborough, conduct two services and then walk back again. He did more than anyone to preserve the history and records of nineteenth-century Roadwater.*

Right: *Selina Mear (née Court) (1873–64), lady's maid in a Cambridge college and Menabilly House, Cornwall, she was widowed young. She served as postmistress from 1920–54.*

The Court family. Left to right, back row: Christopher Mear, Selina Mear (née Court), Lewis Court, Lucy Harrison (?) (née Court), Harry Calloway (workman); middle row: Bessie Court (wife of Lewis), William George Court, George Grinslade (whose 90th birthday was on 31 October 1905), Kate Court (née Grinslade, George's daughter), William Court (Kate's husband); front row: Lily Murrell (née Court), Matilda Court ('Tilly').

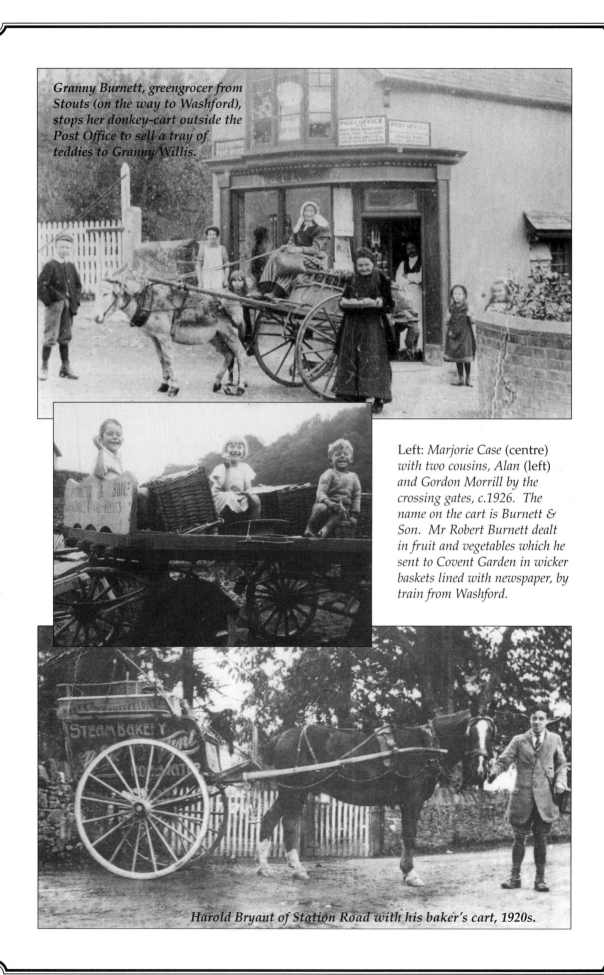

Granny Burnett, greengrocer from Stouts (on the way to Washford), stops her donkey-cart outside the Post Office to sell a tray of teddies to Granny Willis.

Left: *Marjorie Case (centre) with two cousins, Alan (left) and Gordon Morrill by the crossing gates, c.1926. The name on the cart is Burnett & Son. Mr Robert Burnett dealt in fruit and vegetables which he sent to Covent Garden in wicker baskets lined with newspaper, by train from Washford.*

Harold Bryant of Station Road with his baker's cart, 1920s.

Chapter 9
The Early-Twentieth Century

Memories of the Early-Twentieth Century

Bertha Routley

I was born in 1911 and came to Roadwater with my parents Jack and Susanna Marlow. My father had been in the Army in India and was very proud of his service – we always had to have everything spick and span. I got 3d. a week for cleaning my father's boots!

After my father came out of the Army he became the postman. We lived up the Mineral Line at Lower Hayne next to Mrs Willis. My other neighbour, Hettie Rowe, worked for the Salamans at Treborough Lodge and was the first to bring news of our success with the play The Lesson. *I remember Miss Shaw the vicar's daughter coming to visit Mrs Rowe.*

When I was about 16 I went into service into various farms in the neighbourhood which were often spartan and very cold. However, once, while working for a well-to-do family at Porlock, I was a waitress at a big reception. The gentry were dressed up to the nines in lovely gowns and the gentlemen in evening dress! We were kitted out in black and white outfits for the occasion which was great fun for us!

Dorothea Shaw

Dorothea Shaw.

Dorothea Shaw was a daughter of the vicar of Leighland, Revd Charles Shaw, who came to the parish in 1903. Dorothea is well remembered for the many activities in which she took a leading or helping role. In addition to keeping house for her father, and assisting with church and choir duties, she ran not only the Guide company, but unusually for her time, the Scout troop! She went everywhere on her bicycle and the account books of Mr William Court's cycle repair business at Washford record many a puncture and brake repair. Sadly, on the death of her father in 1931, Dorothea was obliged to leave Leighland and take a position as housekeeper in London. She died aged 60 and there is a lectern dedicated to her memory in St Giles' Church.

Joan Corfield

I was born at Manor Mills in 1922. It was a working mill then and farmers used to bring their horses and carts into the yard laden with sacks of grain. There was a hook on a chain hanging down from the loft at the top of the building and the sacks were hauled up. The inside of the mill was out of bounds – my mother was strict and we never disobeyed. I remember one old man who used to work there – his name was Mr Doble and he was very crippled. He lived with a relative called Mrs Perry in one half of the cottage later owned by Mr Priddy. [The mill ceased working in the 1950s and became derelict. It was sold to Walter Taylor in 1964.]

There were three cottages at Manor Mills [one house in 2004], and next door were two old ladies – Miss Radford and Mrs Cridland. The latter was a kind soul – she used to bring her teapot in every morning and share

Joan Corfield.

a cup with my mother. The Smith family who ran the bakery lived in the middle cottage – the bakery was in a lean-to building at the back.

There were Guides in the 1930s – they met at the Temperance Hall which was rather run down. The ladies who ran it were the two Miss Normans from Washford.

Joan Collins

Sid and Walter Lile of Tacker Street traded as 'Tailors and Breeches makers' from about 1925. Sid continued until about 1950. They had customers all over the Brendon Hills. The Lile brothers were musical and played for dance bands, with Fred Bond and my mother, Ivy. They practised on a pedal organ in the Bond cottage. Sid sang or played the fiddle, Walter played the piano, Mr Collins (my father) the banjo, and my mother the cello or bass viol. My first musical memory is of 'Alexander's Ragtime Band'.

Madame Lile Collins – Dressmaker and Costumier (Ivy) specialised in making habits for side-saddle riding. The garments were cut out in Sidney Lile's tailor's workshop. Lizzie Lile was trained as a milliner. She was employed in Cardiff at James Howell's department store, in charge of 'Manchester goods'– i.e. bed linen. Lizzie sailed to Wales and back every week on Campbell's steamers from Minehead. She married Herbert Piper of Vale Mills.

I remember the pony and cart that carried the mail being driven at breakneck speed through the village to catch the train at Washford. The postman doubled as a fish merchant, for which he changed hats – from billycock to a straw boater!

When I was a child in the 1920s the Valiant Soldier seemed to me to be a very rough place full of drunks. Granny Burnett had a shop in the square (Belle Vue) – she made toffee and twisted it into shapes on the door handle! Granny Bond next door always wore a man's cap except on Sundays when she wore a bonnet!

Val Hole (born 1935)

Schooltime – children walked to Leighland along the muddy pitted line, and then up the 'rocks,' carrying their sandwiches of bread and jam or bread and lard. Many children lived in old cottages where oil-lamps were the only lighting, and cooking was done on the range. Cohorts of black beetles, lurking in warm corners, waited for darkness to fall...

Water came from outside taps, or even a running spring at Hayman's Cottages, and privies were often shared with a neighbour.

Shopping was never a problem (apart from the cost!), as there were two or three butchers delivering as well as a fish man, and two bakers in the village. Mr Bryant of Station Road employed several men and had three vans delivering bread and cakes!

Many a rabbit found its way into a village cooking pot – and the skin would fetch a few coppers when the rabbit man came round.

The wireless! What a lifeline! But the radio did not run without an accumulator, so a visit to Mr Dyer's at Westmont for recharging was a 'must' once a week.

Entertainment was mostly home-made but varied – in summer you could swim in a pool 'up the moors' i.e. where the modern Roadwater fishery is located. Cricket was ever popular – but mind those sheep droppings on the outfield! There was no mechanical mower in those days. In winter football, billiards and snooker ruled, and it was a race to be first at the snooker room, while the older folk played whist.

A Time of Change: The First World War and its Aftermath

The widely held belief that after 1918 the world was never the same would certainly have been shared by some Roadwater people whose dear ones – fathers, sons and brothers – were lying dead in Flanders or the Middle East or had been swallowed by the hungry sea. For them the old life was gone forever. But for most people life had not changed unrecognisably. Although hemlines of dresses had risen to calf-length (and in places such as Minehead, naughtily higher, to the scandal of some returning ex-servicemen), for men in town the three-piece suit with hat or cap was still the wear, while the farm worker laboured as he had done before the war, in flannel shirt, waistcoat, corduroy trousers and hobnail boots, with a sack flung over his shoulders in heavy rain.

Yet somehow the atmosphere had changed a little. Even before the war the social reforms brought in by Lloyd George, such as old-age pensions and national insurance, had thrust the heart-breaking poverty of mid-Victorian days out of sight and given men and women a hope of avoiding the shame of the poorhouse in their closing years. Indeed, many of them looked forward to a gradual improvement. Then they were plunged into war and the light of reform went out.

When peace returned, the 'land fit for heroes' seemed slow to break free from wartime rhetoric, and perhaps no one believed in it any more than the politicians. Injustice and ill-rewarded labour were woven into the very pattern of English country life, but having fought or endured 'the war to end all wars' people were given cause for renewed hope. Farm wages had nearly trebled from 9s. or 10s. a week to 28s., and the halving of the value of money had not quite cancelled out the gain, so that very soon bicycles, bought at William Court's Post Office and store on the Bridge for 30 weekly half-crowns, were appearing up and down the village; Shanks' pony was gradually put out to graze.

W. Reed, Devon Regiment.

Jack Quartly Bishop.

Left: *Harold Gooding as a young cadet officer.*

Treborough men who returned from the First World War. Left to right, standing: ? Bishop, ? Bryant, Perce Baker, ? Baker (in top hat); seated: ? Griffiths, ?, ? Griffiths, ?, ? Hole. In 1920 the men returning from the war were honoured at a special gathering at the school. Mrs Salaman made 'a graceful little speech' and the rector Mr Jenoure presented ex-Private Baker with a top hat, which that gentleman had vowed to wear if he collected sufficient funds for the memorial. Mr E. Dyer then played his accordion and the evening concluded with dancing until the small hours.

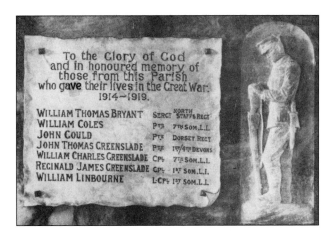

Above: *The Treborough memorial.*

Right: *Roll of Honour in St Luke's Church. These
certificates were mass produced and sold to parishes.
Several of these names also appear on other memorials,
notably the parish memorial at Dragon Cross,
and at St Andrew's Church at Old Cleeve.*

Below: *Leighland memorial in St Giles' Church.*

Yet life was still a struggle against poverty, with
the spectre of unemployment always lurking around
the next corner. People found that no catastrophe, not
even a world war, had the power to overturn or even
change a social order established for 850 years – and
indeed, such a revolution would have disconcerted
them entirely. The pre-war pattern of work and order
reasserted itself without effective protest – when the
big houses opened their doors again, a sizeable
number of village men found work on the estates and
farms and their wives and daughters in domestic
service. 'A job at Nettlecombe is a job for life' said one
father to his son. Meanwhile craftsmen and traders
served as part-time ancillaries, so to speak, and hoped
to be paid in due – or overdue – course.

All in all, by a happy combination of circumstances
these things worked out better for this neighbourhood than most people might have expected. It was
not merely that in the first years of peace all three big
houses changed hands – for new brooms can choke
their wielders with resentful dust. But whereas the
mansions and estates in the neighbouring parishes
have remained in one family for hundreds of years –
the Luttrells at Dunster, Trevelyans at Nettlecombe,
Wyndhams at Orchard and Stream – few of the nineteenth-century owners or residents of Croydon or
Treborough had remained for more than a generation
or established an overbearing presence and authority.
In addition, by the 1920s Golsoncott, once a manor,
was simply a large house in a village.

Fortunately, wielding feudal authority did not
enter into the ways of the new occupants of the

houses: the Reckitts of Golsoncott, Captain Bridges of Croydon Hall, the Salamans of Treborough Lodge and the Pecks of Treborough Quarry House, who all arrived in the neighborhood in or around 1920. Their authority was exercised for the next 20 years rather more subtly – and undeniably for the good of the village. Their several and notable contributions are recounted elsewhere (in Chapters 12, 13, 14, 15, 16 and 18), but in 1940 another world war, of even greater cataclysmic dimensions, brought to an end the way of life that was represented by these estates. Soon afterwards Captain Bridges and the Salaman family moved away, but Mrs Peck, though widowed, stayed on at Quarry House, and Miss Reckitt remained at Golsoncott for another 50 years. Happily, despite the long years, not all contact with the exiles was lost, and something of the life of those houses is recalled in the sections on Golsoncott and Treborough Lodge by two well-known authors, Penelope Lively and Nicholas Salaman, who were privileged to enjoy them half a century ago.

While they lasted the estates could only provide work for a minority of the people of working age, and by no means everyone relished that kind of employment. Plenty of ex-soldiers in 1919 like Kipling's Irregular cavalryman, had 'learned their trade / In the place where the lightnings are made', and more prosaically, had been pushed around for four years and barked at without the right of barking back. They would not willingly slip back into a social situation that all their sacrifice since 1914 had left essentially unchanged and feudal, no matter how mild the control. Their tragedy was that the coming of peace brought economic depression and no work to serve as a fitting reward for all they had endured. And for many a West Somerset man born and bred, emigration, even if it could be had, offered little attraction.

A few men found work at the Watchet paper-mill – it paid at least as well as farm labouring – and the 20-minute cycle ride, lit by a carbide lamp in winter, was no great trial. Others cycled to Minehead to work with Dewars or Burts or other building firms, while still more ventured to Gliddons in Williton, and one or two went by train to Taunton, leaving their cycles in a disused barn opposite Washford station. As already stated, not all of them could buy their cycles outright, but paying by weekly instalments set them on the road. The era of hire purchase had started, a complete break with the thinking of the past that said 'if you can't afford it, do without!'

The shortage of proper housing was eased a little in 1922 when the District Council built eight houses in Broadie. Most of the old cottages continued to be without indoor sanitation, bathrooms, mains water or electricity. Housewives drew water from the stream, where steps still lead down, from the pump (where the telephone kiosk stands in 2004) or from a tap set in the river wall opposite Hayman's Cottage.

The lack of a school in Roadwater nettled the mothers of the village and in 1928 they sent a petition to the Education Authority arguing the case. An official visited the village but the request was turned down and things continued as before. Children attended school from age 4–13 (later 14), either at Leighland if they lived around the Bridge or above, or at Washford if below. Those children going to Leighland had to walk up the Mineral Line to Higher Hayne and then up the steep, slippery rocks to crowd into a dank or stuffy classroom under the stern eye of Ernest ('Foxy') Reynolds. It was half as far again to the school at Washford, where Frank Pratt was the strict but fair headmaster and kind-hearted and rotund Miss Palmer was his assistant. There was always the chance of hitching a lift some of the way home on a farm cart, and if you could afford the ha'penny, a tube of liquorice and sherbet from Tom Burnett's at the foot of Station Hill to help you on your way.

Every year one boy and one girl gained a scholarship to the grammar school; the boys either attended the Secondary School in Alcombe or Taunton School and the girls went to Bishop Fox's. For the remainder, however, unless their parents could save up the £3 or £4 tuition fees and buy the uniform, full-time education stopped at 13. Indeed, many children – and their parents – were glad to be out earning.

Cricket and football flourished during the 1920s and '30s and were taken up vigorously again after the war. Players from nearby villages were welcomed into the teams, and in 1951 Roadwater won the West Somerset Championship. Men's football ceased about 1980 but cricket is still going strong, and a ladies cricket team was formed in 1998 under Sally White.

Cricket statistics have no place in a book of this kind. It is interesting to see, however, that many of the players associated with a particular match in the 1930s were people who played and supported the team right through to the middle of the century. Roadwater were playing away at Brompton Ralph and went in to bat. The stars were Dennis Smith with 98 and Harold Gooding with 100 not out, but also playing were Leslie Blanchard, Roy Davis, Tom Reed, Reg Smith, L. Willis, Bernard Coleman, Noel Evered (of Washford Mill) and Frank Noyes (from Pranketts). Bernard and Dennis bowled out the opponents for 65.

Roadwater people joined whole-heartedly in the national events which took place during the depression of the 1930s, especially George V's silver jubilee of 1935 and the coronation of George VI in 1937. Each year saw the celebration of Empire Day on 24 May, with the pretty sight of maypole dancing. With the onset of the Second World War, however, further changes were inflicted upon the village.

Right: *The Murrells, left to right: Will (became a builder in Minehead), Lewis (salesman in London, FEPOW, grocer in Minehead), Marion (died aged 20), with cousin Kathleen Mear (later Lile) (postmistress).*

Above: *Albert and Alice Case of Langridge Mills. Mrs Case (née Pounsberry) had been a governess. One of their grandsons is Rowley Ford, the well-known Master of the Hunt.*

Left: *Christine Murrell (née Baker) and Kathie Mear, in the court of Oatway, 1928.*

Below: *William Tompkins and his bride Mary Jane Lovell married in 1899 at Old Cleeve. William and Mary were Queenie Taylor's parents.*

Bottom left: *Emma Bishop and Harry Richard, c.1905. The Bishop family has farmed at Treborough for over a century.*

Above: *The Gooding family, c.1902. Left to right, back row: Claude, Arthur, sister-in-law Stone (?); front row: Dorothy and Fanny. The Gooding family ran the shop – the old Post Office and Sunbeam House – selling everything from ladies' clothing to paraffin. They only had to cross the road to visit their relatives in Mill House where this photograph was taken. Arthur played the church organ for more than 50 years.*

Parish Personalities, 1900~1950

Clockwise from top: *John and Mary Reed and family outside their home where the Village Hall stands in 2004; this picture may be of the Burnell family as it is signed 'Eli and Kit' and addressed to Messrs Case, of Glasses, c.1916; five smart young men at Vale, c.1939, left to right, standing: Peter Taylor, Arthur Takel, Albert Burge; seated: Bob Reed, Jack Warren; Wallace Nethercott, c.1920; a charming bridesmaid – Lily Gibson of Lower Roadwater in 1915.*

Above: *Gathering of the Court family in Station Road, 1925.* Front to back: *Leslie Kemp, Ronald Court (later the owner of the men's outfitters 'Gurds' in Station Road, Taunton), Ida Court, Alice Kemp, Emily Burnett, Katie Morrill, Lottie Burnett, Mary Jane Court, Wallace Court, Henry Morrill.*

Above: *One of the Bishop family emigrated to Grenada c.1890, married twice and had a large family. In 1979 there was a coup in Grenada, and the Prime Minister, Mr Bishop (possibly a relative), was assassinated. This young man (left) came to the UK to serve in the Forces during the war, and is seen here visiting a cousin, 'Old' Tom Bishop, at Lower Court, Treborough, 1940s.*

Right: *Frank Taylor with his 'Stop me and Buy one' ice-cream tricycle and a happy customer, 1930s.*

Below: *George Takle next to the pump at the garage on the site of the present shop, 1940s.*

Above centre: *The Sowden family of Leigh Cottage in 1941. John James and Eliza are in the centre.*

Below: *The Bond family at Manor Mills. Left to right: Bert, Mabel, Walter, Dorothy Patton, Florrie Patton (Bristol), Joan, Mr Patton.*

Chapter 10

The Second World War Remembered in Pictures

For King & Country

Top row, left: *Joe Nethercott;* right: *Pam Butler (later Thomas) in the ATS.*
Middle row, left: *Revd H.T. Matthews, vicar of Leighland, served in the Royal Navy;* right: *Alick Sowden.*
Bottom row, left: *Vi Griffiths (later Burge) in the ATS;* second from left: *Bob Reed in India;* second from right: *Dennis Parsons was an RAF gunner serving with 107 Squadron – he was shot down over Northern France in August 1943 whilst returning from an operation to disable the Gosnay power station near Bethune – his grave is at Auchy-au-Bois near Agincourt;* right: *Frank Parsons, Royal Tank Corps, was torpedoed in the Mediterranean on his way to the Middle East, in January 1943 – his name is on the memorial at Medjez-al-Bab, Tunisia.*

The Home Front

'The Three Joans' (Bowden, Burleigh and Burnett), land girls, walking down the Mineral Line. Originally from London, they all married local men and settled in Somerset.

The girls hoeing thistles in 1942.

Above right: *Mr Fred Carpenter as a Special Constable and Mrs Ethel Carpenter in St John's Ambulance uniform.*

Right: *Firewatching at County Hall, Taunton, 1942. This photograph was taken on the roof of the building. Joan Keene is seated front right.*

Below: *Marjorie Case married Jim Moir of the Royal Navy, in July 1945, just after the end of the war in Europe. The beautiful wedding dress had been kept in store by the photographer in Minehead since before 1939.*

Below: *Otto Kun was an Austrian refugee who arrived in Somerset in 1939. He was taken in by Mr and Mrs Reckitt at Golsoncott and is seen here aged 16 wearing a suit handed down by Basil Reckitt. Otto later joined the Pioneer Corps and after the war made a successful career in the motor industry. He died in 1999.*

Above: *These two boys, Roy Huntley, aged four, and Alan Huntley, aged seven, arrived in the village as evacuees the day after war was declared on 3 September 1939. They were billeted on Mrs Frank Keene of Golsoncott Lodge, and stayed until the end of the war.*

GI wedding, 18 June 1945. A popular local girl, Dorothy Warren, daughter of George Warren, married Charles Davis of Portland, Oregon. She later joined Charles, travelling by train across the United States via New York and Chicago with a party of other GI brides. Charles and Dorothy had three children before Charles died in 1969. Dorothy kept in touch with her friends Amy Davis and Queenie Taylor in Roadwater, and came over for a visit in 1996. Left to right, back row: *Mrs E. Smith, Mrs D. Beaver, Mrs L. Coles, Frances Hole, evacuee, Pam Burnett, evacuee, Mrs D. Hole, Mrs E. Bryant, Mrs A. Poole, Mrs N. Appleyard, Mrs M. Hemmett;* middle row: *Mrs R. Burnett, Mr Harold Gooding, Mrs Dorothy Gooding, Mr G. Takle, Mrs M. Bennett, Miss Fry, Mrs Lang, Mrs Hemming, Mrs Gibson, Charles Pike (best man), Biddie Maddock, Charles Davis (bridegroom), Revd Dr R. Beazeley, Mrs Amy Davis, Dorothy Warren (bride), Miss Maddock, brides cousin, Mrs Bessie Ford, Mrs A. Gooding, Ted Burge, Geoff Carpenter, Mrs F. Carpenter, Mrs Audrey Rose;* seated: *Avril Pike, Mrs Edie Pike, child, Reg Davis with a child on his lap, May Gibson and Pat Davis (bridesmaids), George Warren, Mrs Emmie Burge, Richard Burge;* children in front row: *Bobbie Gibson, Mavis Lang or Evelyn Smith, Alan Hemming, Jenny Ford.*

Left: *When the Americans came in the spring of 1944 and camped on Treborough Common, life changed for everybody. There were dances in the Village Hall, the pubs sold out of cider, and many local people entertained GIs in their homes. This snap is of Anthony (Johnny) Volpi of Philadelphia who was befriended by Frank and Daisy Hole.*

Nicholas Salaman remembers:

When the Americans came... they came to dinner and gave parties, and made much of the women of Treborough (Mrs Salaman, her companion, daughter and daughter-in-law, who all lived there during the war.) They gave wonderful open days at their camp, regaling us with Coke and steak sandwiches!

Gordon and Jack Harris remember:

During the war Dad was in Civil Defence and we were in the Scouts. We had a lot of fun doing emergency rescue practice. I had to fall off my bike on the bridge so they could try out first aid on me. We also practised being hoisted up on pulleys in George Warren's yard. When the Americans were camped up at Treborough we used to cycle up there with bread and buns from Bryant's to sell to the troops. They gave us chewing gum and chocolate – smashing!

Above: *Now a listed monument, the pill box at the top of the village was designed to look like a cottage orné. Pictured here is Sid Case, a former Home Guard member, posing in the 1970s for Jack Hurley's book* Wartime on Exmoor.

Left: *A Christmas aerogramme sent to Joan Keene from her fiancé, Bob Bosley, serving in North Africa. The letters were photographed and reproduced from film.*

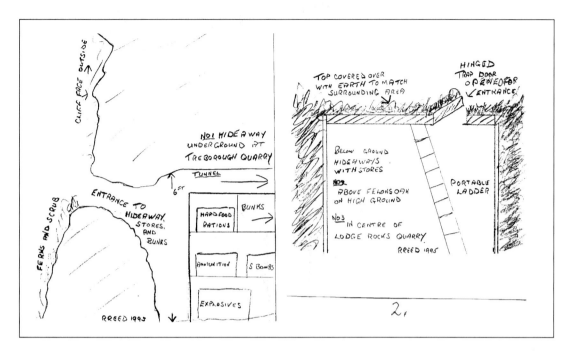

Above: *Bob Reed's sketch of the dug-out in a disused tunnel at Treborough quarry, the base for the 'secret Home Guard' unit. Supplies of food and ammunition were stored here. There were similar dug-outs at Lodge and Rodhuish.*

Right: *Just some of the members of the local 'secret Home Guard'. In 1940 when the threat of invasion was very real, Winston Churchill ordered the formation of a force of men to be trained to use guerrilla tactics against the enemy. The men were recruited from the Home*

Guard and were sworn to secrecy. This group of men was snapped while training in Treborough quarry. Col Adrian Peck remembers as a boy seeing the men at shooting practice there, and Nicholas Salaman, a small boy at the time, recalls picking up a 'dull metallic tube with fins' causing great consternation among the grown-ups. It was a mortar bomb! Fortunately the bomb didn't go off. Left to right, standing: Jim Beaver, Leonard Coles, Walter Taylor, Wilfred Parsons; seated: Stan Beaver, Charlie Burge.

Left: *Topsy Takle in the taxi outside Sunbeam House – an Austin 12 – in the 1940s. Topsy was well-known in the district as a driver, and during the air raids on Weston during the war she ferried members of the Civil Defence force from Roadwater to the scene of action and back again in the small hours.*

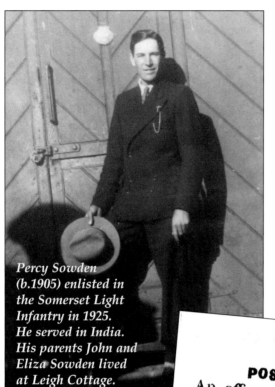

Percy Sowden (b.1905) enlisted in the Somerset Light Infantry in 1925. He served in India. His parents John and Eliza Sowden lived at Leigh Cottage.

One Family's Story

At Sunwai, India, 1930.

Below: *This photograph was taken inside the camp at Lamsdorf, Stalag VIIIB. Percy is the fifth man from the left in the back row. By this time he was nearly 40 and his hair had already turned grey.*

ROADWATER

POSTED AS " MISSING "

An officer of the Queen's Royal Regiment hash informed the parents of L.-Corpl. Percy John Sowden that he was posted as "Missing" on May 20th last. In a letter conveying this intimation, the writer stated, "It is with the deepest regret that I have to inform you that your son has been posted missing. Your son was one of the section commanders of my platoon, and in expressing my sympathy to you I would like to say how useful he was to me in command-

Above: *When war broke out his unit was posted back to Europe. Percy was captured at Dunkirk while serving with the Queens Royal Regiment. The West Somerset Free Press reported the news in June 1940.*

Percy Sowden
6121
N-Stammlager VIIIB.
Deutschland (E 433)

Left: *While Percy was a prisoner his mother wrote to him regularly and sent photos. These were all censored and bear the official stamp.*

This picture: *Memorial on the site of the Lamsdorf camp, photographed by Mr G. Cairns of Dumfries in 1978.*

To.
Percy J. Sowden
Prisoner of war
Germany
=

Above: *In 1944, Eliza died. John Sowden sent his son an incompletely addressed memorial card. Amazingly, Percy received the card – in the same POW camp that fellow Leighland man Charley Routley also spent time, Lamsdorf in Poland.*

Right: *All servicemen received a welcome home certificate. After his return, Percy settled down and became an active member of the Roadwater Football Club.*

The Inhabitants of
ROADWATER & DISTRICT

Welcome Home

PERCY J. SOWDEN

from the WAR of 1939–1945 and ask acceptance of the accompanying small token of their pride and gratitude.

Left: *In 1938 Vernon Bartlett, a foreign affairs expert on the* News Chronicle, *fought a by-election on the need to stand up to Hitler. He served as an Independent Progressive MP until 1950. Here he is on the Bridge with Mrs Bartlett in the 1945 general election. The picture includes: Harold Schofield (agent), ? Shopland (Golsoncott), Peter Burnett, Harry Burnett, Joe Webber, Mrs Bartlett, Vernon Bartlett, Mrs Chidgey and Colin, Mrs Kathleen Lile, Mrs Bertha Western and Evelyn Furse.*

Roll of Honour: Men from Roadwater District Killed in the Second World War

Adam Salaman, Pilot Officer, died while on active service in Lincolnshire and is buried in Treborough churchyard.

Major Gilbert Peck of Quarry House, Treborough, was lost in North Africa in November 1942. His name is recorded on the El Alamein memorial in Egypt and in Treborough church. He was serving in the 3rd Kings Own Hussars RAC.

Ernest Bowden of Sticklepath died in an accident and is buried at Nettlecombe.

Sam Wright of Roughmoor died as a POW in a Japanese camp in 1942.

Frank and Dennis Parsons.

Jack Smith died after returning from war service in Burma and is buried at Leighland.

Dinner in the Village Hall for veterans from Roadwater district and Luxborough, 1945. George Takle is seated with leg outstretched on the left and Miss Laugher is seated front right.

Chapter 11

Farming and the Countryside

Clitsome Farm

John Fouracre was born at Clitsome Farm in 1920 and lived there until 1932. He was educated first at Yarde and then Minehead and Wellington Grammar Schools. At the age of 18 he joined the Somerset Light Infantry and served for 29 years. At the time of writing he lives in Porlock. His memories of the farm and village are given below:

David Case at Glasses Farm, 1920s.

Clitsome Farm was about 200 acres and was owned by Sir Walter Trevelyan. The agent was Mr Tarr who lived at Yarde. We had four cart-horses, calves to store cattle, one cob and trap, which was the only means of transport, six cows, about 200 ewes, two sows and two pigs for fattening. My father grew wheat, oats, barley, mangolds, swedes and turnips. The shepherds were Fred Taylor and George Lockey, while Walter Bond looked after the horses and Jack Tarr and John Howe (from Leighland) were labourers. Mr Duddridge farmed up Slade Lane. He also worked at the mill in Watchet.

We never had bulls, although Mr Quartly of Beggearnhuish had shorthorns. Devons were bred at Roadwater Farm where they held a North Devon herd. Boars were kept by Ivor Palmer at Stamborough. I remember once my brother Hubert and I were sent up to Stamborough with two sows to be served. It was a long walk up the hill, and on the way home the sows started to get tired. They flopped down in the road by the old chapel and refused to budge. My brother and I were very annoyed as we just wanted to get home!

Pig killing was done by Mr J. Jones of Williton. I remember when a pig had been killed, Mrs Lockey used to clean the entrails. I can see her now standing over a big pail of water with a string of chitterlings in her hand.

Shearing took place at Escott Farm where they had a large shearing shed.

When we moved to Thorne St Margaret in 1932, Mr Dascombe took over Clitsome.

There were two pubs in the village – the Valiant Soldier and the Roadwater Inn. Mr Mead, an ex-policeman, owned the former and George Takle had a garage behind the pub. Charley Ford had the

Carting mangolds at New Close, Glasses Farm, c.1905.

Left: *Loading the cart while haymaking.*

Below: *Ready to go!*

Below left: *Frank Fouracre leading the horse home.*

Right: *Making the rick.*

Below: *Frank Fouracre gathering the sheaves.*

John Fouracre (foreground) and Walter Bond.

Left: *Refreshment in the field –
home-made cider. Walter Bond
is on the right.*

Below: The *West Somerset Hunt meet
at Clitsome with Charlie Back, 1920s.*

Below left: *John Fouracre in front of
Clitsome Cottage, c.1928. The cottage
is derelict in 2004.*

Above: *A nice snap, taken with Mrs
Fouracre's Box Brownie, of the children
with Phyllis Purchase, a guest from
Wellington.*

Left: *Children in the yard with summer
visitors. Left to right: Barbara Cowley,
John Fouracre, ? Cowley with hen,
Mary Fouracre, Margaret Fouracre,
Hubert Fouracre.*

Badger dig in Langridge Woods.

Frank Fouracre examining the sheep for foot rot at Clitsome, 1920s.

Roadwater Inn for years, and his wife ran it after he died. (One son Cecil later had a garage by the hall and the other took over Yeaw Farm.) They used to make their own cider in the big barn (since demolished). We made cider too, and my father gave an allowance to the men. I can remember once one of them swaying around on top of a hayrick after helping himself too generously. We all wondered if he would fall off.

Mr Badcock of Badcock & Evered lived at Lowood at the bottom of the village. The cottages (on the corner, since demolished) were occupied by Fred Taylor and his mother, Tom Webber and his mother and Mrs Howe. George Masters collected the rabbit skins.

I remember the stonecrackers' place behind Nethercotts. It was at the entrance to the sheep dip, alongside the river opposite the sawmill. The man carried a big hammer and wore two thick sacks and eye protectors.

Mary Wickstead's memories:

My parents Frank and Eva Fouracre came to Clitsome Farm after their marriage in 1919. They rented it, I think, from the Nettlecombe estate. One thing that stands out vividly in my memory is Sir Walter Trevelyan's funeral. We all stood by in silence as the hearse with the coffin passed by on its way to Nettlecombe church.

I have very happy memories of my childhood. As Clitsome is in Nettlecombe parish, our school was at Yarde – a three-mile walk there and back. We loved the house and farm. I remember Walter Bond and Fred Taylor working for my father. The neighbours were kind and cheerful – I was sorry for poor Mrs Nethercott in Riverside as they were continually being flooded out, but she was resigned to it I think. My mother was kind and used to send milk and eggs to families that were in need. I remember her looking after Sidney Lile's children when his wife was very ill. She also used to visit a handicapped boy who lived

in the cottage on the site of the present Corner View.

We took visitors in the summer and some of them were very nice people. The editor of the Daily Express *came every year with his family. Also a poor artist from St Ives whose name I've forgotten – he spent his days painting.*

Memories of 1950s Chidgley

Mike Roberts

In 1947 my uncle Arthur Walker came to Chidgley with his wife Freida as a tenant of the Nettlecombe estate, after Mr Burnell. In the mid 1950s he bought it from Mr Garnet Wolseley. As a schoolboy I spent my holidays on the farm and have many happy memories. People who worked there were Fred Dunn (stockman), Ern Moore (tractor driver) and Ernie and Walter Bowden of Sticklepath.

Visitors included Tom (baker's boy), Mac the vet, the milk-marketing lorry, mobile library, and Nethercotts, delivering sawdust for the hen house. Mr Macauley, a churchwarden, lived at Nettlecombe Lodge, followed by Bill and Olive Reynolds, Dennis and Betty Reed. Later the Tuckeys and Wills were at Hook Hill. Will and Ivy Hole lived just down the road. Dr Hardman started his surgery in a cottage at Hook Hill when Roy Thorne left. The Newtons lived at Timwood, Bert Calloway at Comberow and Alf Takel at Colton. The Brewers farmed Wood Advent and ? Cooke farmed Huish Barton. Another farmer I remember was Bungey Barnes. Mrs Preece kept Raleighs Cross Inn and we always went up for the annual sheep sale.

Fred Dunn taught me a lot of local history – one thing was that mariners used Kingsdown Clump as a navigation aid for finding Watchet Harbour.

In 1960 my uncle and aunt retired and the farm was divided. Albert Willson had Chidgley Hill Farm and the West-Sadlers bought Chidgley farmhouse and land to the east of the road.

Clockwise from top left: *The Dunns' cottage; Arthur Walker with his dogs and Ferguson tractor; Ken Dunn with Mike and Arthur Roberts at Chidgley; Arthur Roberts driving the tractor; Tom Bishop judging sheep at Treborough; Arthur Walker was a keen horseman and while at Chidgley he bred a colt, Neil, which was eventually purchased by the Metropolitan Police and in 1969 ridden by Her Majesty the Queen at the Trooping of the Colour; Jean Walker and Arthur Roberts with hand-reared calves.*

Left: *Harry Bishop ploughing the field overlooking the Luxborough valley in 1947. Harry is using an iron plough and this was the last time he ploughed with horses. It was probably safer than a tractor on such a steep slope.*

Above: *Reed making, c.1985.*

Right: *Threshing at Lower Court.*

Above: *Present generation at Lower Court, 2003.*

Chapter 12

Vale House

Vale House, 1930s.

Vale was originally a fulling mill, where locally produced cloth was treated to have the grease removed with fuller's earth, after which the cloth was 'tucked' (hung up to dry on the racks or terraces on the hillside in the fields known as Rack Cleeve – perhaps Tacker Street was originally Tucker Street). When ready, the cloth was taken by cart or pack-horse to market, most likely in Dunster or Bampton.

This trade had ceased by 1839, when the 'Mill and Factory' were described as 'unoccupied'. The house became a private residence and was no doubt improved and modernised, probably by Amos Tudball, who died in 1878, or by the Pritchards, who came there from Quarry House, Treborough, after a spell in Treborough Lodge. William Pritchard senr died in 1882. When Mrs Pritchard gave up the rental of Treborough quarry and moved away in 1888, Harry Cording from Kingsbrompton took over and, it seems, restored the mill for corn. However, by the time of his death in 1918 it was not in very sound shape.

About 1920 Charles Wingfield Figgis moved in and ran Vale as a guest-house and took an active part in the musical life of Roadwater. He found the mill to be in a dangerous condition so demolished it and William Court used the oaken vanes of the wheel to make a staircase for his new house in Washford. In 1938 Harold Gooding moved to Vale from Fern Bank and kept his benevolent eye on the fortunes of the village until his death in 1978.

In the 'Sea Lion' year of 1940 a machine-gun pillbox, disguised as a shingle-roofed summer-house, was built at the top of the drive. Recently the ivy which had grown over it has been removed and the shingles have gone, but the present owner of Vale House, James Evers, hopes to be able to restore the building to its earlier condition.

Recollections of Vale

Michael Figgis

Vale House, just west of the Valiant Soldier, was the dilapidated house my father, Wingfield Figgis, bought after his return from the Western Front. There, from

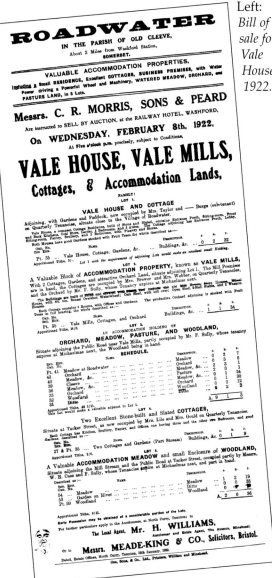

Left: Bill of sale for Vale House, 1922.

we could spend the dinner hour together in the tool shed; he told me tales of animals and country lore. Weathered, stocky and strong, he could accurately throw a stone 50 paces. His corduroys below the knee were tied with straps he called yorks 'to keep the rats out' he told me. With a rake on his shoulder, you would see John jogging along the river bank towards some crisis or another – the ducks in danger of the waterfall or my own yells having fallen in the forbidden mill-race.

Mr Gooding (Claud and Harold's father) in a brown overall kept the well-stocked village store, living in the immaculate house kept by Mrs Gooding next door. I learnt to love the sight and stench of all that went on in the nearby smithy, the ringing anvil and the heavy horses holding up their hairy feet in a shower of sparks.

Village concerts organised by my father brought folk crowding into the hall by the church. He entertained with the songs he accompanied himself. Sometimes he also performed with the BBC in Cardiff or at Savoy Hill in London. On such occasions one was lifted from a warm bed to join those downstairs who were 'listening to his master's voice' on headphones. Local talent in Roadwater could also be augmented by a professional conjuror or singer my father had known in his concert party days in France. When this was all the entertainment available, village concerts were popular occasions. So, too, were the contributions made by the Roadwater Brass Band my father helped to revive, with Tom Ridler as bandmaster, supported by his sons and many other local people, a tradition of brass instrument playing being strong, especially among families living along the Mineral Line. Practice sessions took place in a room behind the Valiant Soldier, or sometimes at Vale House.

These were quiet years before the social revolution began in the 1950s. Horses worked the farms, and the local roads were virtually empty. With dogs and a pony, not to mention John Milton and my parents, Vale House gave me a marvellous boyhood.

about the age of six, I spent the early years of a splendid boyhood in the mid-1920s. The romantic old house, cob walled and slate flagged, could be flooded in winter by the trout stream which normally passed through pools and shallows two sides of the house before reaching the pack-horse bridge, over which cloth had travelled from the mill and across the gorse-covered hills to Watchet. The mill was derelict and unsafe, so we took it down.

After the First World War, time stood still. No television or radio. In fine weather my bearded grandfather pottered on his stick. His wife, my Quaker-bonneted grandmother, travelled in a Bath chair, often propelled by friends on their cycles. Primitive cars occasionally brought dust clouds to the valley road, one or two friends calling at our petrol pump, which mainly supplied the T Model Ford truck that was our workhorse.

John Milton, my first friend, was the gardener who walked up from the Mount each morning with a straw shoulder bag containing his bread and cheese and a bottle of cold tea. I had a smaller but similar bag so that

Michael Figgis and friend at Vale House, c.1928.

Chapter 13

Croydon Hall

The estate around Croydon Hall stretches for approximately one mile and forms the boundary to the village at the southern end on the west side. The purchase of both the Vale House estate and the Escott Farm lands that border the village by Captain John Bridges RN probably restored to the original Croydon estate something of its former expanse. Documents show that it formed part of the large tract of land known as Crowedon or Croydon Hill, extending from Timberscombe for five miles or more to the valley at Roadwater and from Carhampton and Withycombe on the coast to Luxborough. A considerable portion of its high land carried common rights for landholders in these parishes. In Saxon times the holdings of the lords of Rodhuish, Dunster, Timberscombe, Withycombe and Earl (later King) Harold's Cleeve no doubt reached up into the broad range of Croydon Hill, and the land of Carhampton mentioned in King Alfred's will took in much of the hill extending to Timberscombe. At the time of the Norman Conquest it became one of the ill-gotten gains of the Mohuns along with the Lordship of Dunster.

In the fifteenth century it belonged to Cleeve Abbey, and in 1517 the abbot could claim from the holding a dinner and supper once a year for himself and 20 men at Croydon manor-house, later to become Croydon Farm, and possibly Croydon Hall. On the dissolution of the abbey Henry VIII granted its possessions to the Earl of Sussex (1538) and a successor sold them to the Boteler family. An agreement dated 1605 between Robert Boteler and George Prowse, gentleman, both of Old Cleeve, records that in November 1599 Robert Earl of Essex sold the grange and farm called Croydon, with Croydon Wood and Smythes Wood, to George Prowse for £2,000.

Left: *Croydon Hall when it was a manor farm, 1880.*

Below: *Croydon Hall after renovation by Cyril B. Tubbs.*

Cyril Tubbs' car, a Delaunay Belleville registered in 1908.

Croydon Hall club house, in a picturesque and distinctive local style (compare Hazery, Couple Cross and the cottage at the foot of Jumper's Steep, Luxborough), built by Cyril Tubbs for the estate workers, c.1905. It burnt down in 1931.

The Prowse family were prominent hereabouts in the sixteenth and seventeenth centuries, with properties at Minehead, Dunster, Withycombe and Old Cleeve. The old name of Proud Street for the modern Station Road must surely reflect their ownership, and a title deed dated 1771 shows that the site of the Methodist church was Prowse land.

In 1801 James Bindon was in possession, and a generation later, in 1839, Richard Bindon was farming 162 acres, of which 140 were arable. The farmhouse was an imposing building with large wings, set in a compound of two acres. It was much the same, though now dignified with the name of Croydon Hall, when James Pile, from Brendon, Devon, took it over in 1879/80, but as agriculture had plunged into decline and he farmed the now 175 acres with only two workmen, he cannot have had much spare cash for enlargement, nor would the next owner, who took over the property in 1888.

In due course a new breed of landowner, mainly wealthy members of the professions or industrialists, took up residence. The first was Cyril Bazett Tubbs, nephew of Henry Wills of Bristol, the 'tobacco king'. He worked in Datchet as an architect and surveyor and took over Croydon Hall in 1901. He entered into his new role with gusto. Over the next seven years he used his skills to transform Croydon from a large farmhouse into a semi-palatial gentleman's residence. He converted the court into a garden and relocated the farm buildings to the north. He was also a zealous patron of St Luke's, arranged a baby show in the gardens and ran one of the first cars in the neighbourhood, a magnificent 28hp Delaunay Belleville limousine finished in dark green with red lines.

But it was under the next owner, from 1909 to the outbreak of the First World War, that Croydon Hall attained its hour of glory.

Count Conrad von Hochberg

His name lingers on in popular memory, and his story is worthy of inclusion here because of its high tragedy, and each telling is no more than a slight attempt to do justice to an ill-used man. Like many millions of people living in this period, the Count was a victim of war but few can have suffered the pain of divided loyalties as acutely as the Count.

The Count had Englishness in his blood, even though he was a cousin of the Kaiser and a reserve captain in the White Cuirassiers of Potsdam. His elder brother, Prince Henry of Pless, and his younger brother Friedrich both married in England. Count Conrad took Croydon Hall in 1909 and although Cyril Tubbs had done much to make it a gentleman's residence, the Count, familiar with the ducal traditions of Central Europe, spent freely to create a stately residence of which the cultured among his ancestors would have approved.

He rapidly made a place for himself in the agricultural and sporting world. He was President of the Dunster Summer Show and the Winter Show of 1912, and after the latter he presided at dinner in the Luttrell Arms, proposed the royal toast and addressed a few pleasing remarks to the company – he was an entertaining conversationalist –

Count Conrad von Hochberg (right) with his private secretary, Captain J. Whitehead, for whom he built Golsoncott House.

whereupon Mr Hill, of Chargot, proposed the Count's health and said it was up to them 'to keep so good a sportsman in their midst.' The Count replied that since coming here he had 'met with such kindness that he felt quite at home and hoped it would always be the same.'

In his daily life the Count was courteous as well as a considerate and generous employer. Living in considerable style, with more than 20 horses, he needed a large staff and paid them well. He attended the Parish Church most Sundays and, of course, expected the servants to go as well, but allowed them to take the car while he walked! Some years after the war, to combat the foul libels that had been printed about the Count, his chauffeur Charles Criddle, said:

He was more like a friend than an employer. His tastes were simple – those of a country gentleman. He was extremely fond of stag-hunting and fox-hunting, [but] he did not care for hare-hunting. Passionately interested in gardening and highly cultured, he was in every respect one of nature's gentlemen.

A visitor from Taunton in 1914 found Croydon Hall wholly enchanting:

Very charming is the prospect, and the architecture of the residences of the responsible workers on the estate is in keeping with the scenery. On the left is a picturesque thatched residence, once a club, and now a mission hall, fully licensed for services, this being provided through the generosity of the Count. In an adjoining farm, which might be described as a model one, lives Mr Butler, the farm bailiff. On the other side of the entrance lives Mr Perceval, the gardener, who is a skilful artist in the laying-out of grounds; a walk through a miniature avenue of lofty trees, and unexpectedly the Hall lies before one, ensconced in a little dell... The residence has been entirely rebuilt since the Count purchased it five years ago, and it possesses every convenience, being lighted throughout with electricity.

In the garden the herbaceous borders made a wealth of colour, and a rock garden is in the course of formation. A very pleasing effect is secured by the lawn and flower beds on a natural mound, and one of the glories of this side of the house is a group of hydrangea. At the rear of the house the gardens are laid out in the Italian style. Everything was in apple-pie order, and the arrangement of the garden has been to make the best of natural surroundings.

On the Minehead side of the drive the feathered world was very prominent, Indian game being the chief breed of fowls, while the ducks are the finest we have seen for a long time. Glass houses and poultry sheds are in great variety, and the Count this year has spent several hundreds of pounds on glass. One house is devoted to carnations. The farm is quite up-to-date, and this brief description will give an idea of how thoroughly the Count has entered into the life of a country gentleman.

Croydon had never been shown to greater advantage, nor had the social scene appeared more brilliant, than on 24 July 1914; one might almost view the day's event as a grim and Euripidean parable of prosperity waiting for destruction and chaos. By 24 July the shadows over Europe were lengthening, but not everyone – certainly not the Count – could believe that the night was about to fall. On that day he gave a garden party, and a large number of people accepted his hospitality. Altogether there were 45 motor cars, 15 carriages and three saddled horses accommodated in the stables. Maynard's of Taunton – still remembered by some – provided the catering. (With his passion for gardening, while Maynard's staff were preparing in the house, the Count was going round the garden doing little odd jobs such as cutting off dead flower buds.) The guests were informed that immediately after the party their host would be leaving for five weeks in Scotland. He left for London and a week later Austria declared war on Serbia. The next day the Count attended his usual London church in Belgravia and told the congregation that war would mean his returning to Germany. They heard the news with sadness and he was quite affected by the warmth of feeling shown him when he left.

On August 3 he left England for ever. Then the rumours, lies and vilification began – he was a spy, he hoarded thousands of rifles and tons of explosives, he was a recluse with only German servants. These were the mildest of the insults, and even when one considers the frenzied atmosphere of those days, one can only feel shame for the dishonour heaped upon the name of this good man – and for our failure to make proper amends to his memory ever since.

The universal paroxysm of the next four years made it impossible for him to return to England. He had attempted to work in Germany with the Red Cross for British prisoners of war but even that was denied him. All he owned in England was lost. He lingered on, broken in health, until 1934, and in his will directed his funeral to be conducted by the rites of the Church of England and only English hymns to be sung.

Captain John Bridges

His successors at Croydon Hall, Captain John Bridges RN and his daughter Anne, shared Count Hochberg's outdoor and sporting interests and attempted with fair success to keep up the tradition. Actively interested in the well-being of his estate, the captain restored three distant but substantial cottages at Hazery, Couple Cross and the foot of Jumper's Steep in Luxborough. In 1928 the people of Roadwater benefitted from his generosity as he donated Day's Meadow to be their recreation-ground – a gift whose value they show by constant use.

The catastrophes of 1940 dealt more heavily with Croydon and the society it represented than even the

Captain Bridges and the hounds at the Carhampton kennels, late 1920s or early 1930s. The kennel men are probably Charles Back and Harry Holt.

Below centre: *Hazery, near Luxborough, on the Croydon Hall estate, renovated by Captain Bridges in 1939.*

Below: *Captain Bridges' chauffeur, Geoffrey Bates, with the Rolls Royce at Albert Terrace, Washford.*

Below: *Workmen at Hazery, left to right: Foreman Taylor, Bill Venting (Golsoncott), Jack Summers (Bilbrook), George ?, Frank Rowe (Old Cleeve).*

The lovely back garden at Croydon in 1940, the last year of this kind of gracious living.

First World War had done, and the return of peace could not bring it back to life, for the source of labour had dried up. In January 1940 girls from a school in Bristol were evacuated to Croydon Hall, Captain Bridges moved out, took the post of Master of the Kilkenny Hounds and some time after the war emigrated to Australia and took a farm. His daughter Anne stayed in England and moved to Exford, but, sadly, was killed in a car accident in 1994.

Croyden Hall was occupied by different boarding schools until nearly the end of the century. In 2004 it is a centre for meditation and holistic therapy, with conference facilities.

Croydon Remembered

Marjorie Moir

I remember the 1920s quite well. I was born in 1922 at Glasses Farm – my parents were David and Vera Case. Glasses Farm remains bright in my memory – a big kitchen with a black-leaded range, scrubbed table and benches, big black settle, flagstone floor and the zinc bath in front of a roaring fire.

I went to school in Leighland for a short time but I hated it so my mother sent me to Llanberis school in Minehead as a weekly boarder. I travelled on the open-roofed bus. We had to walk to Dragon Cross for the bus. The lanes were scary in the dark – I remember owls hooting and bats whizzing past.

My grandfather Robert Burnett was a dear – he was a strong chapel man and used to read me Bible stories. He thought the Sunday paper was a 'work of the devil' so grandmother used to hide the News of the World

Miss Margaret Davies, head-mistress, in the office at Croydon Hall School, c.1950.

under a cushion until he had gone to chapel! The privy at my grandparents' house (Watersmeet, Station Road) was an ordeal as it hung over the river – it was terrifying going in there with the river swirling below.

Croydon Hall has memories for me too. My grandmother knew Johnny Walker and he was sometimes left in charge when Captain Bridges went away to play polo, or on a longer trip to Australia for the winter months. I was allowed to go into Miss Anne's nursery (but not to touch anything). She had a big rocking-horse, dolls and playthings, much better than mine!

Pam Thomas

Bill Butler, Pam's father, came to Croydon Hall in the early 1920s as a 'Jack of all trades', but by 1940 was estate manager. Pam remembers:

Captain Bridges had a sister who was married to a Luttrell at Dunster Castle. When I lived at Croydon until 1941, it was quite a busy place. There were two chauffeurs, Geoff Bates and Tom Smith, a butler, Mr Evans, about four gardeners under Mr Webb, including Mr Coombs of Peterswell. There were cooks, chambermaids and estate workmen. The odd job man was Johnny Walker. Every Christmas Captain Bridges held a party for the children living on the estate, each child receiving a good present.

During the war a lot of the employees were called up. A school was evacuated to Croydon Hall under Mr Webb, and Captain Bridges moved into the farmhouse. About the end of the war he left Croydon and eventually settled in Australia.

During Miss Davies' time Croydon Hall was famous for its plays. From 1949–65 the school put on three productions a year: a summer pageant, a historical play and a nativity play. The plays, written by Miss Davies, included Harold of England, Salute to Elizabeth, Caedmon of Whitby *and* Travels of Marco Polo. *The play shown here,* The Sheepfold in the Hills, *was an imaginative reconstruction of the early history of Croydon Hall.*

Miss Winifred Deas, matron, in the garden with Oliver Davies, Miss Davies' nephew, 1949.

Left: *Golsoncott, c.1900.*

PHOTOGRAPH BY RUDOLPH NETHERCOTT

Below: *Gordon Hayes (Kingsbrompton) married Marjorie Bragg (Golsoncott) at the Methodist church, March 1954. Left to right: Ruby Hayes, Stanley Hayes, Gordon Hayes, Marjorie Hayes (née Bragg), Olive Woolway, Pauline Burnell.*

Below: *Golsoncott, 1930s.* Left to right, back row: *Fred Beaver, Rosie Hockey (née Beaver), Ellen Beaver, Harry Hockey;* seated: *Daisy Hockey, Gladys Hockey. Beaver brothers Fred and George were born in Buckinghamshire and moved to Roadwater in the 1890s. They are in the 1901 census as 'fish and rabbit dealers'. One brother built Rose Villa and one was licensee of the inn at Knap. Gladys Hockey married Benjamin Elliott, and their son Henry emigrated to Sydney, Australia, in 1962. This photograph came from an album they took with them, and was emailed to Joan and Jim Beaver; it has travelled 20,000 miles!*

Right: *The inn sign of the Valiant Soldier was made from sheet aluminium by Rachel Reckitt in 1935.*

Above: *Rachel Reckitt (1910–95), artist, sculptor, rider.*

Chapter 14

Golsoncott

How well the Celts and Saxons sited their hill-country settlements! Although they were situated high up, they were not on the very hilltop; never skylined but set down a stone's throw from the lash of the wind, where men and women need not wear four layers of wool merely to venture out of doors. That is the setting for Golsoncott, and whether or not it pre-dates Roadwater, it has the feeling of a place immensely old. It might, with fingers crossed and a touch of imagination, claim an entry in the Domesday Book, for there is a 'Gilcote', once belonging to Edwin, placed with Combe and Aller in the lands of the Norman usurper Roger de Courseulle. However, Gilcott Wood stands near Oak, two miles from Golsoncott, and Coinbe, Aller and Rodhuish come between. Still, it had half a dozen acres of meadow, 15 acres of woodland and 60 of pasture, enough for the listed '2 cattle, 1 pig, 11 sheep and 11 goats' to munch all day long.

A thirteenth-century deed mentions a Goldsmithcote, which seems more like a sly farmer pulling the leg of an uninformed lawyer than a genuine name; but at least it shows that for seniority 'Golda's son's cote' definitely rivalled Roadwater, and may have been years ahead.

By 1880 it had grown as large as it was ever likely to be, given the room on the ground. Nowadays immersed in its quietness, it is hard to imagine 60 people bustling around in it, but there were – a dozen families crammed into eight or nine dwellings:

John Hill, labourer and his wife Ellen;
John Risdon, farmer, wife, 2 sons, 4 daughters and a maidservant;
Robert Prideaux, road contractor, wife and 5 children;
Robert Lewis, shepherd and wife and daughter;
George Cooksley, carpenter, wife and 3 children;
William Symons and his wife;
Henry Taylor, shepherd, and wife Ann, a dressmaker;
William Stone, blacksmith, wife Elizabeth and 4 children;
John Slade, labourer, son and grandson;
Frederick Taylor, labourer, wife and 5 children;
James Yeandle, labourer, wife, 4 sons, 1 daughter;

Peter Yeandle, lime burner, his wife, 1 son, 1 daughter, 2 lodgers.

Golsoncott, like Roadwater, had no 'big house' or patrician family to keep it in order, and was none the worse for it. The nearest approach was when, as recounted elsewhere, Count Hochberg built Golsoncott House for his secretary, Captain J. Whitehead. A decade later it became the home of Norman and Beatrice Reckitt. They and their family figured large in the activities of Roadwater for 75 years.

Norman Reckitt was an architect and, in 1928, he designed a village hall after the style of a Somerset pillared barn and gave it to Roadwater. Mrs Reckitt put much of her energy into organising the Women's Institute and supporting St Luke's. Their daughter Rachel, born with a remarkable artistic talent, developed it and worked untiringly all her life, attempting one medium after another and excelling in them all: painting, pottery, metalwork – iron, copper, aluminium and pewter – woodcuts, engraving, welding, statuary, wrought-iron work; and from each of her great loves, the country, horses, dogs and foreign travel, she continually brought something new and original to her art.

Rachel's work never kept her tied to the studio or the smithy, and almost every day, rain or shine, until she was well into her eighties, she would ride down from Golsoncott and trot or canter along the street on a very mettlesome horse, with a high-spirited dog in her wake. She always offered a word of cheer as she passed by. Penelope Lively has kindly contributed these reminiscences of her aunt, Rachel Reckitt:

My aunt Rachel spent her entire adult life at Golsoncott, and died there in 1995, aged 86. She worked there in her two studios, the indoor one for painting and the outdoor wooden hut for sculpture and metalwork, both of them unheated and freezing cold in winter. Her daily routine hardly changed over the years that I knew her, from the time when I spent my school holidays at Golsoncott in the late 1940s, until her old age, which never really seemed to be that, since she continued determinedly to do what she had always done. In the mornings, she would ride, exercising both horse and dogs at the same time; afternoons were sacred as she spent them in the studio.

Riding – and hunting, until her later years – was central to her life, and many older West Somerset neighbours will remember that familiar figure trotting briskly down the lane, or through the farm, on Roland or Juno or Gaiety Girl or, finally, on an evil-tempered retired polo pony called Fury. Decades of riding and hunting meant that she knew the area with intense intimacy, from her own immediate locality to the wider reaches of Exmoor. She knew every field, every track, each piece of woodland; she was a good botanist and a keen ornithologist. And above all she was interested in people; she could tell you who farmed where and who lived in which cottage, and who was related to whom. She had a great capacity for friendship, and a natural empathy that made people warm to her; she has godchildren scattered far and wide.

But Rachel's horizons stretched well beyond Somerset. She was an intrepid traveller, relishing annual forays to obscure corners of Europe in pursuit of remote Macedonian monasteries and other esoteric scenes that would then inspire paintings and engravings when she got home. Many of these journeys were made in the battered old Land Rover that will also be long remembered in Somerset, dashing through the lanes with a couple of barking dogs in the back, usually one Alsatian and one crossbreed (preferably with a good dash of collie).

The war years took Rachel to London, when she was still a young woman. She worked at Toynbee Hall in Stepney, as one of those responsible for evacuating women and children from the blitzed areas. One of her first actions was to send a wire to her mother informing her that, as of the following week, Golsoncott would become a war nursery, and that she should expect a consignment of six children aged under five, plus a matron to oversee them. My grandmother turned over half the house to her evacuee brood, some of whom stayed for several years. Rachel distributed children, around the entire area, and local residents with long memories will recall the ones who became so imprinted on West Somerset that they returned, year after year, for holidays, eventually with their own offspring. The evacuee experience could be a rewarding one.

For Rachel, those years changed her perspective on life. Like many others, she witnessed for the first time the urban poverty of the mid-twentieth century and was shocked. She became a socialist, and voted Labour for the rest of her life, somewhat at odds with her mother's staunch conservatism.

Rachel's interests and involvements were legion. She supported and exhibited with the Somerset Guild of Craftsmen; in her later years she worked for the Samaritans in Minehead. Much further back, she and her mother together took the weekly mobile library to the tuberculosis sanatorium that was then at St Audries. She was deeply concerned with the chapel of St Bartholomew at Rodhuish, where she and her mother worshipped and which is enriched with work by both of them. Equally, she was always active in the affairs of Roadwater Village Hall. And all this alongside her commitment as an artist, one who worked in several different media, from wood engraving to large-scale metal sculpture.

Fine examples of her work can be seen in several local churches, projects which were especially important to her. It is particularly apt that Roadwater's own Rachel Reckitt work – the Valiant Soldier inn sign – should be one of her very first pieces of metalwork. It was created when she was quite young and just starting out on her life as an artist and as a popular and energetic local resident.

As the above account suggests, in 1940 the outside world thrust itself into Golsoncott as never before, and here Marjorie Hayes (née Bragg – she married Gordon Hayes in Roadwater chapel in 1954, see page 110) whose father William Bragg farmed at Golsoncott, takes up the story:

My father W.H. Bragg brought his family to Golsoncott Farm in March 1941 from Colton, after a cold snowy winter. I have vivid memories of spectacular raids, bombs dropping on Wales which we saw clearly from Birds Hill. Incendiaries and bombs were often 'dumped' on the hills as the German planes flew back towards France.

Although we did not know it at the time my brother Hubert was in the 'secret' Home Guard and used to disappear on a course now and again. They had hidden dumps of grenades in various places. We had evacuees billeted on us almost as soon as we moved – Yvonne and Shirley Smith. Their brothers Ivor and Brian were in the village.

Every hand was needed on the farm and I worked hard milking, etc. I also kept rabbits – up to 100 – for the meat and fur. Our farming neighbours at Golsoncott were Mr Beaver and his three sons. Mr Babbage was at Escott.

I joined the St John's, the two Mrs Goodings were in it, also Betty Heath (née Slade) from Manor Mills. We formed a cadet unit, which a lot of local girls joined, and I was honoured to walk ranks with Lady Mountbatten when she came down to inspect us.

Golsoncott House after renovation.

Chapter 15

Leighland

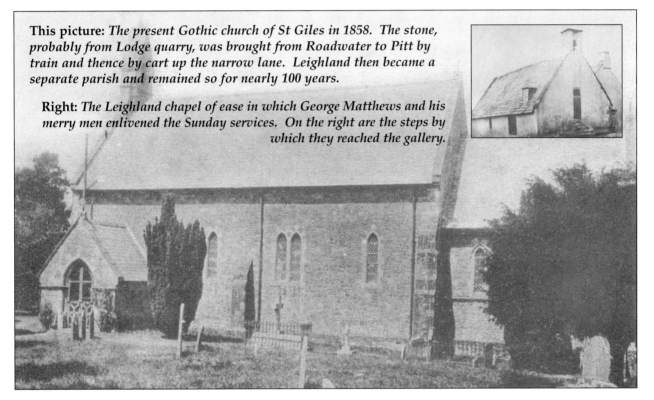

This picture: *The present Gothic church of St Giles in 1858. The stone, probably from Lodge quarry, was brought from Roadwater to Pitt by train and thence by cart up the narrow lane. Leighland then became a separate parish and remained so for nearly 100 years.*

Right: *The Leighland chapel of ease in which George Matthews and his merry men enlivened the Sunday services. On the right are the steps by which they reached the gallery.*

The chapel of St Giles of Leigh may have been of ancient foundation, probably dating from Saxon times, when it was probably known as Legh. It may even have rated an entry in the Domesday Book. It was certainly present before 1320, when the vicar of Old Cleeve was:

> *... charged to attend the chapel of St Giles of Leigh, and there to read the gospel, and administer consecrated bread and water, and to celebrate mass there three times a year.*

The size of the old chapel was 46 feet by 19 feet with a small bell cote and ringing loft. It was linked to 'the farm or grange of Leigh', which, even now, has a field called Giles' Ground and Giles' Rock in the middle of a copse called Cliff Wood.

There was no road connecting the abbey with Leigh and the vicar, who would have been under the control of the abbot, would probably have travelled on horseback. He would have used narrow tracks through the few houses which constituted Roadwater, up behind what is now Oatway House, along the top of Road Wood, passing small groups of cottages at Traphole and Lower and Higher Hayne. At this time the village of Leigh was listed in the abbey rentals as having 18 tenements and land and watercourses worth £11.8s.5d. out of a total of £164.7s.9d.

After Henry VIII suppressed the monasteries and disbanded the monks, the abbey church was destroyed and its other buildings were used for farming purposes. Eventually the King granted the estate, including Leigh and its lands, to Robert, Earl of Sussex. The Protestant vicar or rector of Old Cleeve took on the duties of the visiting monk, or at least paid a curate. But Leighland folk seem to have clung to the old religion and rejected the new one for many years, judging by an outburst from Robert Evans, rector of

Lewis Burnell and Horace Burnett, churchwardens for about 40 years.

Old Cleeve, 1598–1608, who denounced Leighland as 'the place where the idol hath been'. At any rate, when Philip Powel, the Benedictine chaplain to the Poyntz family of Leigh Barton, conducted the services, or more probably read mass, and visited the sick from 1627–42, nobody, as far as is known, tried to stop him, nor did his parishioners suffer the penalties of the law.

In the 1830s and '40s Parson Newton, who normally went about in a far from clerical looking outfit, used to come from Old Cleeve on Sunday afternoons, riding in a farm cart and seated on a bale of straw. This was the cart he used for collecting his tithes. It was said that he practised necromancy, and many people at that time believed in witchcraft and the powers of a parson in connection with the occult. Some say that it was Parson Newton who, by 'conjuring', discovered the man who was guilty of stealing the club chest.

In those days, Leighland had seven cottages in addition to the chapel. One of the cottages sold cheap beer, and during the services, as recounted in Chapter 4, members of the orchestra and choir would slip away for a mug and a chat, returning in time to tune their instruments again after clambering up the stone steps that led to the singing loft.

The old cottages which were adjacent to the chapel have since vanished. Both had little shops selling groceries and sweets, and here children went to buy 'a ha'porth of dumps'. The two old ladies who kept the shops were business rivals and not friends. One was a spinster, while the other had buried three husbands. She always declared her willingness to marry a fourth, but this was not fulfilled, although she outlived her third spouse by several years.

According to 'The guide to St Giles, Leighland' supplied by kind permission of the churchwardens:

Unfortunately the ancient chapel of St Giles was demolished and replaced with the present-day church at a cost of £1,200. It is built of stone in the early-English style and consists of chancel, nave, south porch and bell cote containing one bell. The stained-glass east window was erected in 1889. The register dates from 1775 and the population in 1891 was 317. Leighland was formed into an ecclesiastical parish on 4 April 1865 but the patronage of the living still belongs to the rector of Old Cleeve. [A proposal in 1929 to sever Leighland from the ecclesiastical parish of Old Cleeve was strongly opposed and the idea was dropped.]

In more recent times Mr Walter Williams played the organ for 57 years, for which he received an appreciation from the Archbishop of Canterbury. Others who have given devoted service over many years include Miss Laugher, who used to live in the old Stationmaster's House at Comberow, and who worked the kneeler for the altar rail and many other matching tapestries; Horace and Joan Burnett, who held the positions of Treasurer and Secretary for more than 30 years; and Hetty Routley, followed by her daughter Joan, who kept the church spotlessly clean for many years.

Three wall-mounted memorials record the names of the men of the parish on active service in the First World War, with those who did not return, and of the three who died in the Second World War. Most

Right: *Leighland choir outing to Blue Anchor, c.1920. Left to right, back row: Frank Willis, Revd C. Shaw, Harold Langdon, Jim Tomkins, Bill Westcott, Walter Williams (organist) Charlie Langdon, Percy Poole; third row: Freda Poole, Emily Tomkins, May Northcom, Violet Ettery, Mrs Williams, Miss Harris; second row: Jack (?) Langdon, Harry Evans, Frank Willis, Bob (?) Webber, Ted Tomkins; front row: Ernie Bowden, Bert Langdon, Ted Routley, A. Webber, Walter Bowden.*

remarkably, in a rare act of homage, the name of nearly every man in the earlier conflict is followed by his regiment or corps, the place, month and year of his death, and his age when he died – the youngest, at the gates of Jerusalem aged 18, the oldest, in France, aged 35, and the two Furse brothers only a week apart.

All of them, not too many years earlier, would have been found in the church school, which had been built in 1878 and largely paid for by Joseph Gatchell, who farmed Leigh Barton. It was attended by nearly 100 children who walked there from miles around – from Chidgley, Hook Hill, Brendon Hill, the Mineral Line hamlets and of course Roadwater (children from Sminneys and Cold Harbour attended school in Treborough).

All sorts of reasons might keep them away from school: a Band of Hope procession, a Sunday-school outing, whort-picking or haymaking, turnip carting, 'teddy' lifting – any casual farm work to earn a few pence to help the family through the winter. When winter came snow sometimes blocked the lanes and kept them away, and if they struggled through, six or seven hours in damp clothes did them no good at all. After 50 years of the school's existence, Roadwater people, perhaps roused by a letter from 'A Mother' in the *West Somerset Free Press*, petitioned County Hall for a school of their own. County Hall decided that since Blue Anchor children had to walk just as far to school in Washford over more exposed roads(!) Roadwater was no worse off and would have to make do.

The school employed a headmaster and two female teachers, but in the early years none remained very long until Edwin Reynolds arrived on the scene in 1903. 'Foxy', aided by his wife, remained for nearly 30 years. He ruled with a firm hand, taught his pupils in practical ways and encouraged those who really wanted to learn. By the 1950s numbers had dropped to only 11 pupils and a headmistress, Grace Albiston, and the school closed in 1957.

Leighland School Logbook. Excerpts, 1874–1957

1874

4 May: Miss L. Larcombe took charge.
8 May: 45 children present on the first week.
15 May: Many more children present. Began to teach the first class compound multiplication.
22 May: Very small attendance on Tuesday, attending fête at Roadwater by the Good Templars.
29 May: Holiday on Monday it being Roadwater Club. Attendance fair the rest of week.
12 June: Not so many scholars. Children carrying food to parents in the hay fields.
3 July: Attendance very low this week. Great many children gathering whortleberries.
17 July: Some still gathering whortleberries. Taught first class compound long division.

31 July: Mr Gatchell called. Gave children a treat on Wednesday. Broke up for harvest holidays.
28 August: Recommenced on Monday 21st after vacation. Very small attendance. Gleaning not over.

1875

8 Jan: Very small attendance. Half holiday on 6th, being 'Old Christmas Day'. Weather stormy.
16 April: Great many punished for not knowing their tables.
22 Oct: Very small all week owing to a great deal of rain and the overflowing of the river.
29 Oct: Attendance poor. Great many children away picking hay corns [acorns?].

1878

7 April: Alice M.M. Lambert took charge. Found the school apparatus very poor. Examined the children and found that Standards II and III knew nothing of notation, and Standards IV and V cannot work compound rules. Attendance today 66.
12 April: Having had cause to leave the schoolroom for 5 minutes, I left the children in the charge of the mistress with orders to see the upper classes continued orderly, and went on steadily with their work. When I returned she informed me that they had been talking and that one girl was impudent to her. I therefore punished the whole class, and the next morning Sarah Jane Bryant's mother came and demanded her copy book, and was very impudent and abusive to me. She has taken away the girl and I will not re-admit her until the mother has apologised for her behaviour towards me.
2 May: Notice received of diocesan inspector on 19 May. Sarah Jane re-admitted and has conducted herself properly since.
9 May: Some girls who stayed into dinner obtained their lesson and dinner bags (through one of them climbing over the boys' offices) and went home without permission because I denied them admittance to the schoolroom through misconduct.

1879

13 Jan: Heavy snow, 6 ins deep in playground.
21 May: Holiday as the mistress was married.
28 May: Gave up charge of the school.
22 Nov: Only 39 present. Many could not come up the hill as it was so slippery.

1883

6 Feb: Shrove Tuesday, a half-day's holiday.
9 Feb: The boy W. Court, on leaving school this morning caught his foot and fell full force on his forehead, thereby inflicting a very nasty cut.
12 Mar: Commenced teaching Standards IV and V the geography of British North America.

1884

11 Mar: Many children going with parents to Old Cleeve Sunday School for the 'Gift Money'. Every

Left: *Leighland School, 1920.* Left to right, back row: *Mr Reynolds, ?, ?, Willie Murrell, ?, Albert Burge, ?, ?, ?, Jim Price, ?, ?;* third row: *?, ?, ?, Frank Willis, ?, Charlie Langdon, Clifford Beaver, ?;* second row: *Hettie Rowe, Freda Poole, ?, ?, Nelly Reynolds, ?, ?, ?, ?, Nesta Bennett;* front row: *Bronwen Willis, Joan Willis, Ivy Willis, Clara Willis, Dorothea Willis, Annie Willis, Winnie Duck, Doris Willis, ?, Dorothy Westcott, Gladys Poole.*

Right: *St Giles playlet, 1988. Children taking part include: Anna, Elizabeth and William White, Charlotte Hanson, Tom, Philip and David Harral, James and Eleanor Moss, Jonathan Riley, ? Sawatzki, ? Pini. Gay Pini (far right) is conducting with back to camera.*

child of the second poor who has not received parish relief and had made 250 attendances at this school or Washford receives a sum (about 2s.).

1887
11 Feb: David Griffiths and Frederick Taylor admitted from Roadwater dame's school [in a cottage adjacent to the Valiant Soldier].
23 Sep: Vicar complained of boys throwing stones at the apple trees and breaking the glass in the green house at the vicarage.

1890
21 Mar: E. Bowden left to go to work though not of the proper age. Tom Smith left to go to work though under 13 and not having passed Standard IV.

1892
9 Sept: Gathering of mushrooms has interfered with the attendance.
21 Oct: Decided to open a night school.
11 Nov: Night school opened with 21.

1894
26 Sept: Arthur Coles, a lad in Standard VI, has left this week having gained an open scholarship in Colston's School, Bristol.

1896
19 Feb: An entertainment by the children at Roadwater caused absence of several girls, they stayed home to curl hair.

1898
25 Feb: Not a child present on Tuesday owing to a heavy fall of snow during the previous night.
18 Nov: The school was closed on Tuesday after-noon to give an opportunity for the children to attend the funeral of a little girl of Roadwater who was beloved by many of the school [possibly Florence Cording, daughter of Mr and Mrs Henry Cording of Vale, who died aged 13 from TB].

1899
16 June: A Druids Fête at Washford drew a number of children on Wednesday

1900
2 Mar: The children were given half-holiday to celebrate the relief of Ladysmith.
11 July: The whortleberry plague has begun.
23 Jan: Miss Keylock resigned and was succeeded by Miss Ash from Poltimore school.
30 Jan: Miss Ash has resigned, she complains of the dullness of the place and the very trying walk to and from school.
3 July: This week brings the school under the County Council.

1905
16 Nov: Mrs Reynolds started a coffee club as many of the children have nothing to drink these cold days, during the dinner hour. The children appreciate it, as over 60 have joined.
21 Dec: Revd C.H. Shaw and Miss Shaw came in and gave an orange to each child.

1906
26 June: At the exam Maggie Griffith, Ivy Lile and Bessie Shopland were placed 1st. Edith Williams and Cecil Williams were commended.
9 Sept: Walter Lile passed in Pitman Shorthand.
15 Sept: Roadwater and Leighland choirs went to Weston-super-Mare.

Certificate for good attendance, 1940. Grace Albiston taught at Leighland school for over 20 years.

1907

23 Jan: A notice sent to the Ed. authority specifying to hold a holiday in the afternoon in order to allow many children to attend the laying of the foundation-stone of a new chapel at Roadwater.

8 Mar: Emily Milton age 12 Standard V went to Minehead to sit for labour examination.

8 Sept: Vera Ridler, age 5, suffering from infantile paralysis, taken to Children's Hospital.

1909

28 Jan: Many attended the funeral of Mr Lile.

24 May: Empire Day – half-holiday.

15 Sept: Prizes presented. Medals given to Henry Shopland, Albert Clatworthy and Edwin Beaver.

1910

25 Nov: Drawing lesson. An engine and a motor car were drawn this week.

1912

24 Jan: Walter Charles Burnett has been successful in obtaining an apprenticeship (value £20) given by the Somerset Society London headquarters.

1914

17 Aug: Great European War developing, scholars following events daily.

9 Oct: Flag staff erected in the playground. List of past scholars suspended on wall for children to see how nobly they responded to K's [Kitchener's] call.

1915

25 Oct: Rodney Ridler, a late scholar, killed in battle near Loos.

1918

32 May: Several boys absent the whole school year, on the land, working.

19 June: I [Mr Reynolds] went to Taunton to be medically examined for the Army.

4 Sept: Took children, Standard II upwards, blackberry picking. Went to Leigh Woods, authorised by C.C., owing to scarcity of other fruits (63lb collected).

13 Sept: Took 21 children to Hook Hill to pick blackberries.

11 Oct: Total weight of blackberries picked 481lb; 14s.8d. sent to the Stranded Sailors Fund, Williton, and 1s.5d. to the Royal National Lifeboat Association.

1922

30 July: Clifford George Westcott placed 2nd in exam for Ellsworth Foundation Scholarship: first for the school.

1923

21 Sept: Willie Murrell won a County Scholarship, is now attending Taunton School.

30 Nov: A magic lantern entertainment.

1924

19 Dec: Closed for Christmas. Children given tea in Temperance Hall by the friends of the WI.

1926

HMI Report: 'Despite the isolated position of the school, the Headmaster manages to keep abreast of the times in educational matters.'

1929

9 Dec: Roads impassable, water 1ft deep. Trees across the road.

1939

1 Feb: Mrs G. Albiston started as headmistress.

1 Sept: School closed by order from head office owing to 'evacuation'.

15 Sept: 9 evacuees left out of 15.

1940

22 Aug: Mr G. Williams of Watchet built a blast-proof wall of sandbags outside the door of the infants' classroom.

1941

5 May: Mr Blanchard, SAO, reported children at Comberow over 3 mile limit.

18 July: Fire and respirator drill.

1945

23 Jan: Heavy snow, 2 boys arrived from Hook Hill but none from Roadwater; school closed.

8 May: Holiday today and tomorrow. Victory in Europe.

1946

4 Nov: Miss Chick commenced as head teacher.

18 Nov: Miss Chick left without notice. Miss Chilcott, assistant, took over.

1950

2 May: Florence Burnett called for interview at Grammar School.
3 May: Douglas Routley ditto.
23 June: Both accepted.

1951

3 Jan: 13 present.
5 Oct: Sanitary Inspector tested drinking water.
8 Nov: Dr Beazeley visited along with a missionary from Burma.

1952

29 Jan: Icy conditions. Only 7 present.
31 Jan: Dr Beazeley called regarding broken window in church; children deny responsibility.
7 May: Mr Gooding called about the Fellowship of St Christopher. Concern expressed by parents over children care, due to sensationalism by school dinner helper.
2 June: Age range 5–11.
8 Oct: Photographer came.

1953

16 Mar: Several children transferred to other schools without consulting head mistress: mainly because transport was provided to Washford.
15 May: Corporal punishment (slipper) given to C.S., 12 strokes, and G.B., 10 strokes, for inattention, disrupting class and insolence.
21 May: Water-supply failed.
4 June: School sports at Roadwater.
20 June: Car bringing children to school, only 6 times punctual this term; letter of complaint written.
23 Nov: County Surveyor examined school regarding washbasins and flush toilets.

1954

15 Jan: School milk stolen: police informed.
1 Feb: School car did not arrive. Only 3 children present.
2 Feb: Ditto. School dinner cancelled. No milk. Pipes frozen.
5 May: New toilets completed.

Golden jubilee party, 2002. Some of those who enjoyed the day are: *Olivia Waters, Cary Ebdon, Margaret Mangan, Sonny Barden, Pat Ebdon, Len Ebdon, Lynne Patterson, Kate Makin, Jennifer Asbridge, John Asbridge, Judy Moss, Edwin Hayes, Toby Hickman, Eve Hickman, Philip White, Steve Cornish, Kate Twine, Ian Bradbury, Mrs Bradbury, John Armson, Jayne Cornish, Rob Brown, Betty Armson, Karen Armson, Gill White, Susan Payne, Janet Taylor, Pat Taylor, David Lythall, Suki Hardman, Maurice Hardman, Philippa Hardman, Alessandra Lythall, Alice White, Sonia Waters, Major George Drew, Jack Waters, Elaine Necchi, Michael White, Nick Necchi, Jan Bennett, Mark Bennett, Flo Croucher, Jack Croucher, Sheila Feltham, Inez Hayes.*

Chapter 16

Leigh Barton

Aerial view of Leigh Barton Farm, c.1960.

Right: *Daisy Hole setting out on her bicycle from Soldier Cottage to feed the chickens at Leigh Barton, c.1950s.*

Above: *Cottage in Leigh Woods, last inhabited by the Sowden family, 1960s. In 2004 it is empty but still standing. Note the straw hives.*

The word 'barton' originally meant only an enclosure for barley, but in time it came to denote a pretty considerable farm, of which Huish and Leigh Barton are good examples.

The Winter of 1962-63

The White family moved to Leigh Barton in 1958. Gill contributes her recollections of the early days of the 45 years that she and Philip lived there:

The most memorable period of time was the winter of 1962–63. It snowed on Boxing Day 1962 and the farm remained cut off for vehicles for the next eight weeks. There was an agricultural student living in the farmhouse at the time who put us all to shame by never even wearing a long-sleeved pullover! The initial problem was that the water pump from the well to the reservoir burst, which we managed to get repaired temporarily, from then on we had to drain it every night. The pipe to the only indoor toilet froze and had to be removed from the roof and thawed in the sun – all 50 yards of it. This was a daily chore. We had two tractors on the farm and one of them had the back wheels ballasted with water and antifreeze. This froze because of the severity of the weather and we

were unable to use that tractor for the duration.

We had 200 hens and because of a time switch for artificial daylight hours 90 per cent of them laid an egg daily. There was no means of getting the eggs to the packing station so they were transported on a sheet of galvanised to Roadwater (two miles) and sold on from there. The return journey was used for dragging back essential supplies; there were no freezers at the time.

We are not suggesting that Leigh Barton was any worse than anywhere else up on the Brendons but it does face north-east and got the full force of the wind and the blizzards, so much so that our overcoats became frozen solid. When the thaw finally set in another problem arose. In the roof of the farmhouse there is an extensive valley, we had previously put frames across this valley to stop snow pressing water under the slates in a thaw. Unfortunately, the weight of the snow on these frames forced the whole lot down, resulting in extensive damage to the rooms below when the water came in. Had another year followed on in a similar vein it is unlikely we would have stayed there for the next 45 years.

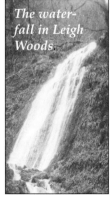

The water-fall in Leigh Woods

Above: *Treborough quarry men, 1875. The following names appear on the 1881 census and some of the men may well be in the picture: Lemuel Gamlin (stone planer), James Gamlin (sawyer), William Bunney (iron stone miner), John Daniel and James Hole (iron miners), George Saunders (iron miner), Richard and John Collins (slate cutters), William Humphrey (slate cutter), William Pritchard (quarry owner), probably the gentleman in frock coat, front right, James Parsons (slate cutter).*

Below and right:
1849 advertisements.

The Pritchard family, c.1870.

Chapter 17

Treborough

Treborough Quarry

Men began to quarry slate at Treborough so long ago that 'the memory runneth not to the contrary' – and it was so easy to get at, so evident to the dullest eye, so eminently suitable for walling, roofing and a dozen other uses, that it may well have been the first organised industrial enterprise in the neighbourhood. By 1456 the quarry was large enough to take on an order from Dunster Castle for 2,000 roofing slates. Another 400 years of work and the quarrymen had turned the hillside into a monstrous hole, a veritable abyss, wide and deep enough to hold a cathedral – if spire downwards – and in 1829 William Savage, in his *Hundred of Carhampton*, reported that the quarry was 'now in full work'.

Nevertheless, slate quarrying, although a modestly remunerative business, was fraught with uncertainty because of the variable nature of the material and the huge wastage – 12–20 tons of rock for every ton of slate produced. Even the most skilful working could not eliminate waste. However, the operators from North Wales who in 1849 took over the running of Treborough, which was Trevelyan property, had bright ideas, and like other entrepreneurs from outside, they knew all the answers without troubling to ask the questions. William Pritchard,

the senior member, thus introduced his company in a prospectus announcing 'Reduction in the Prices of Slate':

PRITCHARD, DAVIES, & Co. FROM WALES, Respectfully announce to Landowners, Builders, and the public generally, that they have engaged (for a term of years) those excellent SLATE WORKS, known by the name of the TREBOROUGH QUARRIES, late in the occupation of Mr N. Ennor.

The antiquity and good qualities of the Treborough Slate is too well known to require description, notwithstanding the unskilful manner in which it has hitherto been worked; and with the improvements which are now being introduced will be quite equal to any offered in the market.

P., D., & Co., have suitable machinery at work on the premises – are assisted by the most competent workmen from Wales – and being themselves practically acquainted with the several branches of business, hope, by pursuing a straightforward course in all business transactions, by strict attention and moderate charges, to merit the support of a discerning public.

Slates of all sizes for Roofs, Floors, Cisterns, Chimney-pots, Tomb and Head Stones, Ridge and Coping Stones, Angle and Stable Drains, &c., made to order, and marked so as to be put together without trouble.

Cutting shed and bench.

The spoil tip.

Drilling level with railway and truck.

Unfortunately for Pritchard, Davies & Co., they had not realised that the Caernarvon slate they were used to was more workable and durable than the Treborough kind, and presumably yielded a higher profit. The incomers miscalculated and before long they had to invest in works and machinery more heavily than they had anticipated. They remained in business for 40 years, however, employing more than 30 men at a reasonable wage by local standards.* William Pritchard kept his promise over the prices. The slates ranged in size from Duchesses (24 inches by 12) retailing at £7.0s.0d., to Small Doubles (12 inches by 7) at 12s.0d. per thousand! Many a carter must have grinned when he ordered a load of Small Wide Ladies. Brought down to units, the most expensive roofing slates cost less than 2d., and the cheapest worked out at almost ten a penny. Paving slabs, water tanks, window-sills, pigs' troughs, polished head-stones guaranteed to withstand all weather, even coffins, and mantelpieces worked by oil and water to look like black marble were offered at low prices.

Even with money worth a hundred times that of today, the profit on these products demanded a modest lifestyle and, as local people saw it, William Pritchard had 'big ideas' (a withering judgment!) and was 'cutting a dash' when he took over a wing of Treborough Lodge. (Daniel Badcock, the Taunton banker, lived in the other wing.) Besides, they reasoned, did he really need three servants for himself, his wife and two children? And what about the fine clothes and the carriage and pair – could he stand the expense? Apparently he could, but in 1882 he died, aged only 57. His widow and son went on with the business until 1889, thus completing 40 years. They then gave up the lease and all work was suspended. But in a decade when, even in this depopulated area, new houses were being built, a slate quarry could not be left idle, and the Trevelyans decided to work it themselves. They appointed Thomas Voss as manager. For three generations down to 1944, when Harry, in the stress of wartime, fell from the roof he was mending, the name Voss in Roadwater meant mason and builder.

Production reached a peak of 1,000 tons in 1904–05 but even this did not yield a good profit, and five years later the quarry closed again. With a spurt of postwar building in 1920 work restarted to supply local needs, but it became obvious that, as had happened with the iron ore 40 years earlier, Treborough could no longer compete with Wales and Cornwall. The only quarrymen still working were Eli Vickery and his two sons, and September 1939 put an end to 700–800 years of another productive local activity.

For a few years the quarry served as the head-quarters of the local platoon of the unacknowledged guerrilla force trained for sabotage if German forces invaded – the 'secret Home Guard'. Thereafter it lay unused and untenanted except by rabbits and other wildlife for nearly 20 years. Ferns and brambles began to grow over, and silence returned to the ravaged hillside, broken only when a car or tractor passed or when a passerby paused for a moment and, for old time's sake, tossed a stone into the abyss and counted the seconds until it struck far, far below.

The old workings, however, could not be left for Nature to reclaim or for local people to use in their own way. The council realised that it might still serve a purpose, and for 20 years (1966–87) heavy tipper lorries, overflowing with the rubbish of the growing town of Minehead and its holiday camp, thundered through Roadwater, shaking the houses and residents' nerves, to regurgitate their loads into the quarry. In addition, around this site were deposited a vast number of wrecked cars – incredible ugliness in the Exmoor National Park. Now they are gone, and coarse grass covers the quarry; and while who knows what arcane changes are being worked below, it is worth preserving from 100 years ago a record of something we shall never see again:

The face of the workings had some very interesting features. Here and there in a block of slate were white lines of gypsum running through, and the lines, ramifying in all directions, seemed like a delicate piece of filigree work. The slate rocks lay in irregular masses, or belts, piled one above the other, sometimes dark in colour, and at other times coloured with red marl, and the geologist might have read here some portion of the hidden history of the formation of the earth.

* For a description of the layout and working of the quarry, see the article by Chris Tilley in the *Exmoor Review* No. 34 and *Notes by the Way* by Glyn Court in the *West Somerset Free Press* of 30 April–14 May 1993.

Treborough Woodland

When this was a working quarry, a tunnel was excavated from the main site, under the road, through which slate was brought to the new cutting sheds. Here the machinery was driven by a large overshot water-wheel. It is this area, along with the surrounding woodland that was bought by the Revd and Mrs Allan Bowhill in 1973.

This picture gives an idea of the strain felt by the people of Roadwater when lorries thundered through for years bearing the waste of Minehead.

Opening of the nature trail. Left to right: ?, Allan Bowhill, Beverley Bowhill, the Rt Revd John Bickersteth, Bishop of Bath and Wells, Mrs Bickersteth, Noel Allen.

A group of young campers enjoying a meal by the camp fire with Alan Dean, 2002.

Camps were run for youth groups and a nature trail, devised and set out by the Exmoor Natural History Society, was completed, and opened by the Bishop of Bath and Wells on 19 June 1982.

After the death of Mr Bowhill in 1995 Mrs Bowhill married Alan Dean. The nature trail was closed in 1997 for the safety of young campers, but camping facilities have been greatly improved in recent years, thanks to Alan's outstanding practical skills. The woodland is now being managed to bring it back to its former coppiced rotation and to encourage biodiversity. The practice and teaching of woodland crafts is carried out in the summer months, and campers of all ages enjoy the abundant wildlife and tranquillity of this beautiful ancient woodland.

Treborough Lodge

Of the three 'big houses', that is, houses for country gentry, in our immediate area, two came belatedly on the scene. They were designed to be pleasant and comfortable country residences for gentlemen of modest rank and adequate fortune, rather than hearts and administrative centres of manorial estates. Their owners might own enough acres to qualify them as landed gentry and give them a sense of their importance in the locality, but not so much as to be the source of daily and perennial anxiety and care. The appellation 'Lodge', subtly implied that this little place would do nicely for summer or for sport at any time, but there was another more stately pile waiting up country. (The Trevelyan of the day was lord of the manor and

sole landowner and a stone lozenge on a side wall bearing the inscription 'W.C.T. 1857' indicates that the Lodge was built by Sir Walter in that year.)

The Lodge in its original, unadorned state showed itself as the work of an architect, probably from Taunton, who had learnt his trade in Regency days when elegance and proportion were prized. However, for some years the estate seemed to be unable to hold on to its lessees or tenants. *Kelly's Directory* for 1866 names a Michael H. Williams; in 1872, W.H. Teschemaker (born in Bath), and in 1875, Newell Connop, a student of civil law. In 1883 a respected Taunton banker, Daniel Badcock, his wife, sister, three children and five servants lived in one wing, and William Pritchard, his wife, son, daughter and three servants lived in the other. (Mary Griffith, aged 33, widow, of Luxborough and her daughter Sarah Ann, aged three, were crammed in somewhere else.) None of the early occupiers stayed more than a few years, and one may hazard a guess that, as 'foreigners' in the local sense, they had found Treborough too remote. The Badcocks stayed the best part of ten years, then moved to Kilve Court.

Their successor was the first to give the house an extended run. Joseph Barnes Bagehot (b.1841), ('Bagshot' in the gazetteers, because that was the family's pronunciation of their name) is described in the 1881 census as a shipowner (on shore) who came from the distinguished Langport family which produced the classic writer on the English Constitution. He stayed for nearly 20 years and seems to have been well liked and willing to accommodate benevolent organisations such as the Band of Hope; but the three tenants between 1906 and 1918 seem to have taken short leases indeed.

Then in 1919 came Clement and Dora Salaman. During their time there Treborough Lodge became a second, if miniature, Blandings Castle, with weekend visitors from far outposts of civilisation, but also a source of domestic and estate employment for a good number of Roadwater men and women, boys and girls, even if high-spirited girls sometimes had to straighten their backs and speak firmly to the mistress when they felt their acquiescence too easily 'taken for granted'. Mr Salaman had the Lodge extended and enlarged and the gardens newly landscaped, but it was Mrs Salaman who made the most indelible impression on the village. Backed by experience on the stage, she founded the Roadwater Players and directed them and members of the Women's Institute in a long series of one-act plays, many of local interest, that she had written herself. They achieved more than local success, for in 1928 the Roadwater WI were called to perform *The Lesson* for the WI annual reunion in London, which they did to great acclaim – and three of the cast took part in a revival 50 years later.

Sadly, all but one of the Roadwater ladies who worked for the Salamans have died since 2001. It is a great pity that no formal record of their reminiscences

Above: *Treborough Lodge was built by Sir Walter Calverley Trevelyan in 1857. It is shown here in 1880, before enlargement by Mr Clement Salaman in the 1920s.*

Above: *A pretty wedding between two Treborough families – Jessica Bishop married Edgar Coles, 1920s.*

Left: *Treborough schoolchildren. Back row, fifth from left: Percy Bakers; middle row, first left: Frank Hole; front row first and second left: Tom and Emily Hole.*

Right: *Treborough school, 1925. Left to right, back row: Ivor Sowden, Alick Sowden, Annie Hole, Alice Coles, Florrie Wells, Emily Calloway, Willie Wells; front row: Tom Sowden, ?, Dorothy Wells, Rosie Sowden, Beatrice Dyer, Evelyn Dyer, Percy Hole, Leonard Coles, Roy Bishop. Evelyn remembers Mrs Salaman, a governor, coming into the school to give 'pep' talks.*

Left: *Dora Salaman in Treborough Lodge gardens early 1930s.*

Right: *The schoolchildren are seen here seated beneath the awning adjoining the church door, the day of Barbara Salaman's wedding, 1928. Left to right, back row: ? Sowden, Edgar Bishop, Roy Bishop, Tom Sowden, ? Webber, ?, Percy Hole, Leonard Coles, Ivor Sowden, Willie Wells; middle row: ?, ?, ?, Beatrice Dyer, Eira Griffiths, Evelyn Dyer, Rosie Sowden; front row includes: ? Bryant, Mavis Bishop, Harry Bishop, Violet Griffiths, Olive Sowden, ? Sowden. The teacher is Mrs Griffiths.*

was made. But Nicholas Salaman, grandson of Mrs Salaman, has clear recollections of those summers before 1939, and it is a privilege to have a distinguished novelist add them to this brief account.

Memories of Treborough Lodge

Nicholas Salaman

I came to Treborough Lodge when I was four years old and my brother Clement was seven. My mother, who had divorced my father two years earlier, had lived with us in a cottage in Oxfordshire where we were happy but our grandmother, father's mother, urged us to come to West Somerset, away from the bombs, where the cow and the kitchen gardens would ensure that we would be fed. (I learned later that the cow was tubercular.)

Treborough was a kind of mini-Brideshead in those days. It was a big white Edwardian house surrounded on two sides by trees, with a lawn to one side and laurel hedges shading a slate stairway that led down to a tennis-court, with, beyond, two big fields fringed by huge woods stretching away to (I think) Slowly Hill. Very good mushroom fields they were, because my Aunt Barbara kept horses. Everything Treborough was best, according to Granny, a small energetic and talented woman who had been a successful actress on the London stage, friend of Irving and J.M. Barrie, before she was brought down to Somerset as the bride of Grandfather Clement.

My mother Betty had fallen in love with Treborough Lodge and West Somerset which combined two of her favourite virtues – the Country and Social Life. I think she fell in love with Treborough and perhaps my grandfather more than with Father. She got on particularly well with Grandfather Clement and with his daughter Betty and son Adam. She told me a year or two ago that when she and her sister-in-law Betty were walking up on Croydon (?) Hill one day they came across a distracted young woman near a small and isolated cottage. She told them she was fed up with having

nothing but sheep for company going 'baaa baaaa' all the time. They asked her why she stayed there and she replied: 'Vaughan Williams keeps me here!'.

Granny's energy and talents never seemed to falter. She became the driving force behind the Roadwater WI's drama group. She wrote plays (The Tale of A Cat and After Sedgemoor come to mind) and directed with gusto. In due course, Roadwater won the West of England top award for an amateur production ahead of many a proud and prestigious town.

Treborough Lodge was a house for grown-ups. It was full of beautiful things, paintings by Augustus John who had been a friend of Grandfather's, and all manner of fine furniture and elegant accoutrements like bonsai trees on the veranda. The doors of the rooms were made of costly cedar. Grandfather's brother had been at the Slade School of Art and there was a strong tradition of 'eye' in the family.

Food was important to Granny. She had a magical cupboard room where she kept all manner of preserves and jams and things that smelt delicious. She always made sure that there was a huge saucepan full of the milk from the Jersey cow slowly heating on the back of the aga to make clotted cream. Treborough honey was the best. I think the gardener Jackie Jewell looked after the bees. At teatime, Granny would sit behind the huge silver tea-maker which had a little blue flame burning under the silver kettle, smelling of meths.

I was sometimes allowed to go into the kitchen to see the cream thickening at the surface, or to eat the strips of fragrant crust cut away from the edges of the grown-ups' toast. My special friend was Annie Baker, the parlourmaid, a warm, cuddly, motherly person who I later learned had sad, phantom pregnancies. She had Peter Pan pictures in her pantry (possibly relics of Granny's connection with Barrie). Also in the kitchen was Queenie Taylor and (I think) Topsy Takle. Those two names are very familiar to me. I believe the Takles ran a taxi service in Roadwater.

The summer of 1940 was full of brilliant blue skies. One day I was looking up and I recall two aeroplanes

The house en fête for the wedding.

Above left: *A day or two before the wedding, a party was held at Treborough Lodge for members of the WI, farmers, shooting tenants and schoolchildren. In this group the bride and groom, Barbara Salaman and Gilbert Peck, are standing behind the table with their wedding gift from teacher Mrs Griffiths and the children, a glass salad bowl and servers. Mr and Mrs Clement Salaman are to the left of the table, Mrs Peck by the bridegroom, and teacher Mrs Griffiths front right. The maid (far right) is Queenie Tompkins (later Taylor). A wedding cake was cut and served to all present.*

circling one another overhead. I remember someone saying: 'It's a dogfight'. Sometimes my mother would organise a party for a picnic on the old quarry which entailed a walk up the hill through the woods. The ground up there was covered with slate on which trees, fern, brambles and delicious wild strawberries had grown. There were still mysterious sheds and remains of railway tracks around. I remember picking something interesting up on the quarry and showing it to a grown-up. It was a dull metallic tube with fins at one end. There was a considerable flurry among the grown-ups when I proudly displayed it. It turned out to be some kind of mortar bomb – the quarry had been used as an army range at one stage.

Small children were mostly confined to a nursery wing where they could neither be seen nor heard. They were ruled by whatever nanny happened to be brought in. We were allowed down after lunch to choose a sweet from a big tin kept on one of the top shelves of the library. I remember wondering why the grown-ups – who could reach the shelf – didn't eat all the chocolates.

Outside the house, we were allowed to go anywhere we liked. Here in the gardens, my seven-year-old brother told me about The Frights. I recall one day I made a fuss about having to play French Cricket with him (at which he always won). He said 'You had better do what I want or I shan't give you the sleeping-draught tonight.' I was puzzled and asked why. He explained that he gave me a drop of sleeping-draught which he put in my cocoa at bedtime to make me sleep. The grown-ups must not see it otherwise the worst would befall – about this he was adamant. I pressed him as to why I needed a sleeping draught. He said, 'because if you're awake when The Frights come, they can take you away...' (I wrote a novel called The Frights, based on some of my Treborough experiences, published by Secker & Warburg in about 1986.)

We were never bored at Treborough. We could sail boats in the stream, hide in 'houses' we made in the rhododendron bushes, play games in the woods, go nutting or mushroom picking, or make bonfires with Jackie Jewell, the old gardener with the ancient trousers tied up with string, who showed us how to put potatoes in the embers and entertained us with tales in his potting shed. The other outdoor man on the estate was Tom Ridler. He was a practical and resourceful man who looked after the cow as well as the cars. He was the guardian of the deliciously oil-fragrant generator and presided over the garages down near the stables, a hundred yards or so down the hill from the house.

The stable flat became home to a quite celebrated painter, Robert Bühler and his wife Eve. Bühler being a German Swiss had been threatened with prison for the duration of the war but my uncle vouched for him and he came to live at Treborough for a while.

My grandfather Clement had died in 1935, I believe. He had made Treborough a very social place, entertaining handsomely, and making friends with the local landed families. There was still some entertaining, but of course there was an absence of men. They were away fighting. And so, until the Americans came, there was a marked shortage of adult amusement.

All these women together – Granny, Aunt Barbara, Aunt Marjorie, Cousin Frances, as well as my mother, and not forgetting Cousin Chell (Chelly-Chops as Granny called her) with her huge buzzing portable hearing aid, you could hear her coming round the corner – made for a somewhat uncertain atmosphere. I remember my dear mother falling seriously ill with pneumonia, and I was so worried that I used to lurk by her bedroom door – though I was not allowed in. One day I was lurking when one of the grown-ups came by, possibly Cousin Frances.

'What's the matter, little boy?' she asked. 'Do you think she might die?' Happily my mother recovered so my worst fears were not realised.

When the Americans came, I think to the camp at Watchet or Williton, the mood improved considerably. There was Col Green and Major This and Captain That... they came to dinner and gave parties, and made much of the women of Treborough – not forgetting their children for whom they brought ice-cream. They gave wonderful Open Days at their camp near Watchet, regaling us with Coke and steak sandwiches.

Of Roadwater: I remember the village shop and Post Office which sold delicious strawberry ice-cream. I remember the watercress beds which grew in the stream. (My mother was always fond of watercress.) I remember Betty Slade and the mill with the huge wheels inside it and the splashy mill-stream. I remember the Valiant Soldier with Rachel Reckitt's fine pub sign outside it.

Of Golsoncott: I remember almost nothing except the Reckitt house and its fine garden, and old Mrs Reckitt, and Rachel who kept big dogs, and at one time a dingo which my mother brought down by train from London and which bit her ever afterwards!

Of Treborough village: I recall the Bishop family who lived at Court Farm. Mrs Bishop was the sweetest person imaginable who always gave me and my mother a big welcome in her spotless farmhouse. Tom Bishop himself was also kind and smiley. We would sometimes walk up there for tea. It must have been a tough life for them up there. When they retired they moved down to Minehead, and I think their son carried on at the farm. Treborough has a tiny church whose priest at the time was the Revd Butler. I recall that he had shingles at one point, a term which excited my curiosity.

Some way down the hill from Treborough towards Roadwater there is a turning which leads off to the quarry. Here a house was built between the hill and the woods for the quarry master. It was a white house, like Treborough Lodge, very cool if not cold inside. There was a lawn, perhaps once a tennis-court, fringed by tall rhododendron hedges. The whole place was rather spooky, ominous and forbidding. Here my mother and father lived for a while when they were first married. I don't think it did them any good.

It was strange to think of Treborough Lodge, once so full of laughter – my father's first cousin, Merula Salaman, Alec Guinness' wife, said she 'found the laughter rather forced' – and so charged with personality and personalities, standing empty and dilapidated when I came back to see it in the 1960s.

My grandmother died in 1947 – and no one wanted big houses in those days of austerity – so the place was sold. The man who bought it was Annie Baker's brother, and he bought it for the timber, not the house. He cut down all the trees on the estate, an act of desecration which of course nature has in due course repaired – but even now I find hard to forgive. The house stood empty for a long time, heated only by means of naked bulbs left burning in sockets that had once held exquisite candelabra while, in spite of this stratagem, the parquet floors heaved and bubbled...

I understand Treborough Lodge is lived in now – but I cannot believe there will ever again be the style, the parties, the finery, the fun, and, yes, the pain, that was contained within those pebbledash white walls, all those years ago when the world was younger.

Col Peck

I remember life at Treborough clearly as my home was Quarry House (tel. Washford 283) until I finished school. I used to travel to my prep school (aged 8) all alone by train. I was taken with my trunk by car to Washford, where porter Payne put me on the train. At Taunton another porter transferred me to a different train.

My grandmother Dora Salaman was a remarkable woman. She ruled the big house with efficiency. All dry goods such as flour, tea,

Lt Col Adrian Peck.

coffee, etc., were sent from the Army and Navy stores in London and kept locked up. Each morning Dora would unlock the store cupboard and dole out the allowance for the day to Queenie, Violet or Alice in the kitchen. In addition to running the house she engaged in numerous other activities – notably the writing and production of plays for the local WI. At various times she was a magistrate, an ARP warden, ran the St John's ambulance cadets and was active in Village Hall affairs.

I remember some of the people who worked at Treborough. Charlie Coles was the cowman who ran the farm of 150 acres and we enjoyed the produce. Once a week he would harness the pony and trap and drive down to Williton with the laundry! The two Misses Buckingham dealt with it and Charlie would make another journey to collect the linen the following week.

There were two cars – a Vauxhall DYC 501, and a Wolseley which was laid up during the war. One chauffeur was Mr Baggott – he left at the beginning of the war. Tom Ridler was the head gardener with three boys under him. The postman used to walk up to Treborough with the mail – his round was 15 miles. The head maid was Annie Baker – she stayed for years. There was a cook, an under cook and at least one other maid.

This life came to an end when my grandmother died at the end of the war.

It was a cold winter, the lanes filled up with snow, and transport ground to a halt. Mrs Kathleen Williams (née Snell), who lived in Treborough Lodge Cottage, recalls that they were cut off for over six weeks and had to rely on a sheep that her father had killed for their meals. She injured herself trying to cut greenery for a wreath for Mrs Salaman's funeral.

Treborough millennium group in front of the church, 2000. The picture includes: *Jessica, Jordan, Kathy and Nathan Batts, Georgia, Annie, Olivia, Sarah, William and Mark Weatherlake, Ellie, Holly, Tracy, Mike, Jack, Hannah, Dinah and Richard Bishop, Ellen, Jasmine, Beth, Ben, Alex, William and Kate Bowman, Elizabeth and David Jessup, Sarah Coombes, Lintem and Jennifer Wightman, Robert Edwards, Fiona Monaghan, Ros and Oliver Roulston, Laurie and Angela Heath, Mark, Jodie and Lawrence Dascombe, Jane and Dennis Takle, Carolyn and Brian Wise, Mike Chipperfield.*

The Valiant Soldier, c.1900.

THE VALIANT SOLDIER INN.

Right: *The Valiant Soldier, snow scene, 1991.* DRAWING BY BILL MONTAGUE

Valiant Soldier inn, c.1910. Landlady Mrs Sarah Beamer is standing with three paragons of male sartorial elegance typical of the time (leather leggings, trousers hitched half-mast, trousers bound with 'yorks' or 'yorkers'). The Beamers prospered in the trade, as reflected in the memorials in Leighland church.

Chapter 18

Revelry, Entertainment and Clubs

The Revel and the Club Walk

Roadwater has a long tradition of celebrations and get-togethers. Every July nowadays the village enjoys its fête; but before that there used to be the gala and sports; and before them the 'club walk'; and before that the revel.

One of the main annual events in hundreds of West Country parishes was the parochial feast, held on the festival of the patron saint of the church or on the anniversary of its dedication. Although Roadwater had no church building, while Leighland had, the village was determined not to be without a feast; and as the village, unlike Leighland, had two level meadows able to hold several hundred rumbustious Chaucerian characters with their japes and junkets, both hamlets joined in the fun. The first framers of the feast had the high-minded idea of letting the peasants have a day off from labour, and the more self-interested one of making sure they listened to the parish priest before sniffing out the 'vittles'. This was a day of making-up-for-lost-time gluttony – at least in a good harvest year – and it must have looked very much as Brueghel depicted it two centuries later.

By mid-nineteenth century, however, most of the old work-free saints' days and holidays had been lost. The enclosure of common land had robbed many thousands of countrymen of their independence and turned them into landless labourers, obliged to work always at their master's behest for fear of dismissal. This parish escaped the worst of enclosure and there remained a few yeomen and cottagers with a small parcel of land of their own, sometimes less than a quarter of an acre; but the rest were as badly off as anywhere.

The revel, in mid-September, with the harvest home, had to serve for the lost holidays, and the village made the most of it. The youths were generally up and about early, going out in small parties to pick evergreens and flowers to decorate the village. Here and there poles had been fixed and they were festooned with ivy trails, lilac and wild hops. This was complete by the time the rest of the men had roused themselves from their unaccustomed lie-in. (The women, it hardly needs saying, had risen as early as usual – no rest for them.)

It seems to have been accepted that as 'you never gets nort fer nort in this wicked world, wi'out you pays for 't,' the copious browsing and sluicing at the Valiant Soldier had to be earned, and so about mid-morning many made their way up to Leighland for the sermon. But more solid food was what they were after, and when they returned to the Valiant Soldier, they were given roast beef, 'teddies' and vegetables, followed by more roast beef, with pudding to follow, and all washed down with deep draughts of 'tib', an old-fashioned beer, or cider, until you looked for a fine spray coming out of their ears. By early afternoon the board had taken on the look of a stricken battleship, with her crew barely visible, three sheets to the wind and half-seas under; but a few stout hearts and livers had survived the battle so far, and now they steered hazily down the street to their next port of call.

Football as an organised game had not yet arrived, but wrestling flourished, rough, tough and brutal. On the Sunday before the revel the champion wrestler of the parish attended the church service wearing the tall hat denoting his status and decorated with red, white and blue ribbons and streamers. At some stage in the proceedings he had hung his hat in the church as a challenge to all comers.

The revel had been held since time immemorial in Day's Meadow (now the recreation-ground, which extended further then). Crowds always gathered for the wrestling, many from the surrounding parishes. There were booths that had done duty for years, selling the old comfits and fairings, wafer-thin ginger snaps and white and brown gingerbread men with flakes of gilt tissue pasted on them, sugared almonds and long caterpillar-shaped creations of white sugar on sticks of cinnamon and other spiced substances. The secret of making the ginger snaps and comfits was held by one or two families and jealously guarded, so that they were reputedly the envy of all who were sweet of tooth and young of heart. Everyone who came made sure of a good supply, for they had to be made to last a long time at home; the boy or girl who nipped too often to the cupboard without asking paid for it with a spanking. Even in those hard times there were easy-going parents, but 'taking without permission' and 'fibbing' were sternly forbidden and called stronger names.

Altogether, at mid-century the keynote was simplicity. The wrestling was the great event, and all other interests subsided when the champion strode into the ring. Even without the challenge on the Sunday before, he looked every inch the champion, and his tight-fitting breeches, heavy worsted stockings and cowhide boots with their toe-tips beaten almost as hard as metal made him look trim and ready for battle. And 'battle' does not much exaggerate, for the soles and uppers of his heavy boots had been soaked in bullock's blood and then hammered hard to make them almost like iron.

He shouted his challenge to all or any. As soon as this was accepted he undid his champion's belt, handed it to the umpire and got down to business. He never ran short of challengers, for although the money prizes were elusive, many strong and active young men coveted the honour. Exmoor wrestling was a matter of bodily strength, a firm and relentless hold, and the skill to exploit the opponent's sudden weakening or change of grip so as to bring him to a fall. When the contestants were evenly matched they would have to try all their tricks until one found the other's weak spot, perhaps his only one. They would hold each other round the waist and give and take tremendous, terrible kicks on the legs; many a wrestler bore the scars until his dying day and indeed would roll up his corduroys and show them as eagerly as any veteran of Agincourt. No doubt it was brutal, but it was in the old blood and the rustic temperament responded to it with enthusiasm.

After the wrestling came dancing, and it went on, with intervals, until late into the night: the two villages were conscious that in their music and musicians they had something which, if not quite unique, was very special to Roadwater and Leighland and made them respected by the rest of the world. George Matthews and his men not only manifestly enjoyed themselves, George also had them play dance music he had composed or arranged himself, and what other village in West Somerset could boast of that? Later on in the day a solitary fiddler such as the cobbler Tom Ettery might play for the dancing.

The revel also served as a small-scale market day, for here the workmen could buy or sell their young pigs, and the 'gentleman who paid the rent' was penned quite near at hand and his vocal contribution to the revelry must have delighted the small boys if no one else. Some people, though, may have divined the hidden pathos behind the pig, when the poor labourers had to sell the animal they had fattened at the privation of their own children, to keep the wolf from the door.

Early in the 1870s the revel faded away – or rather, it was replaced by a different feast, one evolving out of an unusual, if modest, prosperity for the village folk and marking a move into modern times. Nevertheless it still gave clear evidence of a community united in purpose. It was the club walk.

Extreme and unrelenting poverty may sometimes crush the spirit, but in many of our village forefathers it bred the determination to fight it, and from their miserable pay they set aside small sums which, when combined with others', might give them some slight protection against the rigours of illness and old age. These associations were known as friendly or mutual benefit societies, or more popularly as clubs, and they came to take an important place in the life of most villages in the second half of the nineteenth century. They provided a touch of colour, excitement and even pageantry in people's lives.

Mid-century Roadwater was home to just one, based at the Valiant Soldier Inn. They met in the upstairs 'club room', paid in their 3d. per week and before long a 'tidy sum' had accumulated in the club chest. One night it was broken into and the money stolen. The club secretary and others tried in vain to find out who the thief might be, and as a last resort he went to Parson Newton and asked for his help. Newton agreed, and on a given day, by means unknown, he 'conjured the thief up into a willow tree behind the public house.' The man was taken, went for trial, was sentenced to seven years' imprisonment, and came back to live in Old Cleeve until he died.

Those were the simple – if puzzling – facts, but the embroiderers got to work, and soon the story went round that the chest had been so heavy that when the members tried to lift it for a wager, it beat them all, until a lime burner from Treborough 'hoisted en up 'pon his knee.' The village poet expressed:

'It zo happened that when the nex' meetin'
  comed round,
Thicky club box, an' all as were in en,
Had clain disappeared, an' could nowhere be vound,
An' they vowed they'd none of 'em zeen en.

Suspicion fell on the lime burner, but he had cleared off and was never seen again.

One of the committee suggested they should call in the witch doctor in Dunster: 'He's the chap as will conjure for we', but the others felt that in such a mysterious case as theirs, 'magical powers' were needed; so two of them waited on Parson Newton, who agreed to serve if they could find two other clergymen to help. They succeeded, and then:

The passuns agreed wan evenin' to meet

In a spot that they choosed on their own.
An' each comed wi' his sarplice right
 down to his veet
An' they mummeled a mournful ole tone,
Zayin' zummat they'd got in a girt black book
What passun to Cleeve had a-took;
An' there, in the dimpse, they practised a spell
An' zummoned Ole Nick to appear.

Old Nick, unable to resist the power of three parsons, told them where the club chest was buried:

An' when they'd a-laid Ole Zatan to ground,
Then off down to Road they all hurried,
An' there in a cabbage-patch, deep in the mold,
Were the treasure, as they'd a-bin told.

By 1870 two other friendly societies had been added, one at the New Inn, the other the Good Templars Lodge, which met in the large kitchen of William Court's home, Oatway House, until 1878, when Sir Walter Trevelyan built them the Temperance Hall, by the standards of the day a splendid one.

The club walk was, on the whole, a beneficial institution. It gave the menfolk the chance of dining, playing and – if so inclined – worshipping together; it gave them and their families a day for reunions, for most people away from home tried to come back if they could. It was also a day for paying bills and receiving money. Men from the hamlets, Comberow, Sticklepath, Chidgley, Hook Hill, Leighland, Stamborough, Hayne, Wood Advent and Golsoncott would call to be measured for their boots or pay the smith or the carpenter, and these in turn laid themselves out for a special run of hospitality. Thomas Popham, the wheelwright, might have a new cart on show in his yard, glowing with fresh paint, and the smiths, Tom Slade and Nathanael Edbrooke, might each have some new implement on sale and the village shop would have some special attraction such as oranges, raisins or Brazil nuts. The women had their share in the feast, too, in renewing family ties and friendships, in acquiring small treasures and fairings, and in donning the old silken dresses which, though heirlooms, had never gone out of fashion in their simple way of life.

On the morning of club walk day all the activity of the earlier revel was repeated, but now the club men walked up to Leighland in procession, led by the band, their brass instruments flashing in the sunlight. They made a brave show.

In some parts of Somerset the men carried blue staves about five feet long with brass ornaments on the tops and the County Museum in Taunton has a remarkable collection of these insignia. Roadwater men, however, had their own ideas and they followed a custom more natural to a rural scene. Most of our cottagers took pride in their gardens and the old-fashioned flowers that grew in them, such as

lilacs and hollyhocks, wallflowers and sweet williams, geraniums and scented ten-week stocks, with roses in their hundreds. The club walk served as a flower show, with the men and their wives competing keenly for the best display. They carefully gathered the flowers, arranged them in bouquets and tied them to the head of the staff with ribbon streamers; they made a lovely sight. At the head of the members, and immediately after the band, young men carried a magnificent garland consisting of a pole some 15 feet long with various crosspoles on which supple withy wands were woven into fantastic shapes, covered with fresh green moss from the woodlands and finished with a decoration of choice flowers. As a variation of this, the garland might be trimmed with tinted paper wrappings and rosettes. The former kind often weighed some 200 pounds and took four to six men to hold in position as they marched; but it formed a fitting crown to the long line of flower-capped staves as they moved in stately procession to the church.

After the service the procession moved back to the inn where, in the loft over the skittle alley, the club dinner was served. At three o'clock the diners rose from the table – or from under it, if they still could – and moved off either for skittles or to follow the band down to Day's Meadow. The garland, which had been placed leaning against the walls of the church and later the pub, was not forgotten but taken along for further display.

Here the booths were still selling the old fairings, but a shooting gallery had taken the place of the wrestling, and the brass band that of the old orchestra. New sideshows had appeared, livelier and more exciting for the young men and boys and girls, stalls selling 'play toys', as they were called, from the city, and for his penny-ha'penny a lad might purchase a tin pistol and box of pink paper explosive caps and feel himself Buffalo Bill, Garibaldi and General Gordon all rolled into one. A tin trumpet or a shining sword would cost no more, while for only another penny or two his little sister might buy a wooden doll, stalky and ungainly, with stiff joints and painted black hair parted in the middle; but all possessions were to be treasured.

More exotic attractions were becoming common: a peep-show in a caravan that showed gaudy pictures of foreign lands and people seen through magnifying lenses, at a charge of a penny a peep; a man with a monkey or a dancing bear; and a primitive round-about with galloping horses swinging round to the music of a barrel organ, both being turned by hand. Once in a while a troop of Christy Minstrels came to entertain, as well as a couple of clowns. In a puppet show crude wooden figures were made to perform curious antics by means of wires and springs, and similar figures in a shadowgraph exhibition 'performed' between a lamp and a linen screen while the proprietor sang ditties appropriate to the subjects.

Above: *Rachel Reckitt, aged 82, opening Roadwater Fête assisted by Dennis Takle (left) and Pat Taylor in 1991.*

Right: *Programme for Roadwater Midsummer Festival, 1986.*

ROADWATER MIDSUMMER FESTIVAL

JUNE 21st/22nd

SATURDAY Special Luncheons at:- from 12pm

White Horse Washford
Valiant Soldier Roadwater
Raleighs Cross Inn

Flower Festival — St. Lukes Church Craft Exhibition & Sale Village Hall 2pm
Tour of Old Roadwater 3.30pm Visit the Roadwater Fisheries 4pm
Wine & Cheese at Magnolia House 5.15pm
Concert at Cleeve Abbey with Exmoor Ensemble 6pm
With cream teas at the Village Hall & Pitt Mill throughout the afternoon and
Tractor & Trailer Rides

SUNDAY Festival Service at St. Lukes 10am with the Choir of St. Audries
Village Picnic in Recreation Ground 12pm — with Games, Raft Races,
Treasure Hunts, Dancing and Gym Displays
Sponsored Cricket Match BEN'S BASHERS v PHIL'S FIGHTERS 2pm
Pony & Trap Rides up the Old Mineral line 2pm, 3pm, 4pm
Cream Teas & Exhibitions open throughout the afternoon

ENTRY By Souvenir Programme of Old Roadwater £1.00
Children FREE
Programme includes a Draw Number.
Prizes to be awarded Sunday 4pm Village Hall

Left: *Dennis Takle auctioning the cakes, 2000.*

Below: *Roadwater Fête, 1995. Watchet Town Band are in the foreground, while Robert Hand and the participants in a Tae Kwon Do demonstration can be seen on the right.*

But most popular of all the shadowgraphs was a prize fight, created by the showman's two hands with the aid of a handkerchief, and the boxing effects were said to be most realistic and whimsical.

Once a pair of mountebanks (charlatans) pitched their tent and did strange tricks with a shaving scene which kept the boys and girls in peals of laughter. The 'barber' brought on stage a big horse-bucket full of lather, which he applied with a mason's lime brush. One slap completely covered the face and head of the man to be shaved. Then the 'barber' brought out a large wooden razor as long his arm and set to work. Suddenly the whole mass of lather turned blood-red and he apologised profusely for having accidentally cut off his customer's nose. All this tragi-comedy was dealt out at 2d. a head.

The club walk was a day of opportunity for the enterprising grocer and general dealer, too, for he owned most of the stalls and looked to make a rich harvest. Among other things he used to lay in a good stock of Barcelonas (Spanish nuts), for the village folk were said to be 'great on nuts'. A measure of these nuts was also the prize at the shooting gallery – a pretty cautious provision at first sight, but some of the lads had a good eye with a rifle and walked away with their pockets crammed with Barcelonas – and for days afterwards the street, the gardens and the church and chapel were littered with nutshells.

Now and again a cheapjack would take advantage of the great days and pitch his caravan – his emporium, he preferred to call it – outside the inn. It was a dazzling display with gaudy pot-boiler pictures, Britannia ware tea services, kettles, pots and pans, American clocks and German cutlery, and he reaped a splendid harvest from the hard earnings of our unsophisticated people.

Sometimes the emporium remained for several nights and the cunning man employed several wiles to decoy the people to the sale: a whistling contest, a baby show, a pudding-eating competition, the last of these the most diverting of all. Some half a dozen young fellows entered. The puddings which were boiled hard and without suet were well spiced with cayenne pepper and taken up all hot out of the boiling water. He who could pick a pudding abroad with his fingers and demolish it the quickest was declared the winner, but unfortunately for him, he bore the nickname 'Pudden' for ever after.

In later years the small independent village clubs, well-intentioned but chronically short of ready cash in a bad year, gave way to national institutions such as the Order of Druids and the Free Foresters, and two of the stationmasters on the Mineral Line, Dicky James at Roadwater and John Taylor at Comberow, were zealous agents for the Foresters. In time the people, in spite of their inborn distrust of 'foreigners' and 'up-country ways', saw that these trusts were well administered and disposed of ample funds, and so the old village clubs were wound up. The members did not lose all the fun and pageantry of the old, for the Foresters in particular took a pride in their spectacular appearance. They participated in processions with Robin Hood and his men on horseback dressed in green velvet jerkins with silver-mounted horns slung across their shoulders. And even the most colourful aspects of the old club walks paled in the light of such romance.

Roadwater Inn

The licensee of the Roadwater Inn (a Starkey Knight and Ford house) in the 1920s and '30s was Charlie Ford. When Charlie died his wife took over for some years. Later Mrs Ivy Bailey became the licensee until closure in the 1960s. Since then the building has been converted to residential accommodation, while still retaining its characteristic appearance.

Left: *Gloria Bailey standing in the door of the Roadwater Inn, 1948. There is a glimpse of the orchard through the open door.*

Below: *The Roadwater Inn. The picture includes: Arthur Bryant, Bobbie Gibson, Harry Jones, Eddie Beaver and Trevor Davies.*

Behind the bar of the Roadwater Inn, late 1950s.
Left to right, back row: *Tony Burnett, George Quinnell, Ivor Bailey;* front row: *Dorothy Quinnell, Ivy Bailey, Peter Quinnell, Gloria Burnett.*

Drama in Roadwater

Roadwater had always had a tradition of home-produced entertainment but under Mrs Dora Salaman of Treborough Lodge the acting prowess of the village WI reached new heights, most memorably with *The Lesson* first performed in 1928. The village ladies travelled to London with Mrs Reckitt to take part in the WI drama festival. Bertha Routley recalls being taken to Madame Tussaud's before going to St George's Hall for rehearsal. The actors would have liked to linger longer in the capital, but Mrs Reckitt had to hurry back for the stone-laying of the hall, which took place a day or two later.

Dramatic activity in Roadwater had lapsed for some years when in 1975, Mr Geoffrey Darke, a well-known and respected surgeon living at Roadwater Farm, decided to try to resurrect the Players. With the help of his wife Elizabeth, and niece, Elizabeth Cosgrove, a group of interested people were invited to meet at the farm. They soon started to make plans. The first production was a hilarious revue, *Up the Mineral Line*. Other productions quickly followed. Membership grew, and the Players were soon organising play readings, quiz evenings and theatre trips. Since those early days, the Players have won many awards in various drama competitions. The pantomimes, of course, are a big annual occasion, and are hugely popular.

On a different dramatic plane there have been West End plays, Restoration comedy and even Shakespeare – all is grist to their mill. May the Players long continue to give pleasure with the variety of their entertainment programme.

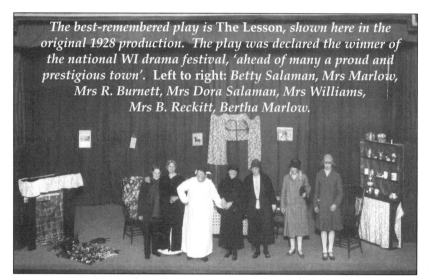

The best-remembered play is **The Lesson**, *shown here in the original 1928 production. The play was declared the winner of the national WI drama festival, 'ahead of many a proud and prestigious town'.* **Left to right:** *Betty Salaman, Mrs Marlow, Mrs R. Burnett, Mrs Dora Salaman, Mrs Williams, Mrs B. Reckitt, Bertha Marlow.*

In 1978 to celebrate the 50th anniversary of the building of the Village Hall, a repeat performance of **The Lesson** *was given, produced by Elizabeth Cosgrove.* **Left to right:** *Gill White, Susan Taylor, Lesley Damerel, Bertha Routley (the only original member of the cast), Molly Gooding, Joan Kerslake, Janice Bond.*

Right: *Certificate awarded in 1933 for* After Sedgemoor. *Roadwater won the cup in the festival. Sidney Lile made the men's costumes and Slades built the furniture.*

Below: *Cast members of* After Sedgemoor. *The photograph includes:* Mrs Salaman, Horace Burnett, Dennis Smith, Harold Gooding, Mrs Tucker, Doris Reed, Florrie Wells, Mrs Coles, Miss Edwards, Miss Laugher, Madge Webber and George Nethercott. *The photograph also shows the cups won in the WI Drama Festival.*

The first pantomime, The Sleeping Beauty *written by Elizabeth Cosgrove, 1975.*
Left to right, standing: *Tina Maddock, Joanne Snell, Claire Bishop* (behind), *Clive Cooper, Jennifer Western, Charles Townsend, Carol Tipper, Barbara Young, Ray Young, Colin Tennant, Jane Chipperfield* (behind), *Lesley Damerel, Sue Taylor, Vivian Gee;* seated: *Sally White, Sarah Bowman, Tonia Tipper, Kate Bowman, Susan Lane.*

Old Tyme Music Hall, 1977. *The players produced a music hall, inviting well-known local guest performers, including the late Ken Almond of the 'Patchwork' folk group, and members of Carhampton Curtain Raisers.* Left to right, back row: *Muriel Damerel, Glyn Court (accompanist), Ken Almond, Albert Tudball (conjuror), ?, ?, Jo Snell, Colin Tennant, Bertha Routley, Carol Tipper, Gill White, Roger Coles, Geoffrey Darke MC, Torquil Cosgrove;* front row: *Kay Sawatzki, Elizabeth Cosgrove, Helen Tudball, Angela Barton, Susan Taylor, Jenny Western, Lesley Damerel, Martin Damerel, Tina Maddock, Diane Beaver, Brian Taylor.*

Right: Outside Edge, 1987. Left to right: *Jan Bond, Gill White, Dennis Evans, Jennifer Hand, Frank Scragg, Pam Scragg, John Holroyd and Martyn Babb. Props were supplied by Roadwater Cricket Club.*

Left: Sing a Song of Sixpence, 1989. Left to right, back row: *Gill White, Sue Newton, Martyn Babb, Heather Roberts, Sarah Pounds, Jeremy Scott, Lucy Takle, Dennis Evans, Robert Hand, Juliet Griffin, Kirsty Tredgett, Kay Ireland, Jocelyn Harral, Al Menzies;* middle row: *Katherine Kingsford, Sarah Robertson, Julie Tredgett, Toby Andrew, Jeremy Babb, Seb Coles, Tom Harral, Jenny Walmsley, Hazel Barron, Julia Kingsford, Joanne Foster;* front row: *Harriet Andrew, Kate Humphrey, Helen Foster, Charlotte Best.*

Left: Hickory Dickory Dock. Left to right, back row: *Alison Maddock, Charles Townshend, Ray Young, Elaine Thorne, Sallyann Lile (Black Imp), Barbara Young, Sue Taphouse, Frank Scragg, Janice Bond, Tina Maddock, Colin Tennant, Tony Pendray, Jacky Hickman, Elizabeth Cosgrove, Dennis Evans, Carol Tipper;* kneeling: *Joan Kerslake;* front row: *Sue Newton, Lucy Takle, Lisa Burge, Kim Taylor, Mairi Cosgrove, Kellie Shopland, Clare Burnett, Angus Cosgrove.*

Right: Lord Savile's Secret, *1990.* Standing, left to right: *Frank Scragg, Charlotte Best, Patrick Daley, Katherine Kingsford, Martyn Babb;* seated: *Rosemary Littlewood, Jennifer Hand, Gill White, Ben Lintott.*

Left: Old Mother Hubbard. Left to right, back row: *Geoff Best, Tom Sunderland, Vicki Sunderland, Stella Rijs, Tina Pendray, Jocelyn Harral, Sue Newton, Julia Kingsford, Laura Walder, Seb Coles, Charlotte Best, Tad Mandziej, Patrick Daley, Rosemary Littlewood, Sarah Coles, Tom Harral, Martyn Babb;* front row: *Alan Babb, Brenda Mandziej, Ben Sunderland, Alec Roberts, Emily Best, Lisa Priddy, Mike Gulliver, Katherine Kingsford* (in animal skin), *Hannah Cullingford, Jennifer Hand.*

Right: The Three Musketeers, *1997.* Left to right, back row: *Robert Hand, Ben Lintott, Colin Hill, Rob Wilson, Chris Flewett, Tad Mandziej, Simon Passmore, Julia Kingsford, Patrick Daley, Carol Hill, Audrey Owens;* middle row: *Jennifer Hand, Charlotte Best, Mo Best, Brenda Mandziej, Jennie Allen, William Wilson, Anne Harris, Kyle Roberts;* front row: *Kieran Roberts, Maya Yianni, Karen Hayes, Vicky Sunderland, Sarah Coles, Megan Hooper, Emily Best, Teresa Passmore, Rhiannon Wilson.*

Clubs, Societies & Having Fun

Roadwater Village Hall

The Village Hall in Roadwater is a remarkable building by any standards. Immediately on rounding the bend by St Luke's Church, the eye is caught by its bold chimney reaching up to the hills beyond. The front of the building is quite plain but on descending the drive to the lower level, a different aspect is revealed. Looking out over the delightful recreation-ground, overhung by the dense wood of Harpers, is a two-storey edifice linked by a flight of stone steps and a verandah for watching the cricket. The lower part is intended to resemble the byre of a Somerset farmhouse with its rounded stone pillars. In 1928, a split-level building such as this one was unusual – today it is a testament to the vision of the forward-thinking architect Mr Norman Reckitt.

The hall was designed and given to the village by Mr and Mrs Reckitt to mark their silver wedding. The latter worked tirelessly for over 30 years to keep the running of the hall flowing smoothly. At the time of writing the hall has been in continuous use for 75 years and inevitably its use has changed with the passage of time. In the early days, clubs and organisations kept the caretaker busy every night of the week – a men's club, billiards, baby clinic, library, the WI and, of course, the dances! The war years saw the arrival of the evacuees with their pathetic paper parcels and strange accents, distribution of ration books, ARP lectures and knitting parties. Early in 1944, America came to Roadwater and for about 10 weeks there was a frenzied round of entertainment.

Inevitably the upkeep of such a large building is a heavy responsibility. A faithful band of workers labour ceaselessly, and in recent years have completed many improvements to bring the hall up to the standards expected in the new millennium. The photographs covering 70 years will give some idea of the central role that the hall has played in village life.

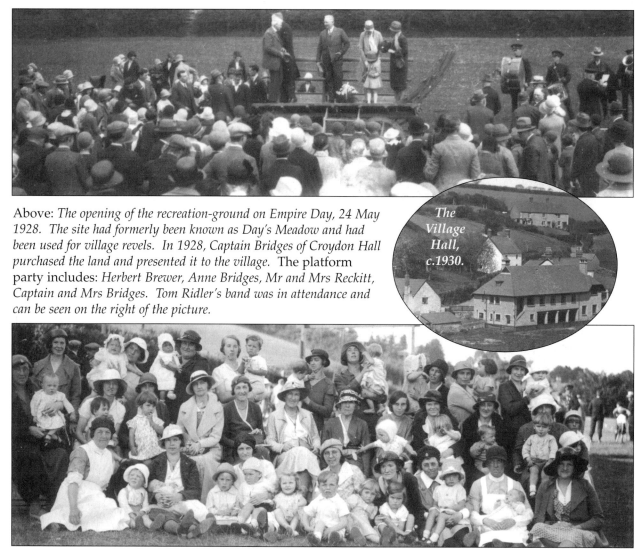

Above: *The opening of the recreation-ground on Empire Day, 24 May 1928. The site had formerly been known as Day's Meadow and had been used for village revels. In 1928, Captain Bridges of Croydon Hall purchased the land and presented it to the village.* The platform party includes: *Herbert Brewer, Anne Bridges, Mr and Mrs Reckitt, Captain and Mrs Bridges. Tom Ridler's band was in attendance and can be seen on the right of the picture.*

The Village Hall, c.1930.

One of the facilities offered by the hall committee was the provision of an infant welfare clinic. The nurse (front row, left) *is probably Nurse Nichols who used to cycle to Roadwater from Old Cleeve. The clinic continued and flourished until the 1950s under Nurse Evans.*

Left: *Maypole dancing on Empire Day, 1930s. Joan Bond is in the frilly dress on the right.*

Right: *Empire Day tableau.*

Left: *Peggy Lile and friends performing one of Mrs Salaman's tableaux. The background is interesting as the event must have taken place in the upper part of Day's Meadow, now part of the Watersmeet housing development. From left to right: Harpers Cottages, glasshouse at Burnett's Nurseries, Larcombe Villa, the back of the chapel.*

LONG LIVE THE KING

Jubilee tea party for women and children (the men were given a hot dinner), 1935. Standing left with patterned frock is Mrs Poole. Winnie Duck is second from right standing at the back. Eileen Coleman is seated front right with two small Coombs children to the left of the pram. Gladys Lile is behind the pram to the right and Mrs Case is behind Gladys. Miss Laugher (hatless) is behind children in the centre of the front row, between two hatted ladies.

139

ROADWATER & LEIGHLAND

Jubilee Celebrations

MONDAY, MAY 6th, 1935.

Thanksgiving Service
AND
PROGRAMME OF EVENTS

ROADWATER & LEIGHLAND

Coronation Celebrations

WEDNESDAY, MAY 12th, 1937.

Order of Service
AND
PROGRAMME OF EVENTS

Above: *The village enjoyed a full programme of events in celebration of the silver jubilee of King George V, 1935.*

Above: *Two years after the jubilee the same programme was repeated for the coronation of King George VI, 1937.*

Left: *Mr Garnet Wolseley of Nettlecombe opening Roadwater Fête, late 1930s.*

Children's fancy-dress competition, one of the events to celebrate the coronation of Queen Elizabeth II.

Left: *Young children's tea party in the Village Hall to celebrate the 1953 coronation.* Included in the picture are: *Queenie Taylor, Mrs Lynes, Mrs Amy Burnett, Mrs George Takle, Molly Gooding, Mrs Carpenter, Mrs Parsons* (in front of Mrs Takle) *with Heather, Mrs Jack Routley, Mrs Doreen Beaver* (in front of Mrs Carpenter) *with Valerie, Smith Twin.* Also in the picture are: *Mrs Priddy* (front left), *Vi Burge with Wendy, Nurse Evans* (standing wearing beret), *Edith Wilcox* (next to Nurse Evans) *and Alan Wilcox.*

Tea party for older children. Included in the picture are: Revd Dr Beazeley, Mrs Hole, Mrs Lynes, Mrs Takle, Mrs Bryant, Mrs Willis, Mrs Duck, Mrs Westcott, Mrs Gooding, Mrs Dorothy Beaver, Mrs Amy Burnett, Mrs Gladys Lile, Mr Gooding, Mrs Reckitt, Tony Hemmings, David Taylor, Gloria Bailey, Joan Wright, Barbara Nethercott, Evelyn Smith, Olive Wright, Margaret Beaver, Jennifer Ford, John Beaver and David Reed, John Tompkins, Colin Chidgey, Robin Hole, Dennis Burge, Colin Routley, Keith Burnell, ? Burge, Eileen Mann with Christine on chair, Philip Hole, Brian Sowden. The girls sitting at the left-hand table are probably from Croydon Hall.

Coronation service in the recreation-ground, with Harold Gooding at the piano, 1953.

Nobby Taylor giving rides in his home-made side car at 2d. a go, 1955.

Tom Webber and Percy Hill on the gate at Roadwater Fête, c.1970. Before the car park was built in 1978 the path to the left of the hall was the way into the recreation-ground.

A WI outing in the 1950s, possibly to Montacute. The Roadwater contingent must have joined forces with another group as it has not been possible to name all the ladies present. The picture includes: Stan Dunn (driver), Mrs Burnett, Mrs Westcott senr, Joan Keene, Mrs Duck, Mrs Westcott junr with Hubert, Mrs Reed, Dorothy Beaver, Molly Gooding, Mrs Carpenter.

Roadwater Village Hall
1928 - 1978
To celebrate the 50th Jubilee of the opening of the Hall, and in gratitude for the help you have given, you are invited to an
Anniversary Supper
at the Hall on Wednesday, October 25th, 1978, at 7.30 for 8.0 p.m.
R.S.V.P. by Sept. 30th to Mrs. A. M. Gooding, Vale Cottage, Roadwater, Watchet, Somerset.

Left: *Invitation to the anniversary supper to celebrate 50 years of the Village Hall, 1978.*

Below: *Hall Committee and guests at the supper. Left to right, standing: Desmond Post, Pat Taylor, Bertha Routley, Philip White, Lesley Pring, Michael White; seated: Janet Taylor, Gill White, Mrs Betty Greeves (née Salaman), Rachel Reckitt, Molly Gooding, Alice White.*

Guests at the supper. The picture includes: Fred Mann, Eileen Mann, Mrs Westcott, Mrs Chidgey, Annette Land, Eric Smith, Sally Smith, Mrs K. Lile, Pam Hole, Val Hole, Mrs Mavis Drew, Major George Drew, Mrs Nell Blyth, Mrs Greeves, Mrs Peck, Col Blyth, Mrs Chipperfield, Mr Chipperfield, Jane Takle, Dennis Takle, Eric Hide, Mrs Hide, Hubert Westcott, Audrey Takle, Arthur Takel, Howard Burnett, Amy Burnett, Mrs Takle, Sally Watts, Rodney Watts, Clare Court, Glyn Court, Derrick Lile, John Hill, Mavis Hill, Mr Newman, Mrs Newman, Trevor Davies, Mrs C. Gooding, Nurse Evans, George Roberts, Shauna Roberts, Desmond Post, Mrs F. Post, Heinz Sawatzki, Torquil Cosgrove, Rene Ryan, Pat and Janet Taylor

'The Mineral Line'

In 1998 Jeanette Fahlbusch and Rob Wilson met to discuss how to bring original music and comedy entertainment to the village. In January 1999 the first concert with Alka Salsa was staged – the event was a sell-out and the rest is history. Performers have since come from India, the Congo, Louisiana, Hungary, Ireland and even Bristol! Each monthly event has a theme with delicious food, cooked locally by volunteers, to match the theme of the evening. The Mineral Line is a non-profit-making organisation.

Tuesday Club

In 1967 a group of young mothers got together and formed the Tuesday Club, with an annual subscription of 25p! The main intention of the group was to hold monthly meetings in rotation at Old Cleeve, Washford and Roadwater. Members wanted to be free of rules and regulations and managed for a time without a committee. The informal atmosphere continues to this day.

Various events soon became popular – such as the fashion show, skittles, and trips to the theatre. Charitable fund-raising also became a regular part of the club's activities, and in 1994 a cheque for £555 was handed to the Children's Hospice South West. The club also supports the annual Macmillan coffee mornings. A chestnut tree which was given to the recreation-ground is fast reaching maturity – a beautiful and ever-present reminder of the work of the club.

Right: *Mineral Line committee in festive mood, 2003. Left to right, back row: Jayne Yianni, Neil Hopkins, Mag Hatton, Jenny Barron, Rob Wilson, Geoff Best; front row: Jude Johnson-Smith, Sue Onley, Mo Best, Mary Coles.*

Some of the members of the Tuesday Club, 2004. Left to right, back row: Sheena Stuckey, Carol Tipper, Elaine Necchi (secretary), Diane Somerfield, Mary Copp, Eileen Burston, Hilary Mills, Flo Croucher (treasurer), Jan Bennett, Margaret Mangan, Phyl Stott; seated: Kay Ireland, Joan Beaver, Joan Clark, Jennifer Asbridge (chairman), Jean Simpson, Ann Cooksley.

Roadwater Scouts

Roadwater Scouts started in 1921 in a tin hut in the garden at Fernbank. Six boys were invested – Hubert Westcott, Cecil Beaver, Thomas Taylor, Edmund Burnett, Clifford Westcott and Carol Lyddon. The first scoutmasters were Mr A. Bell and Mr S. Hayman, assisted by the Revd S. Arthur. The Ambulance badge examiner was Mrs Salaman and the Laundry badge Miss B. North, daughter of the artist J.W. North. Miss Dorothea Shaw took over the running of the Scouts, and did so very efficiently until she left in 1931. Under her leadership the boys went to Wembley for the jamboree, camped every year and won many group competitions.

Right: Rover Scouts at camp in Saltash, late 1920s. Left to right: Revd Sydney Arthur, Curly Webber, Harry Nethercott.

Left: The troop displaying the District Scoutcraft shield won in May 1925. The shield was presented at a fête in July at Treborough Lodge. Miss Shaw is standing back left under the standard, and P. Moles is holding the Union Jack. Boys in the picture: W. Taylor, S. Case, R. Webber, B. Webber, P. Langdon, P. Tomkins, A. Webber, L. Pope, G. Shopland, H. Nethercott, W. Murrell, P. Lovell, G. Pope, D. Burnett, H. Shattock, A. Webber and C. Napper.

Scout camp at Blue Anchor, 1930s. Jack Poole is standing on the right.

Scouts with Scoutmaster Walter Taylor, c.1938.

Roadwater Guides, c.1921. Fourth from left, back row: Miss Shaw; sixth from left: Kathleen Mear.

Village Groups & Sports

Left: *West Somerset Village History Society, founded by the authors of this book in 1986, has expanded to become the West Somerset Village History Society, with 80 members, meeting on a monthly basis in the Community Hall, Monksilver. Here, members enjoy a walk at Wheddon Cross, July 1997. Included in the picture: Desmond Post, Chris Tilley, Hilary Tilley, Malcolm Scott, Colin ?, John Holley, David Court-Smith, Mike Jones, Margaret Bellamy, Barbara Irving, Brenda White, Ralph White, Val Hole, Pam Hole, Gill Tapp, Dawn Giddings, Jonathan Greenhow, Clare Court, Pam Davies and Mary Field.*

Right: *West Somerset Carriage Driving for the Disabled was first established in October 1990 to offer carriage driving for wheelchair-bound and physically disabled individuals who are unable to mount a horse. The group operates at Lowood from spring to autumn with a staff of volunteers working with Margaret Wyatt. Left to right: Nicky Robinson, Jean Brewer, Peggy Sidewater, Wendy Hofmeier, Christine Pershouse; seated in carriage: John Sharman-Courtney and Margaret Wyatt, with Baron ready for the off.*

Inset: *Old Cleeve School at Area Sports, Porlock, 1958. A total of 21 children from Old Cleeve School were selected, including several from Roadwater. Left to right, back row: Peter Stonestreet, Walter Heneage, John Taylor, Sandra McCutcheon, Susan Halliday, Terry Reed, Terry Cheek, Michael Hindon, ? Dickinson; front row: Gerald Beaver, Tina McCutcheon, ? Churchward, Molly Routley, Valerie Beaver, Jenny Beaver* (holding cup), *?, David Harris, Susan Ferguson, Duncan Bell, ?.*

The earliest known photo of sports at Roadwater, 1907.
This event took place at 'Broadie', the field where the council-houses were built in 1931.

Above: *Valiant Soldier Skittles Champions, c.1980.* Left to right: *Eric Mead, Mr Harper, Harry Nethercott, Mrs Harper, Ken Beaver, Bobby Gibson, Roger Coles, Bill Winter, Dennis Takle and Philip White.*

Above: *Valiant Soldier Darts Championship, c.1980.* Left to right: *Pat Taylor, Clifford Beaver, Jim Vaulter, John Burnett, Geoff Tucker, Colin Potter, Dave Burge, Barry Clark;* in front: *Ken Beaver.*

Above right: *Harry Nethercott takes the first roll to open the new skittle alley at the Valiant Soldier, 1983, assisted by pub landlord Mike Twine.*

Right: *Village Hall Snooker Championship, 1978.* Left to right: *Philip White, Chris Priddy (runner-up), Bryan Taylor (chairman, Entertainments Committee).*

Left: *Cricket team, c.1960.* Left to right, standing: *Sid Bircham, Harold Gooding (president), Michael White, Bernard Coleman, John Hill, Geoff Clatworthy, John Baker, Arthur Takel, Sidney Lile (scorer), Harold Male (umpire);* seated: *Tom Webber, Bryan Lile, Derrick Lile (captain), Tom Griffiths, Harry Grimshaw.*

Right: *Roadwater Cricket Team, mid-1970s.* Left to right, back row: *Eric Ide (umpire), Dennis Takle, Keith Burnell, Tom Webber, Roger Coles, Arthur Takel, Philip White, Harry Grimshaw;* front row: *Norman Barnes, Tom Griffiths, Brian Redd, John Hill, Julie Redd (scorer), Chris Anton.*

Left: *Roadwater Cricket Club, mid-1980s.* Left to right, back row: *Mike Hayes, Tim Anton, Harry Grimshaw, Philip White, Dave Sully;* front row: *Tim Harral, David Miller, Chris Anton, Dennis Takle, Brian Redd, Tim Tribe.*

Right: *Roadwater Valiant Soldier v Washford Inn, c.1989.* Left to right, back row: *Mike Twine, Royston Willis, Martin Christmas, Nick Bohun, ?, Bryn Corfield, Richard Needs, Stuart Hall, Nigel Coleman, Neil Clarke, Dave Johnson, Len Harris, Ben Brewer;* middle row (against railing): *Pat Mc Hale, Chris Treble, Steve Ward, Jeremy Lile;* front row: *Bruce Baker, John Baker, Reg Lewis, Mark Willis, Richard Takle, Steve Cornish.*

Left: *Roadwater Football Team, 1928–29.* Left to right, back row: *Tom Taylor, Harry Burnett, Ray Burnett, Tom Milton, Harry Hemmett;* middle row: *Tom Webber, Albert Burnett, Edmund Burnett, Harry Nethercott, Fred Stevens;* front row: *Louie Baggs, Walt Taylor, Hubert Westcott, ? Burnett, Bill Tucker.*

Above: *Roadwater Football Team and Committee, 1933–34.* Left to right, back row: *Tom Reed, Tom Ridler, Charlie Burge, Dennis Smith, Tom Webber, Joe Strong, George Takle, P. Lewis, Tom Milton, Harry Burnett, Will (?) Burnett, D. Lewis;* front row: *Walter Taylor, Hubert Westcott, Hilton Ruddick, Norman Chorley, Harry Nethercott.*

Left: *Roadwater Football Team, mid-1930s. Left to right, back row: ?, George Takle, Ted Routley, ?, Percy Lewis, Roy Davis, Tom Webber, Tom Reed, ?; middle row: Harry Burnett, Alec Davis, Charley Burge; front row: Norman Chorley, 'Nobby' Taylor, Dennis Smith, ?, Hubert Westcott.*

Right: *Roadwater Football Team and Committee (and where they lived), late 1940s. Left to right, standing: George Takle (1 Bridge Cottage), Percy Lewis (Henllys), Harry Emmett (Mount Lane), Geoff Carpenter (Fern Bank), Bob Gibson (Kildare), John Ford (Cottage by Foundry House), Arthur Takel (1 Bridge*

Cottage), Harold Poole (2 Manor Mill Cottages), Stan Westcott (Harpers Cottages), Brian Lile (2 The Crescent), Tom Reed (The Lodge, Golsoncott), Harold Gooding (Vale House), Ted Burge (Strawberry Hill Cottage); front row: Trevor Beaver (3 The Crescent), Idris Beaver (Hayman's Cottages), Bernard Coleman (Vale Villa), Fred Tarr (Egypt), Harry Nethercott (Old Railway Carriage).

Above: *Roadwater Football Team and Committee, winners of the West Somerset League, 1950. Left to right, back row: Perce Sowden, Harry Hemmett, Tom Williams, Gordon Eveleigh, Harry Burnett, Ken Beaver, Derrick Lile, Cliff Milton, Sid Bindon, Jock Murray, Peter Burnett, Tom Webber, Harold Gooding, Alan Burnell; front row: Fred Tarr, Cliff Beaver, Arthur Takel, John Cridland, Bobby Yeo.*

Chapter 19

'This was the News'

Extracts from the West Somerset Free Press

Compiled by Val Hole

11.8.1890

The children of Roadwater Mission Room Sunday school enjoyed their annual treat in a field kindly loaned by Mr Stone, Clitsome. After an excellent tea on the croquet ground, games were entered into with Great Spirit.

29.4.1899

At a well attended meeting held at the Valiant Soldier, it was decided to continue the village cricket club and to accept the kind offer of Mr Case of a field on his farm for the coming season. A hearty vote of thanks was passed to J.B. Bagehot, of Treborough Lodge, for his kind support for the club, and also to Mr H. Lutley, for the use of his field last season.

4.4.1896

A very poor attendance at the annual parish assembly in the Temperance Hall, Roadwater heard that a deficit of some £27 was chiefly due to contributions to better drainage at Washford and Leighland school.

26.12.1896

Roadwater Band of Hope celebrated its winter festival at the Temperance Hall with teas for the children and the public. The Revd F. Hardwidge pleaded with the parents to give up their moderate little drops and help the good cause.

14.5.1898

The junior members of the Christian Endeavour Society gave the last of a series of services of song in the Temperance Hall. The room was full and the audience was most attentive.

5.2.1898

The roller mills at Roadwater were put into action again after undergoing extensive alterations including the installation of an up-to-date automatic roller and wheat-cleaning machine. The flour produced was of excellent quality.

4.5.1901

Walter Willis, a reservist in the Welsh Fusiliers, returned home to Roadwater having served in the war in South Africa. Of the four members of the Washford Lodge of Druids who went to the front, Mr Willis was the only one to return.

6.10.1945

Roadwater councillors decided to ask the Minehead postmaster for a public telephone kiosk in the village.

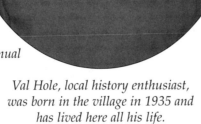

Val Hole, local history enthusiast, was born in the village in 1935 and has lived here all his life.

18.9.1948

The harvest festival was held at the Methodist Chapel in Roadwater, and the Revd J.A. Broadbent, of Cliff College, conducted the service. He seemed to rivet the children with a most interesting address. Mr Broadbent also preached at the evening service but unfortunately the weather proved unfavourable and kept many people away.

26.2.1948

An old time dance was held as a fortnightly dance at Roadwater Village Hall, and once again proved a great success. An enjoyable evening was spent dancing to Mr C.H. Shattock's Orchestra.

Top left: *Topsy with Mary aged about six, opposite Mill House, 1949.*

Above: *Farmer Hake (right) with Eddie Beaver senr and Frances Barnes Hole at Stamborough, 1950s.*

Left: *The opening of Pat and Lon Mc Hale's shop 'Junk and Disorderly', 1988. Left to right: Clare Court (inside shop), Lon Mc Hale, Siobhan Mc Hale, Daisy Hole, Patrick Mc Hale, ?.*

Above: *Walter Taylor (right) and Ted Tompkins rebuilding Queenie's house at Tacker Street, watched by Peter Simpson, 1960.*

Right: *Mrs Margaret Hemmett, Roadwater's oldest inhabitant on her 107th birthday with Beth Nickoles, 2003. Margaret lived in Roadwater for the first 104 years of her life, but then went into care at Randall House, Minehead. Sadly she died in June 2004.* PHOTO STEVE GUSCOTT

Parish Personalities, 1950-2004

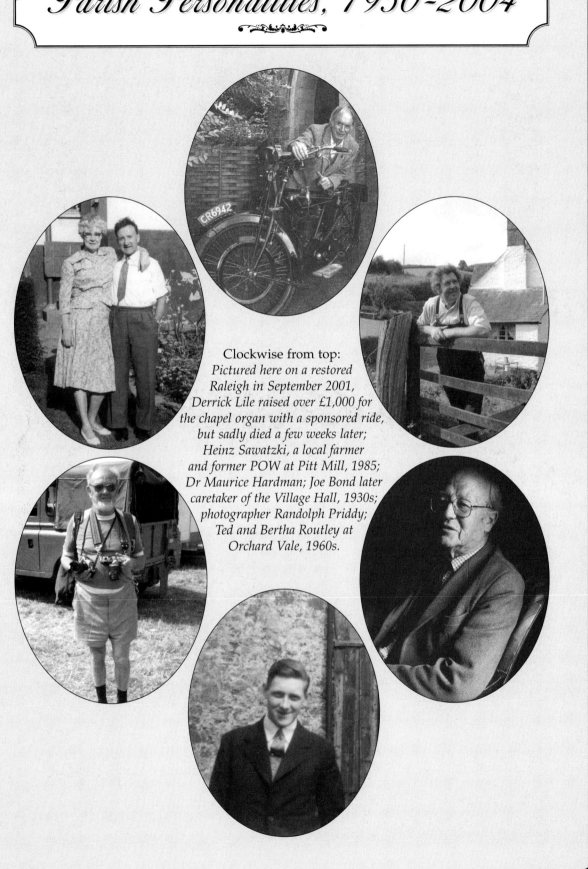

Clockwise from top:
*Pictured here on a restored
Raleigh in September 2001,
Derrick Lile raised over £1,000 for
the chapel organ with a sponsored ride,
but sadly died a few weeks later;
Heinz Sawatzki, a local farmer
and former POW at Pitt Mill, 1985;
Dr Maurice Hardman; Joe Bond later
caretaker of the Village Hall, 1930s;
photographer Randolph Priddy;
Ted and Bertha Routley at
Orchard Vale, 1960s.*

Men's raft race, Blue Anchor to Minehead, August 2001. The Valiant Soldier team consisted of, **near raft, left to right:** *Bryn Corfield, Lee Taylor, Mike Twine;* **far raft:** *Gerald Beaver, Paul Richards, John Cox.*

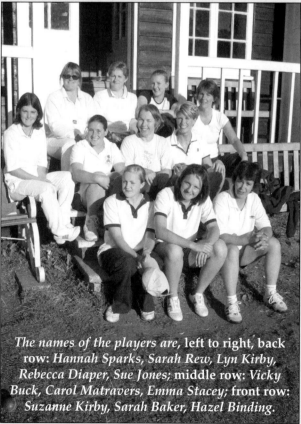

The names of the players are, left to right, back row: *Hannah Sparks, Sarah Rew, Lyn Kirby, Rebecca Diaper, Sue Jones;* **middle row:** *Vicky Buck, Carol Matravers, Emma Stacey;* **front row:** *Suzanne Kirby, Sarah Baker, Hazel Binding.*

Above, inset: *The Tearaways skittles team, weekend in Bournemouth, 2002.* **Left to right, back row:** *Tony Didcott, John Babb, Harry Bishop, Michael Bishop, Chris Henson, Paul Sawatzki, Charlie Pitman;* **front row:** *Bryn Corfield, Mike Twine, Lee Taylor.*

Above: *The Vikings and Tearaways.* **Left to right, back row:** *Andy Madison, Tony Didcott, Sean Hardman, Nigel Grabham, Tom Armstrong, Nigel Coleman, Peter Lyneham, Harry Bishop, Paul Sawatzki, Bryn Corfield, John Babb;* **front row:** *Alex Roberts, Mike Twine.*

Chapter 20

Tailpiece

As I come to this tailpiece and wonder who or what might fitly wag it, I admit to having left two or three old growlers out in the rain, simply for want of a kennel for them. But they wagged their way with their pawky humour into the lore of the old village folk, and for that reason they must have their bark even now.

William and Sarah

William and Sarah's family name has been lost, but they lived rather a cat-and-dog life in a cottage near the mill leat. Ours not to reason why, only to note that they lived on different planes, William a devotee of the quiet life with pipe, pint and slippers in the chimney corner, Sal a vocal trouncer of concert standard and a dramatiser of her woes. William bore her tantrums with a patience which only served to exasperate her until one day she tore out into the garden, shouting, 'Oh, you aggravtin' ole to-ud, you, you'll be the death o' me, you will!' William followed slowly and found her standing on the edge of the leat. Seeing him coming, she gathered her skirts about her as if to jump in and cried, 'I can't stand no more of 'ee, Willum, I can't. I be goin' to drown meself.'

'That's right, me lover,' returned William placidly and unperturbed. 'Drown theeself if thee'rt minded to, but mind thee dissn' wet thee clo'es.'

Some folk, however, thought that Sarah, a house-proud, hard-working woman who gave her 'lazy larrups' of a husband three good meals a day, had good reason to be annoyed. She certainly felt she had, and as time went on she asserted herself more and more forcefully. William let it all flow over him and lived into a green old age. But 'come to last', as they said, even his cheerful unconcern could not stave off the end. He took to his bed and, as his life seemed to be ebbing away, Sarah's conscience smote her for the hard things she had spoken to him. She bent over him with anguished face and cried, 'Oh Willum, me dear, I be sorry 'bout some o' the things I said to 'ee, but I bin a good wife to 'ee, han't I?'

The old man opened one quizzical eye. 'Nort to brag about, Sal,' he said, 'nort to brag about.'

Whether that was how he turned the corner is more than I can say, but from that day he was more his old self and able to face the 'well-wishers'. 'Wull now, Will,' said Harry Cobbledick, 'they said you was purty far gone, but I reckon thee 'rt good for a while 'itt [yet]. Gi'e ee two–dree weeks, maybe, if you be lucky. Miracles do happen, 'sno.'

Mary Jane Luxton, a few days later, was no less encouraging: 'My, Will, you be lookin' so peart as a ruddick [robin], sure 'nough. You'm sure to get better one o' these days, ev'n if you do get wuss fust.'

At length came the day when William pulled himself up in bed and called for his dinner. 'Sal,' he said, 'I be sick an' tired o' this yere invalid's muck. Gi'e I a proper dinner, wull 'ee, wi' teddies and greens an' a bit o' thik gurt ham I zeed ee bring in day avore yest'day.'

'You can have yer teddies an' greens, Willum,' said Sal, sharpish-like, 'but you bain't havin' thik there ham. I be keepin he for the fooneral. You can't have he.'

Tommy Hawkes

Tommy Hawkes, who came selling fish, also deserves a mention.

'Oh Mr Hawkes' inquired a lady, 'how much a pound are your herrings?'

'I don't sell 'em by the pound, ma'am' said Tommy firmly, 'I sells 'em by the heach.'

Silas Locke

And then there was Silas Locke, postman from Washford, who when off duty wore a cloth hat, tweed suit and leather leggings polished mirror-bright. He delighted in cricket and umpired local matches with firmness and good humour, notably one at Roadwater in the 1930s.

'Owzat?' roared the exultant Roadwater bowler.

'Out LBW,' pronounced Silas.

'It weren't LBW and I bain't out,' protested the batsman.

'Now don't ee arguy wi' me, young man. When I say you be out, you be out, an' if you won't have it, look in nex' week's *Free Press*.'

Three Tall Tales

Finally, there were three tall stories doing the rounds in Roadwater more than 100 years ago.

Sam and Bob

Sam and Bob were well into their fourth pint and vying with each other to invent incredible feats and adventures. Said Bob, 'I swum over to Wales las' week, 'sknow.'

Said Sam, ' Giddout wi' ee. Thik idn' nort. I went up in one o' they balloons.'

Said Bob, 'So did I, an' I went fu'ther 'n thee, I went up to the moon, an' druv a nail in en.'

Said Sam. 'Oh ay. Wull, I went right roun' t' other side an' clinted en.'

Ned Fisher

There were two tramps trudging to the next work-house, and they stopped to eat their 'bre' n cheese' at a milestone. One of them peered at the stone and said, 'Well, bless me if this yere idn' where they buried poor ole Ned Fisher, you.'

'Whass mean?' asked the other. 'Ned Fisher? How do 'ee know? Cassn' read, cass?'

'Course I can. Yere 'tis, plain as the nose on yer face: T for Ned an' O for Fisher. I a'ways wondered where they'd buried en to.'

Jack Craddle

Jack Craddle had never learned to read, but he wouldn't let on, and he sat in the Valiant Soldier pretending to read a newspaper.

'Haw! Haw!' brayed some superior person (probably from Minehead). 'Don't you know you've got the paper upside down?'

'Course I do' returned Jack. 'Any vuule can read en the right way up.'

Roadwater celebrates the new millennium.

Subscribers

Betty L. Arthur, Fowey, Cornwall
Glenda Bale (née Western), Watchet, Somerset
George W. Barran, East Ruston, Near Stalham, Norfolk
Hugh P. Barran, Taunton, Somerset
D.S. and J.A. Beadell, Roadwater
Jim and Joan Beaver, Roadwater, Somerset
Wendy and Colin Bell, Derrington, Wiltshire
Mark and Jan Bennett, Higher Hayne, Roadwater
Mary and Andrew Bishop, Roadwater
Mr and Mrs M.P. Botes, The Temperance Hall, Roadwater
Pauline Bowen, Penffordd, Pembrokeshire, Wales
Simon Bowhill, Treborough, Somerset
Allan G. Browning, Victor Harbor, South Australia
B. Joan Browning, Adelaide, South Australia
Gavin D. Browning, Victor Harbor, South Australia
Kevin and Rosemary Browning, Kadina, South Australia
Pauline A. Browning, Bournemouth, Dorset
Miss A.M.P. Bryant, Taunton, Somerset
Gerald and Kathleen Bull, Bishops Lydeard
David and Jean Burge, Minehead, Somerset
Robert Burnett, Hailsham, East Sussex
Dug, Wendy and Sadie Calder, Bristol
Tony and Belle Carpenter, Budleigh Salterton, Devon
Maurice and Joyce Chidgey, Watchet, Somerset
Brian and Nicky Chinn, Roadwater
Joan Collins, Penarth
Sandra Coombs (née Nethercott), Williton, Somerset

Bryn and Debbie Corfield
M. Joan Corfield, Roadwater, Somerset
Michael T.W. Court, Northam, North Devon
Mr Ronald and Mrs Barbara Court, Taunton, Somerset
Alistair and Gill Croucher, Springfield, Wellington, Somerset
Florence J. Croucher, Lower Hayne, Roadwater
Oliver Davies, London
Ursula Davies, Hungerford, Berkshire
Dorothy Davis, California. Family name Warren
Beverley and Alan Dean, Treborough, Somerset
Pete and Jan Evans, Roadwater
Yvonne Evans, Roadwater, Somerset
Barbara P. Feltham M.B.E., East Quantoxhead, Somerset
Elizabeth M. Foster, Dunster, Somerset
Catherine Fouracre
Mr and Mrs Christopher Fouracre
F.J. Fouracre, Porlock, Somerset
Mr and Mrs H.G. Fouracre
Mr and Mrs Martin Fouracre
Mr and Mrs Michael Fouracre
S.J.M. Franklin
David and Diane Geary, Roadwater, Somerset
Philippa Gerry, Minehead, Somerset
Ann and David Gooding, Littleham, North Devon
Jonathan Greenhow
Mr and Mrs E. Hadley, Cardiff
John and Sue Hall, Nursery Cottage, Roadwater
Mrs Jennifer E.M. Hand, Roadwater, Somerset
Dr B.M. Hardman, Leighland, Roadwater
Jocelyn Harral, Huish Moor

Gordon R. Harris, Minehead, Somerset

Jack Harris, Church Cottages, Williton, Somerset

John P. Haynes, Slough, Berkshire

Marjorie Hayes (née Bragg), Minehead

Neil and Jenny Hedges, Roadwater, Somerset

John Hill, Roadwater, Somerset

Nora Hooper (née Westcott), born on the Mineral Line

Harry and Ben Horrobin, Roadwater

Jen Hudson, Harpers Cottages, Roadwater

Violet M. James, Minehead, Somerset

Mike Jones, Taunton

Peter and Gina King, Roadwater

Annette and Pete Land, Williton

Janice Lee, Penarth

Mr Cedric H. Lewis, Watchet, Somerset

Jeremy Lile, The Crescent, Roadwater

Heather and Peter Lineham, Roadwater

Penelope Lively and Family, Forches Garden

Mrs Margaret Mangan, Roadwater, Somerset

Eileen Mann (née Coleman) and Christine Hancock (née Mann),

Ernest Charles Matthews, Eastern Green, Coventry

Ivor John Matthews, Stapleton, Bristol

Edward C. Mear, Blairgowrie, Perthshire

Joan Middleton, Roadwater, Somerset

John Peter Middleton, Roadwater, Somerset

Mrs Hilary Mills, Washford, Somerset

Philip Milton, Brimpton, Berkshire

Marjorie Moir, Wimborne, Dorset

Judy Moss, Comberow, Roadwater

Colin and Mary Nash, Helmdon, Northamptonshire

Mrs Edna Nash, Dinas Powys, Glamorgan

Joe Nethercott, Newport, South Wales

Mrs R. Nettleton, Roadwater, Somerset

Mr and Mrs G.R. Nichols

The Parkes Family, Roadwater, Somerset

Donald F. Parsons, Withycombe, Minehead, Somerset

Derek Parsons, Bristol

Mr and Mrs Ray Parsons, Townsend, Williton

Raymond Parsons, Williton, Somerset

Liz and Tim Pearson, Melton Mowbray, Leicestershire

Lt Col Adrian Peck

Revd Peter and Mrs Muriel Pengelley, Roadwater

Bill Poirrier, Roadwater

Michael and Harriet Proudfoot, Roadwater

M. Reynolds, Roadwater (ex Golsoncott)

Mr W.G. Ridler, Treborough

Charles W. Routley, Leighland, Somerset

Peter Ruffle, Pitt Cottage

Les and Sheila Rush, Washford, Somerset

Nicholas Salaman, Chelsea, London SW10

Barry Sawatzki, Stoney Ford, Devon

Heinz G. Sawatzki, Cullompton, Devon

Paul Sawatzki, Roadwater, Somerset

Richard J. Sawatzki, Alcombe, Somerset

Pamela and Frank Scragg, Chapel Cleeve, Somerset

Mrs Jane E.A.V. Sefton, Bicknoller, Somerset

Roy Shopland, West Hill, Devon

B. and J.M. Skudder, Doniford

Terry Snell, Roadwater

A.G. Snook, Portskewett, Monmouthshire

Christine Somerfield (née Western), Watchet, Somerset

Percy J. Sowden (deceased), Roadwater, Somerset

Phyllis M. Stott, Roadwater, Somerset

Janet A. Strong, Watchet, Somerset

Mrs Sheena J. Stuckey, Roadwater, Somerset

Jack Sully, Llandaff, Cardiff

William and Janet Tindall, Watersmeet, Roadwater

Keith and Joy Towells, Watchet, Somerset

Edward and Carolynn Townsend, The Old Post Office, Roadwater, Somerset

Sandra A. Tucker, Golsoncott

Mike Twine, Valiant Soldier, Roadwater

John F.W. Walling, Newton Abbot, Devon

Edna Western, Watchet, Somerset

Gwyneth White, Penarth

Ralph and Brenda White, Liddimore Farm, Watchet

Simon and Polly White, Coldharbour, Treborough

Miss Annette Wickstead

Mr and Mrs Myles Wickstead

Mark and Kellie Willis, Washford

Margaret Wyatt, Roadwater

Community Histories

The Book of Addiscombe • Canning and Clyde Road Residents Association and Friends

The Book of Addiscombe, Vol. II • Canning and Clyde Road Residents Association and Friends

The Book of Ashburton • Stuart Hands and Pete Webb

The Book of Axminster with Kilmington • Les Berry and Gerald Gosling

The Book of Bampton • Caroline Seward

The Book of Barnstaple • Avril Stone

The Book of Barnstaple, Vol. II • Avril Stone

The Book of Beccles • Pam Hardman and Maureen Saunders

The Book of The Bedwyns • Bedwyn History Society

The Book of Bickington • Stuart Hands

Blandford Forum: A Millennium Portrait • Blandford Forum Town Council

The Book of Boscastle • Rod and Anne Knight

The Book of Bramford • Bramford Local History Group

The Book of Breage & Germoe • Stephen Polglase

The Book of Bridestowe • D. Richard Cann

The Book of Bridport • Rodney Legg

The Book of Brixham • Frank Pearce

The Book of Buckfastleigh • Sandra Coleman

The Book of Buckland Monachorum & Yelverton • Pauline Hamilton-Leggett

The Book of Carharrack • Carharrack Old Cornwall Society

The Book of Carshalton • Stella Wilks and Gordon Rookledge

The Parish Book of Cerne Abbas • Vivian and Patricia Vale

The Book of Chagford • Iain Rice

The Book of Chapel-en-le-Frith • Mike Smith

The Book of Chittlehamholt with Warkleigh & Satterleigh • Richard Lethbridge

The Book of Chittlehampton • Various

The Book of Colney Heath • Bryan Lilley

The Book of Constantine • Moore and Trethowan

The Book of Cornwood and Lutton • Compiled by the People of the Parish

The Book of Crediton • John Heal

The Book of Creech St Michael • June Small

The Book of Cullompton • Compiled by the People of the Parish

The Book of Dawlish • Frank Pearce

The Book of Dulverton, Brushford, Bury & Exebridge • Dulverton and District Civic Society

The Book of Dunster • Hilary Binding

The Book of Easton • Easton Village History Project

The Book of Edale • Gordon Miller

The Ellacombe Book • Sydney R. Langmead

The Book of Exmouth • W.H. Pascoe

The Book of Grampound with Creed • Bane and Oliver

The Book of Gosport • Lesley Burton and Brian Musselwhite

The Book of Hayling Island & Langstone • Peter Rogers

The Book of Helston • Jenkin with Carter

The Book of Hemyock • Clist and Dracott

The Book of Herne Hill • Patricia Jenkyns

The Book of Hethersett • Hethersett Society Research Group

The Book of High Bickington • Avril Stone

The Book of Ilsington • Dick Wills

The Book of Kingskerswell • Carsewella Local History Group

The Book of Lamerton • Ann Cole and Friends

Lanner, A Cornish Mining Parish • Sharron Schwartz and Roger Parker

The Book of Leigh & Bransford • Malcolm Scott

The Book of Litcham with Lexham & Mileham • Litcham Historical and Amenity Society

The Book of Loddiswell • Loddiswell Parish History Group

The New Book of Lostwithiel • Barbara Fraser

The Book of Lulworth • Rodney Legg

The Book of Lustleigh • Joe Crowdy

The Book of Lydford • Compiled by Barbara Weeks

The Book of Lyme Regis • Rodney Legg

The Book of Manaton • Compiled by the People of the Parish

The Book of Markyate • Markyate Local History Society

The Book of Mawnan • Mawnan Local History Group

The Book of Meavy • Pauline Hemery

The Book of Mere • Dr David Longbourne

The Book of Minehead with Alcombe • Hilary Binding and Douglas Stevens

The Book of Monks Orchard and Eden Park • Ian Muir and Pat Manning

The Book of Morchard Bishop • Jeff Kingaby

The Book of Mylor • Mylor Local History Group

The Book of Narborough • Narborough Local History Society

The Book of Newdigate • John Callcut

For details of any of the above titles or if you are interested in writing your own history, please contact: Commissioning Editor, Community Histories, Halsgrove House, Lower Moor Way, Tiverton, Devon EX16 6SS, England; email: katyc@halsgrove.com